apparently on fire from top to bottom, but deftly manages to tell the dramatic stories of many others who watched the flames come on. For those of us who were in the fires, this is a story telling urgent truths of an extraordinary ordeal; for those who didn't see a flame, who want to know what our communities have been through, what can be learned, and what faces us in the future, it is an essential one.'
—**Kate Holden, author of** *The Winter Road*

'A throat-gripping, essential read for all humans. Be prepared. This book reads like a thriller and will haunt like a prophecy.'
—**Jonica Newby, author of** *Beyond Climate Grief*

'A raw account of the Black Summer bushfires, combining vivid eyewitness testimony with a storyteller's eye for detail and nuance. This story matters: not just as a memoir of loss and destruction and ragged weeks under orange skies, but as a warning for next time. Bronwyn Adcock brings this horror fire season to life, forcing us to ask whether the right lessons have been learned. Accounts like this are essential reading if we're to have any chance of preventing a recurrence.'
—**Scott Ludlam, author of** *Full Circle*

CURROWAN

THE STORY OF A FIRE

BRONWYN ADCOCK

dead ink

dead ink

First published in Australia in 2021 by Black Inc.
This edition published in Great Britain in 2022 by Dead Ink,
an imprint of Cinder House Publishing Limited.

Print ISBN 978-1-911585-90-9
Ebook ISBN 978-1-911585-91-6

Cover design by Luke Bird / lukebird.co.uk
Cover image © Lea Scaddan/Getty
Typeset by Laura Jones / lauraflojo.com

Printed and bound in Great Britain by Clays Ltd, Elcograf S.p.A.

MIX
Paper from
responsible sources
FSC® C018072
FSC
www.fsc.org

www.deadinkbooks.com

CONTENTS

For Chris, Tasman and Leyla, and in memory of Atticus

'What is happening is extraordinary. It would be difficult to say there wasn't a climate change dimension. We couldn't have imagined the scale of the current event before it happened. We would have been told it was hyperbole. This is teaching us what can be true under a climate-changed world.'
David Bowman, Professor of Pyrogeography and Fire Science, November 2019

'Unlike the other elements of the Ancients, fire is not a substance but a reaction. It is what its surroundings make it: it takes its character from its context.'
Stephen J. Pyne, *The Still-Burning Bush*

PROLOGUE

THE EVE OF ALL
OUR TOMORROWS

It's 3.00 am on the last day of 2019, and I go from asleep to suddenly awake, heart racing.

I've been waking this way ever since the Currowan fire began. Often nothing in particular rouses me, only a feeling of vigilance: *I'm ready*. Other times it is the sudden recollection of something I lost in the fire that jolts me awake – a vivid image roaring into my consciousness, accompanied by a set of stories.

Oh no, the photo album, the one with apricot-coloured flowers on the cover with the pictures from that first share house at uni.

My god, Grandpa's cane chair; and there he is, sitting in it on his verandah catching the last rays of sun on his face, smiling at six-year-old me.

But most of the time, what wakes me is fear of what this still-burning fire will do next.

I know this is the reason I am awake now. The day is forecast to hold dangerous fire weather, conditions that will almost certainly incite the Currowan fire – anything could happen.

In the dark I reach for my phone. This constant checking for fire updates: another new routine. I look first at the Fires Near Me app, and what I see is so shocking I think I must be dreaming.

I weave my way through the unfamiliar contours of the house we're temporarily living in, bumping against the cardboard boxes stacked in small towers, which are filled with the things I did grab when we evacuated. I haven't unpacked them yet because I'm not confident we won't need to go again. In the kitchen I turn on every light and look at my phone again.

It's not the Currowan fire on the move but another one, about 150 kilometres south. I checked the status of this fire before I went to sleep and it was burning in remote mountain ranges well west of any populated areas – my younger brother lives in the vicinity and we'd been speaking on the phone about how it could mean trouble for him in the coming days. But now the app is showing it's already escaped, with two enormous fingers of red reaching towards the villages of Cobargo and Quaama – one almost on top of the farmland where my brother and his family live. *Are they still asleep? Do they even know?* I text him and he responds within minutes: they're already in the car with kids and animals, racing towards a coastal headland.

Back in early December, not long after this all started, I found out about a webpage where you can click on a link that lets you hear the radio communications of the Rural Fire Service volunteers out in the field. So now I open my laptop and set myself up at the kitchen bench, spending the hours to dawn staring out the window at the slow, gentle lightening of the night sky, accompanied by a soundtrack of unfolding horror.

As usual, there's not enough resources. I listen to the desperate pleas of firefighters, calling for help they know isn't coming.

'There's no bloody trucks, so we're buggered,' says one. Another is calling for an ambulance because he's pulling children from a burning house and their little bare feet are scorching on the ground. I hear a firefighter, panic just suppressed in his tight, strained voice, saying he can't protect the homes in his hamlet anymore and that he's retreating to the fire shed to try to save the lives of anyone who makes it there with him.

I'm hunting for scraps of useful information to pass on, something I've already spent countless hours doing over the past month. So when I hear a firefighter say he thinks the blaze is heading towards the headland where my brother and his family are – and there are no fire trucks on site – I know what to do. I google *what is the safest way to shelter from fire in a car* and call my brother. Over time I've become much better at the task of imparting information to someone in imminent danger, and so with a tone of casual enquiry – as though asking if he has milk in the fridge – I relay what I've heard and ask if he has a woollen blanket in the car, just in case.

I step outside to stand on the front lawn, nausea rising. The sun is up now, belting down heat from a cloudless blue sky. I'm in the little coastal village of Bawley Point, our cottage just a few doors up from the beach, and I watch as a stream of holidaymakers amble past me towards the sand, towels on shoulders, small fluffy dogs trotting alongside – people who've somehow made it through the constant road closures, unde-terred that we are surrounded by fire. I'm aware that I could be coming across as unhinged – still in pyjamas, staring into space – but I don't care. I'm living so deeply inside this relentless, never-ending fire story that it's like a pane of glass is separating me from anyone not trapped by it too.

It's still before breakfast when I get a call telling me that fresh smoke has been spotted coming from our property. Before the fire, my family and I lived in a forested, semi-rural area about ten kilometres northwest of Bawley Point. While fire went through our place weeks ago, the Currowan fire has a way of lingering, even as it continues a steady march across the landscape. Fires are behaving in such extreme and unusual ways this season, I worry we could suffer the same fate as the North Coast village of Wytaliba. It got hit by fire twice: first in October, then a second, worse bite in November that took out nearly half the homes.

I need to go and investigate, but can't decide what to do with my two children, aged six and eleven. To take them into the bush, towards smoke, on a day of extreme fire danger seems risky; but so too does leaving them home alone, with the possibility we could be separated if something happens. I've seen roadblocks go up quickly over the last month and know they are strictly enforced – one man I know was arrested and charged for trying to get through one.

Resolving that we'll stay together, I head west with them. As we enter the dirt road that leads into our property, I grip the steering wheel and focus. Once this was a sedate drive through a forest of spotted gums, grey and pink trunks holding up bouquets of green, a darting wallaby or a lazy diamond python the only hazards; but now it's a sparse, blackened wasteland, full of peril. Many trees have already fallen, others dissolved into ash on the forest floor, but there are some that look only tenuously upright, and I drive with one eye to what's above, accelerating past any that tilt.

I pass a hand-painted sign one of my neighbours has attached to a blackened trunk: *Sightseers not welcome*. I'm glad for the sign. It's a bonus that it's polite. Other places have ones that say: *You loot, we shoot*.

On our property I soon find the source of smoke. The trunk of an enormous gum, so large four adults would have struggled to hug her girth, has snapped in half – it must have been smouldering inside for the past month – and now flames are leaping out of the fallen trunk, sending a dramatic display of plumes up into the sky. It's in a patch that was once rainforest – but the delicate ferns, spiky cycads and ancient bangalow palms that once dropped their fronds to the ground like a skirt are all gone. While I can see why the smoke is worrying the neighbours, who are still in their home further up the hill, I know it will be short-lived: there is nothing here left to burn.

As we walk back to the car, past the twisted metal of sheds, bicycle frames and a melted swing set, I smell something terrible. I send the kids on ahead and follow the odour to the chicken pen, where I discover the first wallaby I've seen in a month. Blowflies swarm its emaciated corpse.

I can't believe this creature's misfortune. All month I've been diligently leaving out water and food supplied by a local wildlife carer at a feeding station just 50 metres away, but instead of finding this, the wallaby has pushed its way in here and become trapped. I wonder if I should bury it, but then remember we don't have a shovel anymore.

A wave of despondency threatens but doesn't get a chance to settle, because the weather is turning. The forecast nor'wester has kicked in, bringing with it squalls of blackened leaves. I start half-running towards the car and yelling at the kids to get in. As we drive away, the temperature gauge on the dashboard reads 42 degrees.

The highway is abnormally deserted. When I round a bend, I see two police cars parked in the middle of the highway and officers putting up barricades for a roadblock. 'Where's the fire?' I ask, anxious to know what's going on, but all they'll tell me is the highway is closed.

When I get back to Bawley Point, the power to the entire village is out. There's also no running water because the pumps run off electricity. I get on my phone to find out what's happening, but I've got no reception and nothing will load. A light haze of smoke is wafting through the air.

I take the kids – no indecision about that now – and drive a few streets to a friend's place, where a small group of people are standing outside talking. The word is that the Currowan fire is now running to our south. A woman I know pulls in. She's just come from her job in the large town of Batemans Bay, 30 kilometres south. She tells us she had to evacuate because the fire was coming in. I'm so shocked, I'm almost disbelieving: 'A fire in town?' I make her tell me again. This time she pulls up her sleeve to show me a small red mark on her arm where she was hit by an ember outside Bunnings.

The following hours I spend alternating between sitting on my friend's back step, watching our kids and others from the neighbourhood turn cartwheels and bounce on the trampoline in a yard bordered by already burnt bush – gulping in lungfuls of sepia-coloured haze as they play – and walking out to the headland to try to find mobile-phone reception. Along the smooth, warm rocks of the point, there are lots of us holding out phones at odd angles, climbing onto boulders, rushing to cluster on a spot when someone yells, 'I've got range!' Cars are pulling up, some already packed – tourists wanting to escape this holiday from hell.

Snippets of information filter through. By lunchtime, we know the Currowan fire is also running to our north. My friend gets a text from someone in the little hamlet of Conjola Park: *There's fire in my yard*. When Facebook momentarily loads I read that fire is in the playground of the little primary school my nieces attend in the town of Milton. As the day goes on, the stories about Conjola get worse; I hear forty houses are gone, then I hear half the village. I hope it's not true.

We are safe enough here, we think, but there's nowhere else to go anyway: we are locked in. The Currowan fire is to our south, west and north, the Tasman Sea the only clear front.

For locals, these places to our north, like Conjola, are part of our broader community – our children go to the same schools, people work together, friends and family are scattered between. Nearly everyone has a mental roll call of those they're worried about. I've been trying to ring my parents all afternoon, and when I finally get through late in the day they tell me they watched from their house as a fireball swept through farmland at a place called Little Forest. They assure me they're safe, but still I hector them: *Are you packed? Is the car pointed in the right direction? You must be ready to move quickly if you need to.*

That night, New Year's Eve, no one has the heart for celebration. But we need to eat and want company, so in the evening I gather with friends over candle and torch light for a communal meal, made from the rapidly perishing food we've all pulled from our fridges. As the clock draws closer to midnight, the volunteers from our local Rural Fire Service brigade who headed north into the melee that afternoon have still not returned. Several of us have loved ones on board, but no one speaks their fears.

Waking on the first day of 2020, it feels as though there's been more than a simple turning of a calendar year; I have entered an entirely new world.

On New Year's Day, the power is still out, telecommunications sporadic, and word is spreading that the entire South Coast is running low on fuel. Hearing that any purchases are now cash only, I take the money the kids' grandparents gave them for Christmas from their envelopes and drive to the petrol station on the highway. The queue of cars stretches out of the servo and so far down the highway I can't even see the end; I give up, figuring I'll ration my usage instead. When I return to the village I run into our local RFS captain. As I recount what I've just seen, he panics they'll sell out of diesel, leaving nothing for their fire trucks, and is gone before I finish my story.

When phones do work, they bring hard tidings. The names of locals who lost their homes yesterday are passed on in hushed voices, almost unspeakable news. I hear that one person has died, possibly more; small communities being the way they are, it is likely to be someone I know.

By the second day of the year, looking at my near-empty pantry, I start to think seriously about how I am going to source food. Those who've already tried say there is no point trying to drive up the highway to the nearest large town of Ulladulla, because the road is in a permanent state of gridlock. Tens of thousands of tourists are trying to flee the South Coast – authorities have issued an evacuation order – but all roads are still blocked by fire and fallen trees and no one can get out.

A friend hatches a plan to use his boat to travel by sea to Ulladulla – he's never taken it that far in the open ocean before, but reckons he'll be right – but we aren't even sure if anything will be left at the supermarket. Reports are that panic buying has broken out, people filling trolleys mountain high, and shelves aren't being replenished because delivery trucks can't get through.

In the midst of this comes the warning that *another* dangerous fire day is imminent – it's time to brace again.

PART ONE

A SEASON
OF FIRE

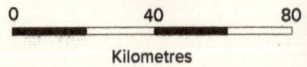

CHAPTER 1

THE GATHERING STORM

The year 2018 starts with a heatwave, coming down upon southeastern Australia. On the first Sunday, just after three in the afternoon, the temperature in the western Sydney suburb of Penrith slides up another notch, hitting 47.3 degrees Celsius – making it officially the hottest place on Earth. Temperature readings are taken in the shade, though, and across the city at the Sydney Cricket Ground, where the final Ashes test is being slogged out, a heat-stress tracker on the sideline measures what anyone out in the sun is experiencing: it peaks at 57.6 degrees. Incredibly, just one player, the English captain, finishes the day in hospital. At an international tennis tournament at Sydney Olympic Park, the heat shuts down three courtside cameras. Further south in Victoria, it bubbles and melts bitumen on the Hume Highway, slowing holiday traffic to a crawl.

This blistering start proves just a prelude. Above-average temperatures continue throughout summer and into autumn. Another heatwave, this time stretching across the entire country, strikes for ten days in early April. Dozens of towns in New

South Wales experience consecutive days above 35 degrees; the ninth day is the hottest Australian April day on record. The Bureau of Meteorology describes what's going on as 'abnormal'.

The heat is not the only extreme weather event underway. The amount of rain falling across eastern Australia started diminishing from late 2016, and by 2018 decent rainfall is almost a complete stranger to the land. New South Wales has its driest autumn in more than a century. By winter, 100 per cent of the state is drought-declared.

This is supposed to be the year Greg Mullins finally starts relaxing. It is his first full year of retirement after a thirty-nine-year career with Fire and Rescue NSW. He'd served the last fourteen as commissioner, in charge of one of the largest urban fire and rescue services in the world – the only man who stayed longer in this position died at his desk. But Mullins is watching the landscape wither under the extreme heat and drought, unable to escape a growing sense of unease that the conditions are being set for a catastrophic fire event.

Mullins knows as well as anyone that Australia has always been bushfire-prone. Growing up in the bushy outer suburbs of Sydney with a father who was a volunteer firefighter, he was schooled in the realities of helping his mum and siblings protect the family home when fires were nearby and Dad was out on the truck. He fought his first fire at age twelve, and countless more over the course of his professional life. But he fears that what's coming next is right off the scale of anything this country has ever seen.

For the past decade, he's been observing significant changes to the rhythms of fire that Australia has always known. No longer just a feature of summer, bushfires are appearing in other seasons, the big ones coming closer together, their behaviour more extreme. Mullins, like most professionals in the emergency services field around the globe, sees these shifts as harbingers. He knows the science says human-created climate change is making the planet hotter and drier, which in turn will make bushfires worse.

The warnings have been coming in for more than a decade, becoming stronger with time. In 2005, Australia's national science agency, the CSIRO, said southeastern Australia would face an increased fire risk in the future. By 2008, a report commissioned for the Australian government put a date on it: 'Fire seasons will start earlier, end slightly later and generally be more intense. This effect increases over time, but should be directly observable by 2020.' The following year, a government-funded research organisation warned 'our current knowledge and practices on bushfire management' would not be adequate in this new era of climate-change–fuelled bushfires. In 2017, a major study examined historical records of 'fire weather' in Australia going back sixty-seven years. Using the Forest Fire Danger Index – the combining of meteorological data such as heat, wind and humidity, along with dryness, to come up with the degree of fire danger on any given day – it revealed Australia was already experiencing more days of dangerous fire weather, with increases in the frequency and magnitude of the extremes.

By 2018, Australia has been warming at an accelerating rate since the 1950s, with each decade hotter than the one before, and cool season rainfall has been diminishing in southeastern Australia for twenty years: key ingredients for this more dangerous bushfire era to eventuate.

But it isn't simply fear of a bad fire season that is keeping Mullins from enjoying his retirement. His years on the inside, working closely with successive governments, have convinced him that those in power have failed to confront what is happening. As a result, we are not prepared for this new epoch.

Mullins largely blames the so-called 'climate wars' for Australia's state of unpreparedness. A decade of lost time, where a persistent campaign was waged by vested interests in the fossil fuel industry, supported by politicians from prime ministers down and segments of the media, fanning scepticism about the existence of climate change. It was so successful that instead of being a question of science and how we prepare, it became a heavily politicised controversy.

Because it was so political, Mullins says – and he is not the only senior Australian public servant to make such a claim – it became a taboo subject, and 'if you're not allowed to talk about something, you can't leverage it'. Over his career the pressure he faced was both implicit and overt. Once, he says, he was privately reprimanded by his minister for linking climate change and fires in a media interview. He learned to self-censor, for example making sure to omit the phrase 'climate change' when putting in a budget submission to upgrade his bushfire tanker fleet – even though this was his rationale for the upgrade.

Mullins starts calling some of his former emergency services colleagues, and learns that he isn't the only one who is worried.

By 2018, it had been just over ten years since I left Sydney and moved to the New South Wales South Coast. It was a homecoming of sorts. I'd grown up in the area, but hightailed it out as soon as I finished high school; first to university, then to work in the city and overseas.

The region known as the South Coast starts around 100 kilometres south of Sydney and runs down alongside the Tasman Sea. Most of the population live in a collection of villages and towns that cling as close to the coastline as physically possible; it's an ocean-facing culture, a place with a preponderance of surfers, fish-and-chip shops and seashell–themed holiday houses.

Sitting to the west of it all, running parallel to the coastal belt, is a long band of green. This area starts with farmland, before merging into a vast hinterland of forests and rivers – a playground for dirt-bikers, hunters and bushwalkers. Further west still lies a spur off the Great Dividing Range, with intricately webbed gorges, sculpted rockfaces and flat-topped escarpments – so wild and remote there'd still be places a foot has never fallen.

Living on a property on the edge of the forest hinterland, near where it starts to give way to coastal terrain, I had a foot in both camps. When I built here, with my husband, Chris, I knew it came with the risk of bushfire. We factored this into everything we did, such as using steel instead of wood to construct the house, installing robust fire hoses on either end and investing in a 100,000-litre concrete water tank, to make sure we always had enough water. We kept a huge area around the house clear of trees, what's called an *asset-protection zone*, and every year spent countless hours beating back the endlessly encroaching bush. When the season was right, we did small hazard-reduction burns on our land.

For years, we discussed to the point of tedium whether a fire might hit – a conversation so frequent it became habit, more than a sense of imminent threat.

But that year, I started to notice a string of curious, unsettling things about the land. Like how even on the odd occasion it rained, a shovel in the ground the next day would still come out dry; and how while we once had legions of leeches, marching relentlessly out of the damp rainforest gullies hunting for a bare ankle to latch onto, now I couldn't remember the last time I'd seen one. I knew the state was in drought, but it was still disconcerting when I went into the local farm produce store one day and saw the owner with a furrowed brow, scribbling with a pencil in a notebook, drawing up a list of local farmers so he could ration out the dwindling supply of hay for hungry animals.

But the loudest herald of all came in the form of a ferocious winter fire that roared into farm country 20 kilometres north of where I lived.

It happened early one brisk winter morning – the time of year you could look outside and still expect to see a frost. Dave Howes had not long left for his job as a logger in the state forests and his wife, Debbie, was at home on the family farm, delaying leaving the warmth of her bed, when she received a panicked call from a friend: 'Do you want me to come and get the horses?'

An out-of-control bushfire was roaring out of Mount Kingiman – a mountain range west of Ulladulla – and heading towards dozens of rural properties. By the time Dave and his adult sons, Steven and Lachlan, got home, the fire front was still a good ten kilometres away but, fuelled by an icy wind, it was already spitting embers into their paddocks. Spot fires were exploding in the dry grass.

Howsie, as Dave is known to his friends, knew better than anyone that the land was in a perilous state. In his forty-seven years he's probably spent more days inside a South Coast eucalypt forest than out. He began working as a tree feller when he was seventeen, following in the footsteps of his father, and the back country has always been a part of his own family life with Debbie and the boys too; mounted wild boar heads take pride of place in the lounge room. He couldn't remember a time the forests were so dry and thick with scrubby understorey, but still, he never expected this.

The Howes swung into action, the boys chasing down spot fires in their utes, Debbie hosing down the house and the stables. The wind was so ferocious it knocked down a powerline over the road and started another fire run. When the front finally hit them, mid-afternoon, it looked like a fireball. 'It was night time before we could get hold of it,' Dave says. They saved the house and animals, but lost half their farm – sheds, fencing, cattleyards and paddocks.

A man of few words, Dave just shakes his head, incredulous, when he recalls the strangeness of that day. 'We were fighting the fire in jumpers,' he says. 'The wind was that cold.'

The Kingiman fire was my first real brush with bushfire on the South Coast. It didn't threaten my place, but I did have to drive through smoke and the overhead buzz of helicopters to my parents' empty house – they were away in their caravan somewhere in Queensland, in oblivious grey-nomad bliss – to let myself in and make a phone call, asking for a decision that in thirty years of living there, on an old dairy farm, had never been required before: 'Don't panic, but I need you to tell me right now exactly what valuables you want me to take.'

It was hard not to feel rattled. Other fires were breaking out further down the far South Coast that week, and the RFS issued the earliest total fire ban on record for New South Wales. So it was with some misgivings that at week's end I went ahead with a long-planned trip to the Snowy Mountains.

The night I left the ski fields to come home, I drove out through an intense snowstorm that followed me all the way to the top of Brown Mountain – the last ridge before the Monaro High Country falls away to the far South Coast. As I crested the mountain and started the descent, the swirl of snow suddenly disappeared, and I could see what looked like orange lights lining the landscape down towards the coast. It took me a moment to realise I was looking at fire. *This is crazy*, I thought.

While I was viewing these events of 2018 as isolated, odd incidents, Greg Mullins was following the reports of the South Coast fires from his home in Sydney and seeing them as part of a larger pattern. There had been another two serious fires that autumn. One was in the town of Tathra, where seventy-nine homes were destroyed in a single afternoon during a period of some of the highest Forest Fire Danger Indices ever recorded. The other was a major blaze in Holsworthy, in southwestern Sydney, that threatened thousands of homes, a military base and a nuclear reactor, taking 100 trucks and fifteen aircraft to control. It was a fire that Mullins fought, having joined his local RFS as a volunteer in his retirement.

What more evidence do we need? he thought.

January 2019 delivered Australia's hottest month ever recorded. Largely thanks to a wild storm season in northern Australia that sent a burst of heavy rainfall south back in spring, the country avoided major bushfires. 'We dodged a bullet,' says Mullins. But he was certain there was no way we would get so lucky again. The brief rain spell had made no impact on the drought in New South Wales, which was now entering its third year.

Mullins again started calling around former colleagues, this time with a plan and a simple pitch: 'The whole premise is we tell the truth, and we need to tell the truth, because this is really, really bad. I'm frightened.'

In April 2019, with Mullins at the helm, a group calling themselves Emergency Leaders for Climate Action (ELCA) launched to the public, warning that Australia was unprepared for worsening extreme weather. There were twenty-three members, all former leaders of firefighting, emergency services and land management agencies from across every state and territory. It was a grouping unprecedented in Australia, the first time former public servants, the most senior in their field, had galvanised so publicly. Each would have known of the potential consequences; falling out of favour with government is a good way to risk opportunities like consultancy work. But Mullins says they took little convincing, and he only had a couple of knockbacks. Now he hoped the group's 600 years of collective experience would make them impossible to ignore. *Good luck debating me about bushfires*, was his attitude.

In a blitz of media appearances, targeted to pressure the government, ELCA members warned that Australia was set up to fight the fires of the past, not the present. They said our approach of relying on shared resources – sending volunteers and fire trucks between states and using planes leased from the northern hemisphere – was no longer adequate in an era when fire seasons were happening simultaneously in different locations. They warned that the burden placed on volunteers, the bulk of Australia's firefighting force, would be too great in light of what was coming.

Mullins called for extra investment in aerial firefighting assets – something he viewed as one of the most serious gaps in our capabilities. He knew that, behind the scenes, the National Aerial Firefighting Centre, the body that coordinates Australia's aerial firefighting resources, was already lobbying the federal government for extra money, but a business case they put forward back in early 2018 was still languishing, unaddressed, in Canberra.

While Mullins won't name names, he maintains his group had the support of some current emergency services leaders, who felt unable to speak out publicly. ELCA asked for a meeting with Prime Minister Scott Morrison, saying that as they were 'unconstrained by their former employers', they could speak more frankly about the 'rapidly escalating' risks.

It wasn't just Mullins' group sounding a warning about the approaching fire season. In August, the official 'Australian Seasonal Bushfire Outlook' was released. A tool to help fire authorities make strategic decisions about the coming season, it stated that the heavily populated eastern seaboard faced above-normal potential for bushfire. Over a period of eight months, the Bureau of Meteorology delivered more than 100 briefings to the Commonwealth, state and territory governments about the elevated risks.

The weather outlook could hardly have been worse. As well as several years of extreme heat and drought, layered atop decades-long warming and drying trends, another two-pronged force was coming into play. Australia is always prone to year-to-year weather variability, due to cycles that arrive and drive extreme weather – El Niño and La Niña are the best known examples. In the second half of 2019, a cycle called a positive Indian Ocean Dipole (IOD) event occurred; it cooled sea-surface temperatures in the eastern Indian Ocean, and this reduced the rainfall over Australia. At the same time, a rare sudden warming event over Antarctica prompted the Southern Annular Mode (SAM) to dip into the negative, reducing cloud cover over eastern Australia and drawing in hot and dry air.

Together, the positive IOD and negative SAM events supercharged the existing heat and drought.

For a land waiting to burn, there couldn't have been a more perfect storm.

As 2019 drew to a close, I could see the land around me crisp-drying. I'd been following Mullins' warnings in the media, and we were continuing to chip away at our fire preparations – gratefully taking on loan a friend's goat to eat down the long, dry grass around the house – but the prospect of a fire coming to my home still seemed largely theoretical.

Elsewhere on the coast, though, people with far more experience of fire than me were seeing a clearer picture of the dangers that lay ahead.

About 40 kilometres south, Ian Barnes was looking around his community and fearing that 'because they have never experienced big fires, they don't know the threat they are sitting on'.

Barnes is a volunteer with the RFS. He's captain of the brigade in Malua Bay, one of several coastal hamlets squeezed between the coast and the bush, just south of Batemans Bay. As is common on the South Coast, the older area is oceanside, but in recent years a sprawl of new residential housing developments has pushed west – with deep gullies of bush running like ribbons through the estates and backyards edging the trees. For the retirees, sea- and tree-changers, and Canberrans wanting a holiday home, it's the perfect combination – you can see a lyrebird out your window and still be in the ocean in minutes. But Barnes views it purely through his firefighter's lens: it's 'urban interface', a transition zone between wildness and human activity, full of risk.

Before he retired a decade ago, Barnes worked for four decades as a professional forester. Sometimes, when he was tramping the coastal forests, he'd spot what he says the 'old-timers' called a Commonwealth Bank tree: a large eucalypt plumbed with hollows, a proliferation of limbs growing low on the trunk – branches everywhere, like the bank. A tree only develops this form if it has open space, and to Barnes, every rare sighting was a reminder of how we've changed the land since 1788. 'To my mind, especially along the coastal areas where Aboriginal people were mostly settled and there was a lot more ignition taking place, the forests were more of an open grassy woodland.'

Barnes believes the Australian landscape needs controlled burns, both to keep it healthy and to make it less prone to destructive wildfire. 'Fire is the default, and you must have a good reason not to have it,' he says – especially if you're going to build homes close by. One of the reasons he retired early from his job working for State Forests – as it was called before it became Forestry Corporation, a leaner organisation, more focused on the business of logging than forest stewardship – was frustration that he couldn't complete enough hazard reduction, because government cost-cutting meant his staff numbers kept falling.

It's a common complaint from Australians who live close to the land – that we don't do enough hazard reduction. Blame is attributed to a range of targets – from 'greenies' to faceless bureaucrats and their red tape. Scientists have pointed to the fact that as the climate warms, the window for safe burning is shrinking. Barnes thinks there's some truth in all these explanations, but essentially it comes down to an inherent laziness in our attitude to managing the land. 'It is too easy not to do it,' he says.

As the summer of 2019 approached, with forests to the west of Malua Bay thick with bone-dry understorey, he knew this was no longer an option – no one in their right mind would light up now. Barnes weighed up his options. With a slight build, spectacles and an encyclopaedic knowledge of local ecology and fire history, Barnes comes across as more like an academic than a firefighter – but he's fought and managed plenty of serious fires in his time, and he soon came up with a plan to prepare his brigade for the dangerous summer.

He devised a workshop, titled 'Fire from the west – our biggest threat'. It was based on the hypothetical scenario of a fire developing in the remote forests west of town and racing into the urban area. It was not pure conjecture; bushfires of decades past have burned through areas that now contain housing.

Over a weekend in October, at the home of the Malua Bay RFS – a pale green three-bay shed that sits on a hill above the village – Barnes delivered the first part to his brigade members. He saw this part of the workshop as mental preparation: getting them to think about what it would look like, what they would do, if the unthinkable happened.

In November he started the second part, taking his team out of town and into the forests to familiarise themselves with the fire trails and to start mapping the locations of static water supplies such as dams and swimming pools.

But Barnes and his team never completed the workshop, because the South Coast was out of time.

CHAPTER 2

IGNITION

On the evening of Monday, 25 November 2019, inside the multi-storey glass-fronted building in south-western Sydney that is the state headquarters of the Rural Fire Service, staff are gazing up at a wall of screens, watching radar images of storm cells roll across the state with growing apprehension. Earlier that afternoon, the Bureau of Meteorology issued a severe thunderstorm warning for large parts of eastern New South Wales, and through the windows they can already see blue-black storm clouds percolating against the city skyline. Outside, commuters racing to get home can feel an approaching mugginess, nudging aside the dry sting of bushfire smoke that's been hanging over the city for weeks.

Thunderstorms in the midst of a fire season are always a dangerous wildcard: they can deliver fire-quelling rain or start new blazes. A lightning-ignited fire is one of the more pernicious – especially in remote forests, it can smoulder slowly inside the trunk of a tree, like a sleeper agent, before exploding hours, days or even a week later.

Right now, these storms are a liability the RFS doesn't need – it is already facing simultaneous fire emergencies, spread out across vast areas of the state.

The 2019 fire season began in the drought-stricken north of the state back in September. The landscape was so arid that fires sparked easily, spread quickly and proved impossible to extinguish. With dams empty and rivers running dry, the RFS struggled even to source water to fight the fires. It brought in machinery to do dry firefighting when it could, so as not to leave the local communities without drinking water. In October, at a meeting of the senior leaders of all emergency services Australia-wide, the RFS commissioner, Shane Fitzsimmons, warned the road ahead was long. The only way out was decent rainfall – yet none was forecast to arrive until February 2020.

By early November, with the north of the state still burning, new fires were igniting further south. Blazes broke out west of Port Macquarie, in the Blue Mountains and to the northwest of Sydney. On 11 November the New South Wales premier declared a seven-day state of emergency, ahead of what the RFS called 'the most dangerous bushfire week this nation has ever seen'. Flames licked at backyards in the northern Sydney suburb of Turramurra and nearly 600 schools were closed due to the dangerous conditions. The RFS issued a stark public warning, the likes of which few Australians would ever have heard before: 'There are simply not enough fire trucks for every house. If you call for help, you may not get it. Do not expect a fire truck. Do not expect a knock at the door. Do not expect a phone call.'

By the night of 25 November, more than 16,500 square kilometres of the state has burned – an area seven times larger than the Australian Capital Territory. More than 600 homes have been destroyed and six people killed. Hospital emergency departments are seeing a spike in individuals presenting with respiratory problems, brought on by the smoke haze blanketing large parts of the state. As RFS headquarters watches and waits to see what these storms will bring, it has over eighty fires already burning, more than half out of control.

A few hours before midnight, a storm cell starts rolling across the remote hinterland of the South Coast. It's an outlier; the forecast didn't have the storms coming quite this far. Before long it's throwing forks of lightning down into the Bimberamala National Park and the Currowan and Shallow Crossing State Forests.

The Bimberamala is as rugged as the terrain gets out here. The highest ridge reaches 570 metres above sea level before plunging into a deep river gorge; it is a place accessible only to the most adventurous bushwalker. This wildness provides shelter for innumerable treasures, such as old-growth forest and patches of temperate rainforest, animals at threat of extinction, the abandoned relics of a nineteenth-century goldrush and an Aboriginal campsite that predates white settlement.

The state forests are a patchwork. The parts that have never been logged are dense with spotted gums and carpeted by dark green burrawangs; gullies run deep with ferns and cycads. The areas recently felled are thin, the larger trees taken away for sawmill logs, woodchips and firewood, their limbs and canopies discarded in stacks on the forest floor. Older logging compartments are thick with young eucalypt saplings busily competing with wattle and weeds to see who will reach the sun first.

What these forests have in common is that they are all desperately dry.

A few intrepid humans live out this way, in clearings with solar power and patchy mobile-phone reception, connected to the outside world by a vast labyrinth of dirt roads and fire trails that are rarely signposted. But the main witnesses to this storm are the nocturnal animals of the forest. A powerful owl, calling to his mate from a nest in the hollow of a centuries-old tree; a sugar glider, slowly cruising the canopies looking for dinner.

It's dark – the last hours of a waning crescent moon – so when a single fork of lightning comes down and connects with a large eucalypt on the southern end of the Bimberamala, it momentarily lights up the forest like a flash from a giant camera. Then, just as quickly, there is nothing.

When Dave Howes arrives for work in Compartment 212 of the Shallow Crossing State Forest at 7.00 am the next morning, Tuesday, 26 November, there's no sign the overnight storm has splashed even a single drop on the parched landscape. A film of bulldust, dragged up by months of heavy machinery and log trucks tracking the dirt roads, still coats the leaves and puffs up under his boots.

When Howes first started out as a tree feller, it was with a chainsaw – his father began with an axe and crosscut saw – but for the past decade the job's been mechanised. Now he operates a 20-tonne log harvester, a machine that looks like a Transformer, with enormous mechanical limbs – a ten-metre arm that grabs the tree, a hydraulically powered saw to cut it and a set of curved knives to delimb it. It's stinking hot with barely a puff of wind, and as he folds his tall frame into the harvester's cab and starts the trundle down the spine of the ridge into the forest, he thinks, *What a rotten day*.

On a high mountain peak about ten kilometres northwest, a pair of eyes is looking down, scanning for signs of fire. Forestry Corporation has a network of fire towers across the forests of New South Wales it keeps staffed during times of high fire danger. Today, as an added precaution due to the overnight storms, it has a couple of vehicles in the forests since dawn, driving the fire trails and up to known vantage points. But they see nothing.

At 12.30 pm, Howes and his crew stop for lunch. A hot westerly has sprung up. It's howling, blowing dust into their cups of tea. At 1.21 pm, a weather station on the coast picks up a gust of 75 kilometres per hour.

At 1.30 pm, Howes has just climbed back into the harvester when the bloke operating the skidder yells, 'Howsie, look behind you!' He turns to his west and sees a huge, billowing plume of smoke coming up from the forest, growing bigger by the second. The loggers radio the Forestry foreman, who races his vehicle back up to one of the lookouts, his frantic voice soon coming back down the line: 'Park your machines, get out of there.'

No one wants to leave this valuable equipment behind. The harvester alone is worth $1.4 million, the other three machines well over $300,000 combined. But even at top speed these machines move at little over walking pace, and the sky is already turning orange. To the west – the direction of the fire – it's purple and black, like a bruise. Howes and his crew know this thing is coming so fast all they can do is save themselves.

Howes parks the harvester in a clearing and leaps into his vehicle, accelerating hard out of the forest. When he walks in the door of his home thirty minutes later, his pulse is still racing. When Debbie asks why he's home so early, he replies with his typical lack of exaggeration: 'We've been chased out by a big red fire dragon.'

A couple of hours earlier, I had emerged from a morning digging away in the archives of the National Library in Canberra for a writing project to discover the nation's capital bathed in a sepia haze. The overnight storm had ignited a new blaze south-east of the city, and I wondered if this could be the source of the smoke – with so many fires around, it was becoming hard to tell. As I started the drive home, passing dry farm country with paddocks the colour of sand, a fierce wind whipped up and the stands of brittle eucalypts lining the road began to throw bark. The mix of dust and smoke became so murky I needed headlights.

About halfway home I pulled over to make a phone call. I'd scheduled an interview for a feature article about the bushfire season I'd pitched a few weeks earlier to a news magazine. It hadn't taken much journalistic nous to realise that what had been happening in the state's north – where my focus lay – was an enormous story. Small regional communities in northern New South Wales had been experiencing a relentless onslaught from fires that refused to be put out, peppered by devastating strikes: Rappville losing forty-five homes, a quarter of the village, in one evening; Bobbin, fourteen homes in one street and the local school; Wytaliba, half of all homes, devoured in just thirty minutes.

Before I dialled I checked the Fires Near Me app. It features a map pinpointing the presence of any fires in your area and is the official platform for distributing bushfire information. By now I had developed an almost Pavlovian impulse to check it on a certain kind of day; where I live, when it's hot and windy, you might pass a neighbour on the road in through the forest and ask 'Have you checked the app?' in place of a greeting. I could see there was a new fire up ahead, near a little village on the Clyde River called Nelligen. I worried the road might close, so quickly sent a text to cancel the interview and started driving.

In Nelligen, I parked my car and walked onto the bridge that spans the river. First, I just saw wisps of white smoke rising behind the caravan park. But then I looked upriver. Coming up from deep in the forest I could see thick, dark smoke pulsing energetically hundreds of metres into the sky, forming into what looked like a mushroom cloud from a nuclear explosion.

What I was looking at was another angle of the 'big red fire dragon' which was that very moment chasing Dave Howes out of the forest.

Around the village I could hear car doors slamming and vehicles screeching out of driveways. Others stood alongside me on the bridge, transfixed, talking loudly into phones, all eyes locked on this monstrous thing. I walked over to the local café to buy a drink, but the lady behind the counter took a few moments to see me even though I was right in front of her – she was somewhere else – and she put up the *Closed* sign as I left.

I went back to the bridge for one last look. Downriver I saw the approach of a helicopter with a water bucket suspended underneath by a long cable. Once it passed overhead it was framed against the towering plume, where it was headed, and seemed to have shrunk to the size of a child's toy.

I drove away feeling deeply unsettled. Not because I was worried about my home – it was still a good half-hour drive away – but because I was struck by the collective sense of fear I just witnessed. It seemed so incongruous in this familiar, pretty little place.

By this stage of the fire season, only four of the seven Large Air Tankers leased from the northern hemisphere had arrived in the country. A LAT is a firefighting aircraft valued for its ability to swiftly travel long distances and drop large volumes of water or fire retardant – upwards of 35,000 litres, compared to a few thousand litres from a helicopter bucket. Australia only owns one, belonging to New South Wales, so we are almost completely reliant on these planes from overseas to deliver firefighting might. Already there had been signs this fleet – ordered under national arrangements, then shared between the states based on need – was stretched too thin; in mid-November, Queensland's premier wrote to the prime minister requesting a LAT to help with fires in her state and was refused. 'We need more national resources,' she said in a media interview.

Throughout November, Greg Mullins – who said the fire season was unfolding 'exactly as we predicted' – continued to agitate for the urgent ordering of more planes. Emergency Leaders for Climate Action had not managed to secure a meeting with the prime minister, or with any senior government minister, and Mullins said in a radio interview that 'had we spoken back in April, one of the things we would've said is to try to get more aircraft on lease from the northern hemisphere'. In a television appearance, he said that even when all seven LATs did arrive, it still wouldn't be enough. 'They can be a decisive weapon. I just came back from California – they had forty on one fire.'

The federal government continued to maintain that resources were adequate to deal with the fires. In late November, Scott Morrison reassured an increasingly worried nation that the 'national coordination and the response effort' to the fires 'has been outstanding'. The summer of cricket was about to start, and in what seemed an attempt to buoy spirits he tweeted a photo of himself with the Australian cricket captain, captioned, 'For our firefighters and fire-impacted communities, I'm sure our boys will give them something to cheer for.'

Morrison dismissed the need to meet with Mullins and the former fire chiefs, saying he was taking the advice of the 'existing fire chiefs', who were telling him they had what they needed.

However – as the government well knew – a different story was unfolding out of view of the public eye. The peak body for fire and emergency services in Australia had in fact repeatedly been requesting funding from the federal government so additional air support could be secured – and the government wasn't acting.

We only know this because the following year a journalist would secure a trove of documents through a freedom-of-information request.

These documents show that back in August 2019, the Australasian Fire and Emergency Service Authorities Council (AFAC) asked the federal government to address the business case from the National Aerial Firefighting Centre – the one first put back in 2018. In particular, AFAC wanted funding for more Large Air Tankers, stating, 'Facilitating increased availability of LATs provides real and tangible support to rural communities, volunteer firefighters and hinterland communities.'

The federal emergency management minister, David Littleproud, supported this submission as 'having merit'. But the Home Affairs department, headed by Peter Dutton, knocked it back, saying the government didn't have the money.

In mid-November, AFAC tried again, with chief executive Stuart Ellis speaking directly to Littleproud's office and writing a letter. In his letter, Ellis told the minister that continued inaction on the 'compelling' business case 'does no credit to the federal government or fire and emergency services'. He said the simultaneous fires underway across the country had already 'tested available resources', pointing out that if the August request had been met, Queensland would not have missed out on a water-bomber when it needed one. He warned that if fires continued to spread, this would 'increasingly stress the adequacy of existing resources' to a point where 'the assessment may be insufficient available'.

If additional funding came through, he said, then more planes were available for lease from the northern hemisphere. 'It's not too late for this season.' He cautioned against delay, pointing out that there were considerable lead times in getting these aircraft into the country. 'We are confident that upfront investment in mitigation [resources] will reduce economic disruption and post disaster/recovery calls on funding,' Ellis wrote.

The minister responded to Ellis by email, reassuring him that the funding 'is under active consideration'. But David Littleproud was also concerned to ensure this stoush did not become public. Ellis had recently given a media interview in which he stated that Australia *did* have enough air support available, and Littleproud said in the email, 'It is reassuring to hear that we can be confident in your opinion that we currently have sufficient resources.' He encouraged Ellis to keep to this line, for the sake of morale. 'To support the Australian people and provide confidence in our collective efforts, I consider consistency in information and messaging most important and seek your assistance in that regard.'

Just how the emergency services minister thought maintaining public confidence would support the fire effort, he didn't say.

At the new fire on the South Coast that afternoon, the helicopter I'd witnessed heading towards the huge plume pouring from the forest was the only aerial resource that arrived on the scene. From above, the pilot could see the fire was already racing through the tree canopy – what's known as 'crowning'.

Burning branches and clusters of leaves were being hurled a kilometre into the sky; spat-out embers were lighting new spot fires ahead of the front.

Strong wind and turbulence made it too dangerous for the helicopter to get close. On the eastern edge the pilot was able to drop his bucket of water over a clearing where people were running around with hoses, trying to protect horses and stables, but his machine was no match for a fire behaving in this way, and he could do nothing to stop the spread.

Over the following hours, in homes and workplaces along the South Coast, the pagers of RFS volunteers started going off. There was enormous confusion about exactly where the fire was – the first RFS truck drove around the dirt roads for two and a half hours before they saw flame. By the time many of the trucks got into the forest it was night, and there was still no clearer picture.

Gary Creer had just knocked off work at the correctional centre in the town of Nowra, about an hour north of the fire, when he got the call. Creer is the captain of the RFS brigade in the little estuary-side village of Basin View. At forty-seven, he's one of the younger volunteers, but he's always maintained that 'while we lean on the elderly side we have a lot of experience', and that night he was especially glad of this.

As he drove with his crew into what looked like 'mountain goat country', he had on board seventy-two-year-old Carolyn Goodland, a twenty-four-year veteran of the RFS who was also an amateur history buff with a specialty in the old gold mines of this back country. In the black smoke-filled night, she guided them with confidence through the labyrinth of narrow dirt roads she knew by heart, hunting for the fire. They came upon it when they rounded a bend, discovering it burning over both sides of the road. With no way of turning around, Creer told his driver to put his foot down and they burst through, getting ahead of the fire.

After reporting back to the RFS officer in charge, Creer was told to put in a back-burn, a commonly used firefighting technique. The idea is to slowly burn a deep line in front of the fire's path so that by the time it arrives there is no fuel left to consume. Night, with its cooler temperatures and moisture in the air, is usually considered the ideal time to light a back-burn.

But as soon as Creer put a touch of flame to the ground, it didn't trickle slowly like it was supposed to but took off at speed, the ground in front of it combusting. He tried a couple more small patches but got the same result; strange behaviour for a night fire. Nervous about starting something he couldn't control, he abandoned the strategy.

There was little else they could do. To chase after the fire would be dangerous and most likely futile. Once it moved off-road and delved into bushland, they wouldn't be able to access it; and even if it did come out to the road, a handful of people with hoses couldn't stop a fast-moving bushfire.

Creer and his crew pulled in near a property by the river to wait – if the fire came to them, they'd help defend the house. But it didn't, so they spent the hours leading up to dawn and their shift's end huddled in their cold truck, trying to nap.

Dave Howes made one last mad dash back into the burning forest late that night. While the harvester he had left behind didn't belong to him – it was owned by the contractor he worked for – he was worried that if it was destroyed, he'd be out of a job. So, along with Debbie and their son Steven, he drove in, passing through fire and falling trees, Debbie saying more than once, 'What the hell are we doing out here? This is ludicrous.' He didn't see any fire vehicles, just beekeepers hammering along the road in their flatbed trucks, hives thrown hastily in back. When they arrived at the logging compartment, every tree was blasted to smithereens and the bulldozer had been incinerated, but the harvester was unscathed.

It was a night of confusion and small wins. Some fire trucks drove around for hours, unable to find the fire; others pulled out early, assessing that it was futile. Some RFS crews helped landholders steer the fire away from their properties, and no homes were lost. But the fire ran as it pleased.

Fires run, but they also rest. And by the early hours of Wednesday morning, 27 November, around twelve hours after it was first sighted, this new South Coast fire had finished its explosive start. At 4.00 am, an RFS plane with an infrared line scanner attached flew overhead and captured its form – a jagged blob on the landscape, measuring around 25 square kilometres.

At the RFS headquarters in Sydney, it was added to the tally.

CHAPTER 3

THE ONE THAT
GOT AWAY

I wake early, uneasy, on Wednesday morning. When I got home the day before, after driving away from Nelligen, I was surprised to see the smoke plume rising up in the far distance beyond the ridge behind our house. The fire was closer than I'd realised.

I start hunting through the collection of topographic maps we've accumulated over years of camping and exploring the back country, laying them out on the dining table and comparing them to what the Fires Near Me app is showing, trying to plot the exact location of the fire. Phone calls and text messages are streaming between the homes in our local area and community Facebook pages are filling with comments. *Should we be worried? Where is it heading?*

The fire is still out in the forests, around 20 kilometres inland from the coast. The RFS has downgraded it to the lowest alert level, which says there 'Is no immediate danger'. But it is still classified as 'out of control'.

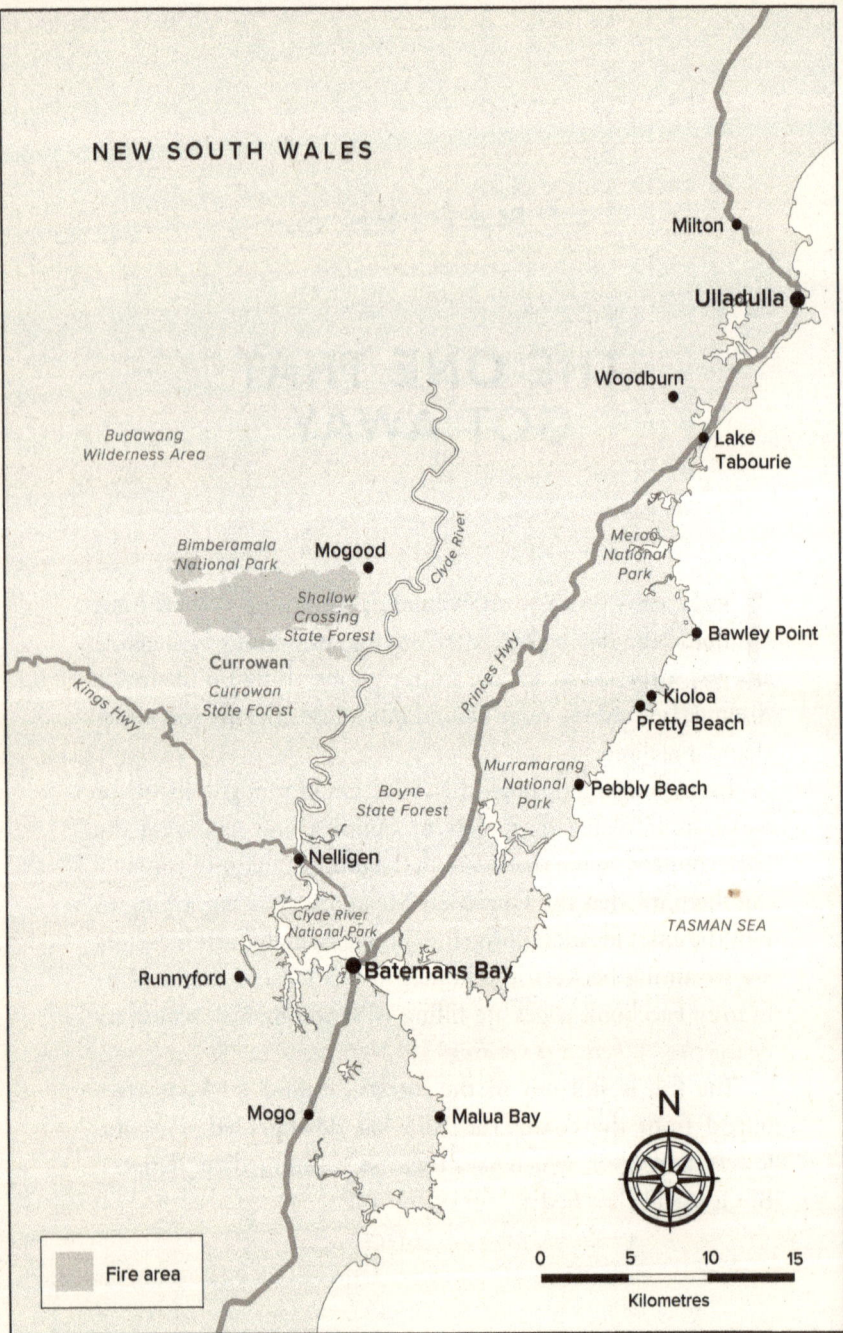

NEW SOUTH WALES

Milton

Ulladulla

Woodburn

Lake
Tabourie

*Budawang
Wilderness Area*

*Bimberamala
National Park*

Clyde River

*Merao
National
Park*

Mogood

*Shallow
Crossing
State Forest*

Bawley Point

Currowan

*Currowan
State Forest*

Kings Hwy

Kioloa
Pretty Beach

*Boyne
State Forest*

Princes Hwy

*Murramarang
National
Park*

Pebbly Beach

Nelligen

*Clyde River
National Park*

TASMAN SEA

Runnyford

Batemans Bay

Mogo

Malua Bay

N

Fire area

0   5   10   15

Kilometres

Many of us are taking solace from the knowledge it is still west of the Clyde River, a long body of water that cuts through the hinterland like a ribbon. We see this as a barometer of our safety and hope the river will stop it escaping from the back country and coming for the coast.

Unlike those of us at home working our devices, Bruce Shea is not the kind to trust what he hears in the media or from authorities such as the RFS: he likes to see things for himself, make his own decisions. Just before dawn that morning, Shea, ruddy-haired and in his early fifties, a self-described 'bushman', had got in his vehicle and driven west to find the fire. He is working as a farm manager for an equestrian centre and horse stud near the coastal village of Bawley Point, due west of the fire, so needs to know exactly what this thing is up to.

There wouldn't be a road or fire trail out in these forests he hasn't been through more than a hundred times before, much of it on horseback. His great-great-grandfather was one of the first white settlers out here in 1860, when a small village named Currowan was being planned for the banks of an estuary of the Clyde, and the original landholding is still in his family. There's no village anymore, but the locality is still called Currowan, as is the adjacent state forest.

The early colony didn't just co-opt land. A census taken by a white explorer in 1842 records 'Currowan' as the name of one of the many clan groups of the Yuin people – the original custodians of the South Coast. The entire region is patterned with place names drawn from the Yuin: Yatte Yattah, Ulladulla, Broulee, Nowra.

It doesn't take Shea long to find an eastern edge of the fire. The hot westerly winds of the day before are gone, replaced by a cool morning with just a hint of a gentle nor'easter, so the fire has lost all rage and speed. He's able to walk right up to it, filming with his phone and narrating what he sees. 'This is her,' he says, approaching a slow, ankle-high fire trickling through the leaf litter. 'Sneaking along doing a lovely job, actually. If it was July, I'd be inclined to let the bastard go.'

Like many of his ilk, Shea is not afraid of using fire to clear the scrubby understories of the forest – he thinks there should be more of it – but he knows now is not the time. He calls his cousin to join him. They've got some shovels and rakes in the ute, good tools for dry firefighting, and together they ponder, *Maybe we should just hook in and put this thing out?*

A vehicle comes down the road. It's a man from Forestry Corporation who tells them they better move on. The fire has been declared a Section 44, which means that under law the RFS commissioner is now in charge of all firefighting operations. His cousin doesn't like being told to leave, but Shea pulls him in. He knows how this works: the RFS won't be using bushies in utes to fight this thing – they're better off going and preparing their own properties.

Ninety kilometres away, inside a warehouse-like building on the edge of the industrial area in the large town of Nowra, RFS superintendent Mark Williams is leading a newly formed incident management team that is poring over maps and studying weather forecasts, trying to plan a response to this new fire, which has now been given a name: the Currowan fire.

While RFS headquarters in Sydney has an overarching role in the coordination of fires around the state, including decisions about releasing additional resources, the day-to-day management of fires comes from regional fire control centres like this one. Under the RFS structure it's the staff, who wear white shirts, who will make the plans; and the volunteers in their signature yellow who will physically fight the fires.

This is only Williams' second day back in the Nowra office, where he's usually based. He's just spent seventy-five days on secondment as an incident controller on the North Coast fires. It was all still going on up there when RFS headquarters tapped him on the shoulder and said it was time to come home, in case fires started on his home turf. A twenty-year veteran of the RFS, Williams initially felt a flash of reluctance – he didn't like walking away from a job unfinished.

But Williams turns his attention to what is before him. The Currowan fire is burning in a remote area, with a perimeter now around 30 kilometres in length. On his side is the weather; the next four days are forecast to be mild, so the fire won't be moving far. What he won't have is any more aerial resources, other than the single helicopter of the day before – headquarters has told him everything is already earmarked for elsewhere.

Williams is neither surprised nor upset by this. He knows that with so many fires burning across the state, RFS headquarters is 'playing chess with all these pieces and you've got that finite resource'. The RFS has a statutory obligation to protect life, property and the environment – and it does so in that order. Williams understands that if he's asking for resources to help tackle a fire burning in remote bushland on the South Coast, he'll be trumped every time by an incident controller elsewhere who has a fire coming towards homes or critical infrastructure.

'You fight the threat and the highest priority level that you've got at the time,' he says of the way the system works. 'So, if life is directly under threat, that's your highest priority, as opposed to something that you know darn well is probably going to bite you in the backside in two days' time, but at the moment it's not at that level.'

Williams and his team come up with a strategy: they will try to box the Currowan fire in by surrounding it with containment lines – many kilometres of back-burns. The idea is to take advantage of the mild conditions to put in the back-burns, so that when the weather turns and the Currowan fire starts running again, the already burned lines of the box will stop it escaping. On its eastern side, they will rely on the Clyde River to hold it back.

Ideally, with a strategy like this, Williams would keep the original fire small by making the box fit as tightly as possible. But he decides he has to change tack because of the exceptional dryness of the landscape. It's so flammable, he calculates the odds of success are higher if he pulls the containment lines further back, to places he thinks have a better chance of holding – for example, somewhere with a wider road to back-burn off. Making the box this big, though, means the Currowan fire will be allowed to double in size before it hits the containment lines.

It will be what Williams calls 'a campaign job'. It's a labour-intensive plan, so RFS volunteers from brigades all over the South Coast are called in, heading out into the forests for twelve-hour shifts, day and night.

Over the following four days, from Wednesday to Saturday, I swing between two vastly different alternate realities – preparing for the possibility of an imminent life-threatening emergency and continuing on with life as usual.

The presence of the fire in the forests dominates our home life. Chris joined our local RFS brigade at Bawley Point as a volunteer a few years earlier. Like many volunteers with day jobs or family responsibilities, he opts for the night shifts – getting on the truck in the evening and coming back from the bush at dawn. For some South Coast volunteers, it's their second campaign of the season. When I speak one morning to a man doing some work on our property – he too having just come off a night shift on the Currowan fire – he mentions almost as an aside that he also fought the fires on the North Coast, and was present when a horrific firestorm hit the village of Nymboida, destroying eighty-five houses.

I start pulling out our bags of stored fire kit – rags to block gutters, fireproof clothing, goggles – and charging head torches. When I go to a local hardware store to buy extra sprinklers I discover others are thinking similarly; there are only a few left and the shop has already sold out of firefighting pumps. I notice the odd burned leaf flutter down onto our lawn, and flinch when I see an ambulance parked near my kids' bus stop – there as part of the staging post for the firefighting operation to our west.

I feel a constant, thrumming anxiety, but I still do the grocery shopping and fret about not having sourced a costume for my daughter's school Christmas carols concert, scheduled for the following week. On Friday night, I drink wine at my neighbour's house, admiring her newly fitted-out kitchen.

I also continue working on my magazine article. I make the phone call I cancelled the day I saw the Currowan fire start from Nelligen. It is to a former senior ranger from the National Parks and Wildlife Service, who now works for one of the unions that covers its staff. National parks employees are a small but essential component of the state's professional firefighting ranks and a valuable source of knowledge about landscapes. He tells me that a recent state government restructure of the organisation has seen them lose dozens of senior staff, including some of their most experienced fire managers. On-going 'efficiency dividends' are being met by not back-filling positions; they started the fire season with nearly 100 vacancies, mostly frontline firefighting positions. He tells me he's just seen an organisational chart for an area that takes in a large national park not far from me, which shows six vacancies. 'If that area lights up, who knows who will be putting them out,' he says.

On Friday I email a woman from a fire-affected community on the North Coast, requesting an interview. I explain to her, 'I'm trying to paint a picture of what the fires were like for those who experienced them first-hand.'

Lots of people that week are trying to anticipate what the fire will do. Phil Butler is living with his wife and son in a little tin shed they have set up as home, on a property out near the Clyde River. He's already been thinking for a while that it is time to move on, but once the fire starts, he decides the time is now.

Butler is a Budawang man, part of the Yuin Nation. Now in his early fifties, he spent most of his boyhood in his Country, but without knowing much about his culture. He lived on a rural property with his dad, also a Yuin man, who worked hard and expected the same of his son. Butler remembers, when he was horse-riding in the bush as a teenager, coming across caves at a place called Burrill Lake, where the walls are adorned with rock art dating back 20,000 years. He was awestruck and told his dad what he'd seen – but his father simply chipped him for skiving off on his jobs.

Decades ago, Butler and I went through the same South Coast public high school, a handful of years apart, and I've got no memories of ever being taught anything about the original custodians of the land upon which we both lived.

Butler left school and the South Coast in his mid-teens. After a couple of decades living away, with good times but also mistakes and a fair burden of grief, he came back home when he was forty, to try to find his way. His father's brother, a respected Budawang elder called Uncle Noel Butler, embraced him with teaching, and for the past decade Butler has been immersing himself in his culture – learning the songlines, dances and language of his Country.

A couple of years ago he took a job with a private landholder, moving out to the property near the Clyde and helping him restore his land, including with cool burning – the kind of hazard reduction work Butler used to see his father relentlessly undertake when he was a boy, now commonly known as cultural burning. But this week, he packs up everything of value he owns – photos, birth certificates, treasured memorabilia – and moves to a new home: a campsite in a national park called Meroo, on the coast.

Meroo Lake is part of Butler's songlines and has deep spiritual significance for him. It's also special because his grandfather camped here as a young man, back when Aboriginal people were still being forcibly relocated around the South Coast. He chooses a campsite close enough to the road in so he can still get his son to school, but also near the beach, in case the fire comes in. Surrounded by his ancestors and culture, he feels recharged and safe.

Meanwhile, out at the Currowan fire, some observers are watching how the containment plan is unfolding with a growing sense of alarm.

The plan drawn up by Williams and the incident management team in Nowra to build a box with back-burns is an enormous undertaking – firefighters have to light up lengths totalling nearly 40 kilometres. But lighting up is only the start of the job. For a back-burn to be effective, it needs time to burn deeply enough that the firefront doesn't just run right over the top of it, and its edges need to be properly extinguished so it doesn't become the source of a new wildfire. As the RFS training manual cautions, 'If a back-burn is not controlled it may only make the situation worse … if conditions are too unfavourable, or there is not sufficient time for a back-burn to create a sufficiently deep buffer ahead of an approaching wild-fire, it may be futile and dangerous for fire crews to attempt.'

Yet in the rush to get these back-burns in before the weather turns, rules are being broken. Because fire reaches its maximum rate of spread once it is 100 metres long, the preference is to light a back-burn in a series of spots or limit it to shorter lengths – but on this fire, many kilometres of continuous lines are going in every day. A number of witnesses – both experienced firefighters and private landholders – observe that the edges are not being thoroughly extinguished, called 'blacking out'. At times, the blacking-out is slapdash, and follow-up patrols – to make sure the back-burns are out – are infrequent. As one observer notes, 'If it worked, that would be lovely, but the bush was just too dry and there were just not enough people, or time, to properly put the back-burns out.'

On Thursday, 28 November, one of the back-burns escapes, breaking out of the western side of the box and heading off unchallenged into an even more remote and inaccessible land-scape. One RFS volunteer who turns up the next morning to work on this section of the line grumbles, 'Whoever was on last night didn't do their job and they allowed the fire to jump.'

Perhaps there was poor technique involved, but the larger problem is that there is too much to do in too little time. On a fire of this size in any other season, RFS crews outside the area would have flooded in to assist, but with so many fires in the state, the South Coast brigades are on their own.

On Friday, back-burning starts on the northern side of the box, lit off a road nearly nine kilometres ahead of the fire-front. Racing along with drip torches – handheld tools that drop flammable liquid on the ground – RFS crews light up around ten kilometres in length without pause. Employees of Forestry Corporation and National Parks are also involved in the fire operation, and some are horrified when they learn the incident management team in Nowra is also sending in a heli-copter to drop incendiaries, to further deepen the back-burn. Knowing this part of the terrain well – they traverse these landscapes for a living – they're not confident a back-burn started in this spot can be prevented from escaping.

So much fire is being allowed into a tinder-dry landscape, both from back-burns and by permitting the fire front to steadily march towards the lines of the box. Some National Parks staff seek to raise their concerns with the incident management team in Nowra but, having lost a huge swathe of their most experienced local fire managers in the recent restructure – individuals who could hold sway – they feel it is harder to get their voices heard. They also think the team in Nowra has been left poorer by the absence of the wisdom of these old hands who know the landscapes best.

A few of the more experienced RFS volunteers are also uneasy about what they regard as signs of disorganisation. Some crews are being sent out without paper maps of the fire-ground, and are having to rely on iPads and mobile phones for navigation, even though the forests are full of communication black spots. A couple of times they're not given a clear briefing or tasked with a proper plan.

The run of mild weather is anticipated to end on Saturday, 30 November – storms and severe winds are forecast. The containment box is about to face its first test.

The wind comes in over the heart of the Currowan fire on Saturday evening, going from dead calm to gale force in an instant. The fire explodes – off and racing. Firefighters' radios crackle to life with the order to immediately evacuate all non-essential personnel from the forests. 'Pull out, pull out, pull out,' is what one firefighter hears – *It sounds like it's all going to custard*, he thinks – before he loses communications altogether when the temporary radio-relay station is overrun. His crew heads west, towards Canberra, to take the long way out of the forests – likely a lifesaving decision.

On a dirt road deep in the forest a couple of kilometres away, Dave Howes finds himself racing for his life for the second time in a week. After the destruction of the logging coupe, he switched over to working with fire crews on 'make safe' operations – using his harvester to clear the roads of the huge number of trees, already stressed by drought, that were toppling like ninepins in the wake of the fire. Now he is being showered with embers and the fire front is coming so quickly there is no hope of outrunning it. He's working with a water tanker and a couple of fire trucks, and together they decide the only option is to make a break for already-burned areas. The other vehicles take off at speed, but there is no way Howes is going to chance leaving the harvester behind again. He's got his foot to the floor, thinking, *This is pretty hairy.*

Gary Creer's brigade from Basin View has two trucks in the forest when it suddenly goes from 'just a bushfire to like all hell had broken loose'. In exceptionally bad timing, the fan belt on one breaks with a loud bang, shattering the radiator. With the truck spewing coolant, the driver nurses it along with grim determination until they make it safely to the river.

The panic escalates when fire starts to spot over the eastern side of the Clyde. This is the most serious breach of the containment box possible: if the Currowan fire takes hold on this side of the river, it will have a string of coastal villages – like Bawley Point and Kioloa – in its sights.

Fire crews rush over the causeway that crosses the river, chasing the flying sparks and embers at a distance from the main fire. But amid the chaos, haphazard things are happening. One senior firefighter comes across an RFS crew with a drip torch out, putting in their own back-burn on the east side of the river. They say it is a tactical burn – something crews can do in an emergency situation without pre-planning – but he is furious, believing it shows poor judgement, and radios into Nowra, telling them to get this crew back to town.

A spot fire does take hold on the wrong side of the river, at a place called the Berry farm. So that night, a cavalcade of fire trucks is sent in to contain this new threat, using a back-burn to stop it in its tracks.

One of the many RFS crews working throughout the night at the Berry farm is from Malua Bay, led by Captain Ian Barnes. Barnes says that while the back-burn is 'effective' in halting the spot fire, the mop-up and patrol is 'woeful'. The main job that night is blacking out, and Barnes says, 'We did our bit. We were slower than most because we did it more thoroughly.' But not everyone is working the same way. 'I saw one truck driving by, just spraying water. That was their attempt to black out,' he says.

As a forester with a background in dry firefighting, Barnes eschews the use of water alone to put out fire. 'You have to get down and dirty,' he says. 'You pull logs down. You have one person with a rake hoe, one with a nozzle, and you must investigate everything, turn everything over. I have always drilled it into my members, blackout is the most important part. Because if you are going to spend millions of dollars of public money and god knows how many hours of volunteers and it gets away from one jump over, what is the point?'

By 6.00 am on Sunday, 1 December, their twelve-hour shift over, Barnes can see that while 'a lot of mopping up had been done, it was nowhere near complete'. He can't understand why there isn't heavy machinery on site: 'In my days you would have had a tractor there as soon as possible to deal with the mopping up.' But still, there are plenty of fire trucks. 'When we left that morning, it was like a bloody traffic jam up there.'

Bruce Shea knows a strong westerly wind is forecast for early that afternoon, and he wants to check where the fire is. Not long after Barnes leaves the scene, Shea makes another foray into the forests. When he arrives at the Berry farm, sometime around 7.00 am, there isn't a fire truck in sight. On his way in he'd seen a large group of trucks pulled up at a petrol station on the highway, getting breakfast at the end of their night shift. But there is no sign they've been replaced, and he can see what he estimates to be a two-kilometre length of back-burn flaring. 'The trees were spitting out sparks, there was fuel up to your waist,' he says.

Certain the run for the coast is now on, he starts hammering back towards Bawley Point, pulling in on the way to an isolated little weatherboard petrol station on the highway. He knows the owner is new to the area, so he asks her what her fire plan is. She tells him she's going to clean out the gutters in a few days and passes him an RFS public information map that a crew has just dropped off, showing the fire still on the west of the river.

'Nuh,' says Shea, reaching over the counter and grabbing a pen, colouring in the new position of the fire. 'This thing is going to be on you this afternoon,' he tells her.

At home this Sunday morning, I'm oblivious to what has been unfolding in the forests over the last twenty-four hours. It is the first day of summer; sun is streaming in through the windows as I colour in with my daughter, contemplating doing something about the weekend clutter of unfolded laundry and discarded schoolbags.

Soon our phones start to ring. Word is spreading that the fire has jumped the river at the Berry farm. The Fires Near Me app is still showing it hasn't – but the app has been problematic all week, oftentimes appearing out of date.

Other fire-threatened communities across the state are having a similar issue with the app. The most accurate way of mapping the path of a fire is with an infra-red line scanner, mounted to an aircraft that flies directly over the fire, capturing an image – a line scan – that is transmitted directly back to operation centres via satellite. This line scan is then used by planners, who can also share the information about the precise location of the fire with the public through the Fires Near Me app. But the RFS only has a couple of aircraft suitable for this task. There is also a shortage of specialist mappers and aircraft observers. At times, smoke stops the planes from flying, but primarily it is a lack of aircraft that means most blazes across the state are only getting a small number of snapshots.

Chris and I choose to believe what we are hearing on the ground. We know that if the fire is coming through the Berry farm with a westerly wind behind it, this is bad news for Bawley Point and Kioloa. But as we are a good seven kilometres north, it doesn't place us directly in the firing line. Still, as a precaution, we decided to pack our valuables and get our children out – I'll take them to my parents' house, about 30 kilometres north.

I pack slowly, mindful of keeping it minimal so it won't be a pain to unpack later. One of our kids has band practice at a house about halfway between our place and my parents' mid-afternoon, so I decide to time our leaving with that.

At 3.41 pm, above the din of four eleven-year-olds playing drums and electric guitar in a small suburban garage, I hear a text message come through on my phone. It is an emergency alert from the RFS for our locality: *Seek shelter as the fire impacts. It is too late to leave.*

I am wildly confused. I run outside and look south to see a churning smoke plume many times bigger than my first sighting of the Currowan fire taking over the skyline. Straightaway, I ring my parents and ask if they can come and get the kids and our belongings, and then I start pulling the boxes of our precious things out of the car and dumping them onto the grass at the end of the cul-de-sac. 'It's fine, it's fine, everything's okay,' I say to my children as I leap into the car and then charge away without them.

There are no other cars heading south with me down the highway, towards the fire. But in the northbound lane, I can see the beginnings of the exodus from Bawley Point and Kioloa. Cars pulling boats and trailers, roof racks packed high with layers of surfboards. I have no idea what I'm driving into and my heart is hammering.

Around the same time, 100 kilometres south, on a sportsground parched the colour of bone, a historic gathering of the Yuin Nation is just winding up.

All weekend, hundreds of Yuin people from along the

South Coast have been gathered here, at the foot of Gulaga Mountain. Organisers say it's been one of the largest comings-together of the Yuin since colonisation; men, women and children, painted and decorated, dancing and singing, playing clapsticks and didgeridoos. The Yuin Elder who called this *bunaan*, or corroboree, said it was to heal the country and call the rain. 'The country is sick,' he said. 'It's time for something to happen, some healing.'

Phil Butler has been there for the whole weekend, dancing and connecting with his mob. It's already been 'the single, most strongest, amazing event of my life', but when he feels a few spits of rain coming down just as he is leaving, he's exhilarated, feeling a real 'buzz'.

The buzz follows him as he drives up the highway towards his campsite at Meroo. His wife is with him, but his son is away with friends for the weekend. As they get closer to home, he starts to notice native animals, kangaroos and wallabies, coming out of the bush onto the edge of the highway, and he begins to worry.

When he gets to the turn-off into Meroo, a fire truck and a national parks vehicle are blocking the entrance. 'It's too late,' they tell him. 'The fire's coming. You can't go in.'

CHAPTER 4

THE RUN FOR
THE COAST

As I pull back into our property that Sunday afternoon, Chris is already on the roof, kitted out in his fire clothing, filling the gutters with water. It's all happening so fast my mind can't catch up with what's going on; when I run outside to help dressed only in summer clothes and Chris yells down that I need to get my fire gear on, I'm momentarily surprised. *Really? Already?*

We can't see any signs of fire, but we fill gutters, close windows and empty the decks of anything flammable. Outdoor furniture, kids' craft materials, shoes and potted plants all get shoved in a pile inside. Once the house is battened down, Chris tells me he's leaving. His brigade is doing a night shift and needs volunteers.

RFS volunteers face split loyalties all the time. But this doesn't mean it comes without stress and pressure on families, and on this occasion I respond less than graciously to the call for sacrifice: 'Are you fucking kidding me?' is some of what I say.

But Chris has checked the maps and the hourly weather

forecasts and says he doesn't think the fire will hit our place that evening; if it does, he'll get back as soon as he can.

That night it's just the dog and me, on watch. I set an alarm for every two hours but never really sleep, padding around the house as silent as a thief. Our home is on the edge of a mountain and I keep returning to the vantage point of the deck; looking across the forests that sweep down towards the ocean and Meroo Lake, and back to the west, at the dark form of the ridge, where somewhere beyond I know the fire is lurking. Having never been in a bushfire before, I'm not sure exactly what it is I'm looking for, or what I'll see if it comes.

I must have dozed off, because around 3.00 am I'm jolted awake to the lights of a truck moving through the trees below. After a moment's confusion, I realise it is a beekeeper, coming to remove his hives out of the forest. I've recently read a news story about apiarists devastated by the loss of their bees in the North Coast fire, so seeing this, I think, *He must know something*. Any uncertainty – lingering hope – that maybe this fire won't happen to us instantly dissolves.

Chris arrives home just before dawn. By mid-morning Monday we still can't see any signs of fire at our place, but just south, the Currowan fire is now well and truly out of its box and running hard towards the coast – coming from the area of the Berry farm, where crews had been working in the early hours of Sunday morning.

It is a devastating blow for those who had worked hard to contain it. 'All that back-burning and effort we put in that night was completely lost, it just disappeared,' says Ian Barnes. 'People will say, *Ah, you shouldn't have back-burned, that's why it got away*. Well, I was there. If we had not back-burned it, it would have got away on a wider front, to be honest. The reason it got away was that we were not able to keep it contained in the back-burn area. And then you have to ask the question, why couldn't we do that?'

The Currowan fire is barrelling out of control towards a string of seven coastal villages, including Bawley Point and Kioloa, where residents are being warned to seek shelter. It is only now that it's heading towards built-up population areas that RFS headquarters in Sydney releases extra resources. Fire crews from outside the region start arriving, as do water-bombing and reconnaissance aircraft. One of the Large Air Tankers flies down from the RAAF base in Richmond, Sydney, laying down lines of pink fire retardant behind the village of Kioloa.

While those of us living outside the villages in the semi-rural areas would love to look up and see planes in the sky, none of us are under any illusion this will happen.

Someone on a property near us sets up a WhatsApp group, and it pings nonstop as more and more people join, sharing the names and locations of those who are preparing to stay and defend their homes.

Our central preoccupation is figuring out exactly where the fire is. We all know there must be escapes coming out of the box from places other than the Berry farm, but we don't know where. West of us, people are driving up to vantage points, hunting for signs of smoke. Fire rarely moves as a uniform wave – it's more likely to come in fingers, reaching across the landscape. Knowing which gully or hill the fire is moving along is a vital clue as to whether it's going to skim the edge of your property or barrel right through it; whether it will be upon you in hours or days.

Chris and I are most concerned about the fire coming through a low-slung saddle on the mountain to our west. If it comes either side we think it likely to move slower, but if it comes directly through the saddle we fear the terrain will serve as a funnel, shooting it at speed in what would be a catastrophic scenario for us.

The Fires Near Me app is not keeping up with what is happening, and on the ground it feels like we are flying blind.

Throughout the day we sharpen our preparation. Chris scrambles up the hill with a shovel to our water tank to heap dirt upon any sections of exposed underground pipes while I crawl on my stomach under the house, sweeping away dry leaves and debris with my arms. But when a hot westerly wind kicks in at lunchtime I lose my nerve and know this means I have to leave.

Really, it's been a foolish gamble staying as long as I have. Staying and defending your home is an enormous decision to make – it's an act that requires both physical and mental fortitude – but it is one I've always prevaricated on. *Maybe I would, maybe I wouldn't.* This indecision itself was a sign I was leaving myself dangerously exposed to a situation I wasn't fully prepared to handle.

As I drive away, I say to Chris, 'Stay on your phone.' He yells a quick goodbye. It is a moment of immense weight; him staying behind to face the danger alone. But we are both so wired with adrenaline neither of us pause to make this anything other than a transactional departure.

Pulling onto the highway to drive north to my parents' house feels as if I am entering a no-man's land. The Currowan fire has closed a 35-kilometre stretch of the Princes Highway, the main route that runs down the east coast. When I approach the police roadblock further north, I stop to ask if I will be allowed to return once I leave. No, comes the answer. It is one-way only, out of the fire zone.

Throughout that Monday night and into Tuesday, I keep tracking the path of the fire. My main tools are our WhatsApp group and listening in on the radio communications of RFS volunteers out in the field, picking up reports of where they are seeing fire and where the triple-zero calls are coming in from. While I can't physically fight the fire, I want to do anything I can to help those I know are still in the fire zone.

On Tuesday afternoon, I am relieved to hear that the school Christmas carols concert is cancelled because of the unfolding fire emergency – I still don't have my daughter's costume organised and have been wondering how I was going to simultaneously listen to carols and the RFS radio channel. But my son has cricket training, which can't be missed, even in case of fire.

After picking him up from school – the fire radio up loud on the car speakers – I pull in at the cricket oval. With the large topographic maps spread out beside me on the passenger seat, iPad propped on the dashboard, notebook and pen in hand, I watch kids run down balls while listening to the sudden dramatic escalation of the fire.

It is close now. I've already heard the last trucks pull out of the forest a couple of hours earlier – 'It's beaten us,' a firefighter said – and now the WhatsApp group is pinging with direct sightings.

It's taken a run up the mountain and spotted across the hwy into back of kennys. Dig in folks

I'm watching major black smoke heading up the hill behind yours

can u see flames?

There is brief excitement when someone thinks they can hear the whirring of a helicopter, but nothing appears.

I'm on a hill in lemon tree and it's hammering it's going to spot like crazy. Go is what I'm saying no bombers no nuthin

Keep the intel coming in

Go now to mine. Go.

The cricket field is on a headland in Ulladulla, about 20 kilometres north of where it is all happening. Looking south, I can see the plumes of smoke above where we live getting thicker and darker. The whole sky is turning orange, and as balls and witches hats are collected, a sepia haze starts drifting across the field.

Back at my parents' home, I speak to Chris several times. He is inside the house, smoked in, unable to see without a torch. I am looking at the paper map, tracking reports of fires starting to break out in a fan shape to the east of our property – which is puzzling, because the fire front is coming from the west. Then I understand. The fire is spotting ahead of itself. Which means that it has to be coming through the saddle with incredible ferocity; our property is about to be hit from multiple directions.

I call Chris, but he doesn't need my theory about what is going to happen. Moments earlier he'd been outside turning on a water pump when a wall of flame suddenly came blasting up the hill through the canopies and he'd had to sprint for the house. Within minutes, fire burst through from all the surrounding forests into the asset protection zone and wrapped around the house, licking at the footings.

When he calls me about twenty minutes later, I can hardly hear for the roar in the background and the heave in his voice, but I hear him say he needs help. I don't know if he's gone outside again, so I yell, 'Get in the house!' before the phone cuts out.

Chris is asthmatic, and I don't like how he was breathing. I call triple zero but end the call not confident they understood the location of our hard-to-find property, so I ring Chris's deputy captain in his RFS brigade. 'We'll get him,' he says.

The Currowan fire has now exploded out of the back country and is descending on numerous semi-rural properties in our area; I can hear the names of familiar locations coming through on the radio. On the WhatsApp group, someone asks, *Has anyone heard from Chris?*

I try his phone a few more times but it keeps ringing out. There is nothing to do but wait.

I turn off the radio – just useless noise now – and shut myself in a room at my parents' house, my brother crouching silently beside me. Through the window, I can hear the sound of my children and their cousins playing outside. After a while, I stand to pull aside the curtain. Watching them in the grey dusk, running and rolling across the lawn in their school uniforms, I know they are oblivious to the precipice it feels like our family is standing on. With all my will, I hope they'll never experience what it would feel like to fall.

The news that the Bawley Point RFS crew has successfully retrieved Chris comes through within an hour, a period of time that feels fathomless.

The first report I hear is that he is unconscious – which is not true – and then that he is okay but being taken out to the staging post for the fire operation so he can be checked over by paramedics. I need to see for myself, so my brother drives me there to meet them.

The staging post is on the border of the fire zone, in a large park that has been temporarily repurposed. It is a place I've spent hundreds of hours at with my kids when they were younger. But in the dark, walking past the barbecues and the children's play equipment, the grassed area now dense with fire trucks and ambulances, it feels like arriving into a scene in a disaster film – though one badly glitching, with images coming in fragments.

When I find Chris and the crew, he's already been checked over by paramedics and cleared; he is *fine*, disliking the fuss. There is no emotional reunion. He seems almost hyper, adrenaline pumping, impatient to get back on the truck to keep fighting the fire elsewhere. I, of course, want him to come with me.

The crew are in a state of deep quiet. They've all just been through a terrifying experience. When the Bawley Point captain, Charlie Magnuson, had radioed his group officer to tell him he was going in after Chris, he was told, 'Charlie, I strongly recommend you do not go up there, but if you are, I wish you luck.' When they arrived at the long entrance to our property, the forest was already burning on both sides of the road and it intensified as they drove. When they pulled up at our front gate, fire roared out of a gully below, licking over the truck.

Chris had pulled hoses into the house and had been fighting the fire from a small internal deck. When Charlie yelled at him to come, he was reluctant to abandon the house but knew he had no choice. He ran down to the truck, scrambling in on his hands and knees, sucking on an offered Ventolin. Charlie told the driver to put on the truck's external sprinklers for the nearly two-kilometre drive through the burning forest, and as they pulled away our shed was going up in flames, paint cans and gas bottles exploding with loud bangs.

At the staging post, someone – I think it is Charlie – takes me aside and tells me our home probably will not make it. Until now, I hadn't even considered the house; I just feel numb.

As Chris and the Bawley Point crew are all getting back on board, ready to drive away, Hendrick Boon, a giant of a Dutchman, the driver who had navigated through the burning forest, comes over and draws me into an enormous bear hug. 'Don't worry, we'll look after him,' he says.

I don't sleep much that night. Churning through all the consequences of losing our home, my mind leaps with no sense of order from the unfathomably large questions – *how on earth will we ever start again?* – to the smaller dilemmas: *how will I tell my daughter I forgot to grab the cage with her guinea pigs when I raced out the door?*

When my phone rings early the next morning – a number I don't recognise – and Chris gets on the line and tells me he's been back and our house is still there, I can hardly speak for relief.

The Currowan fire continued with its pummelling of our area. On the afternoon of Thursday, 5 December, after steadily encroaching for days, it made a sudden strike from the north towards Bawley Point. Residents who'd decided not to evacuate came out with their hoses, while others fled to the headland. Dozens, including children, sheltered inside the village fire shed.

Bawley's captain, Charlie Magnuson, had been put in charge of the local brigades, plus three Fire and Rescue NSW strike teams and several other RFS trucks that had arrived in the village. As the fire raced in, he issued the order to protect 'life and property only' – a firefighter's call of last resort. When he told one of the strike team leaders to get his team on protecting the fire shed, the man asked jokingly if that was where the beer was kept. 'No, it's full of women and children,' Charlie said. Two helicopters arrived and started bucketing ocean water onto the wall of flames coming into backyards.

I was at the dentist in Ulladulla when I received a Face-Time call from a friend in Bawley. She told me flames were cresting 20 metres above the trees behind her house and she'd just escaped towards the headland. I could see the orange glow behind her. When I yelled, 'Go further! Go further!' in the crowded waiting room, no one batted an eyelid. This was our community's new normal.

In Bawley Point, watching the wall of flames approach, Charlie had every truck available to him spread out along two roads. He was calculating that the best-case scenario he was facing was losing only a third of the village, when suddenly, 'like a gift from heaven', a southerly change hit. Within minutes, it forced the fire back on itself and away from the village.

But five kilometres further north, the southerly change that helped saved Bawley was now sending fire hurtling through the Meroo National Park towards the village of Lake Tabourie. The RFS had warned people days earlier to leave if they weren't well prepared to defend, but many had stayed, and were out with garden hoses as fire reached the doorsteps on the southern edge of the village.

Out of the dentist and back listening to the scanner, I heard the name of the street under threat. In a panic, I went through my phone contacts and texted my friend Vince, who lived there. *Are you out? Fire is about to hit patersons close.*

The reply came back swiftly. *Wrong Vince I think Bronwyn.*

In my haste, I'd texted someone I'd worked with years ago.

On the northern end of the village, a friend who'd decided to stay was on his roof, kitted out in an ad-hoc firefighting outfit: snow goggles, a leather jacket with the synthetic lining ripped out and a bandana over a particle mask. Watching the 300-metre-wide front – with flames twice the height of the eucalypts in the national park – barrel towards the far end of town, he was thinking it was probably time to make a break for the beach when he noticed a subtle change in the wind. A surfer, he picked it immediately: the southerly was shifting to east-south-east. It was just enough to stop the fire hitting Lake Tabourie dead-on, instead shooting it parallel to the village and through more bushland. Yards were singed, sheds and cubby houses destroyed, but all homes and everyone in them were unharmed.

Over these few days, the onslaught in the semi-rural and forested areas around our place was unrelenting, requiring constant vigilance and sleepless nights. One by one, the people in our WhatsApp group faced their turn.

Ok flames are here 80 metres from house. Driveway cut off now. Here we go. See you on the other side peeps.

It's ripped through my place heading south bound. I can hear it down the valley though, heads up guys down below.

We called 000 and no one. Not enough resources they say. Fuck paying tax anymore.

Right across the state, there were simply not enough resources. Earlier in the week, the minutes from a state situation meeting for the National Parks and Wildlife Services noted, 'No point asking for large new strike teams as there is no one left to send.'

Meanwhile, evacuees from the fire zone were floating around the towns to the north like exiles: wearing borrowed clothing and clutching phones; sleeping on the couches of friends' houses and in cheap motel rooms. In Target in Ulladulla I ran into what seemed like half the population of Bawley Point in the change rooms, stocking up on clothes as the lockout dragged on. When I went down to the sea pool on the edge of the harbour, piles of blackened leaves were heaped on the shore, washed up from our beaches down south.

People in the fire zone were running low on supplies, so I gathered a list of things they needed – mainly food, ice and

Ventolin – and met Chris at the roadblock. At the line, which was being vigilantly policed, I exchanged the supplies for a forgotten homework book and two guinea pigs that smelled like smoke.

Ulladulla's library and civic centre had been converted into an evacuation centre. One of the first through the door was Phil Butler. The blast of fire that had come through our place on Tuesday night had continued down to the water's edge at Meroo Lake, incinerating not only everything he owned, but most animals and plants. With his wife and son, he was given temporary accommodation in a local motel.

On Friday, 6 December, I went to my kids' school assembly and was surprised by how many parents were there; the community-wide trauma seemed to have driven people in, not away. As I walked in, a woman came up to me and thrust a school uniform and a set of cricket whites into my arms – in case I needed spares.

The children were subdued. We all knew by then that several had lost their homes and many other families had lost land and livelihoods. Around 730 square kilometres of the place we all lived in had been burned. When the principal took to the small wooden stage, he started by confessing he'd evacuated from his home in Bawley Point five days ago without any socks, so he'd been wearing the same ones all week. True or not, the story worked – the kids dissolved into laughter. The principal said he knew we were all sad and put up a PowerPoint showing images of beautiful South Coast landscapes – the beaches, the mountains, the lakes – urging us to not lose sight of what we loved. He said that if we wanted, we could give the person next to us a hug. For the first time all week, I began to cry.

By the end of the weekend, after eight days of lockout, word got around that roadblocks were easing and people from the coastal villages were being allowed back. Lines of cars took to the highway. In Bawley Point, a hand-painted sign saying *Welcome Home* greeted the newly returned.

I had mixed feelings about seeing our property; it felt like an unwanted yet necessary task. Because our area was still closed to residents – there was too much active fire around – I met Chris at the roadblock and walked over to his vehicle, planning to say 'I'm under RFS escort' if I was stopped. Which was more or less true – Chris still hadn't left the fire zone. He'd taken leave from work and was permanently on call for his brigade.

As I headed down the highway, the familiar landscapes soon became unrecognisable. Passing through a ten-kilometre stretch of blackened forests, the signs bearing the names of local creeks and turn-offs to villages all bubbled and distorted, I experienced a feeling similar to one I'd had decades earlier, when I was living in Sydney and came home to discover our house had been burgled and ransacked.

The destruction along the road into our property was even more complete. The fire had burned so intensely here there was barely anything left of the forest – in parts it was just bare earth, and I could see contours of the land I never knew were there. We paused briefly at the place where the road leads off to our neighbours' properties. When the sweep of fire came over the saddle it took three houses; only two of us were left. It seemed incomprehensible that the place I drank wine and laughed in just a week ago didn't exist anymore. But there was no way I wanted to look.

Entering our property to see our house sitting there, unscathed, surrounded by blackened grass right up to its footings, I felt sheer amazement.

Everything else was gone. No trace of the shed where we housed our solar-power battery system. The carport, once filled with bicycles and hanging racks of surfboards, was just a twisted pile of metal. There was a green puddle of sludge on the ground where once a water tank stood.

I didn't know how the house survived, but I suspected it was a combination of things. Chris got a lot of water on and around it before he left; the steel footings were impervious to the flames; and even though fire came into the grass in the asset protection zone, having less to burn no doubt reduced its intensity. Anything closer to the forest, like the sheds, had completely dissolved. But all it would have taken was a single ember sneaking in somewhere, so I didn't discount the role of luck.

Exploring the property, I discovered our underground waste treatment system was now an open gaping hole, the fire having chased through plastic pipes, deep into the ground. The concrete water tank, cracked and leaking, was still too hot to touch. I pulled open the doors to the shipping container we used for storage – a repository of treasures like old diaries, paintings I'd been meaning to hang, a Turkish rug I'd lugged across a continent. It now gaped like a black mouth, empty. The only relic left amid the ashes was a garish ceramic water filter – a wedding gift I'd never liked but felt obliged to keep.

The inside of the house was smoky and dank: strewn with hoses and the toppled piles of things I'd brought in from the deck when we were preparing for the fire's arrival. The breakfast dishes from a week earlier, the day we got the emergency alert, were still stacked on the sink.

The whole time, I kept hearing the sound of trees crashing down in the forest and I could see numerous wisps of smoke. On edge, I was relieved when Chris said it was time to go.

*

The next day – Monday, 9 December – the NSW Rural Fire Service commissioner, Shane Fitzsimmons, announced that fires across the state had burned through 27,000 square kilometres – an area greater than the country of Wales. Nearly ninety fires were still burning, with thirty-nine listed as out of control.

Northwest of Sydney, in Wollemi National Park, five blazes had coalesced into what was being described as a 'megafire' – a new lexicon for Australia. The Gospers Mountain fire was burning over an area of 3,200 square kilometres, menacing populations from the Blue Mountains to the Central Coast. Southwest of Sydney, another major fire was threatening the dam that accounts for 80 per cent of the city's water supply and striking into small villages not far from the urban fringe.

'We've got fires effectively stretching now from the Queensland border right down to our far South Coast area,' Fitzsimmons said. Firefighting crews were feeling the strain. 'They've been flogged now for months, particularly up in the north … and with the fire activity extending further south, we're literally rotating through thousands of people every day, every week.'

Across the nation, the tally of homes destroyed had now topped 1,000.

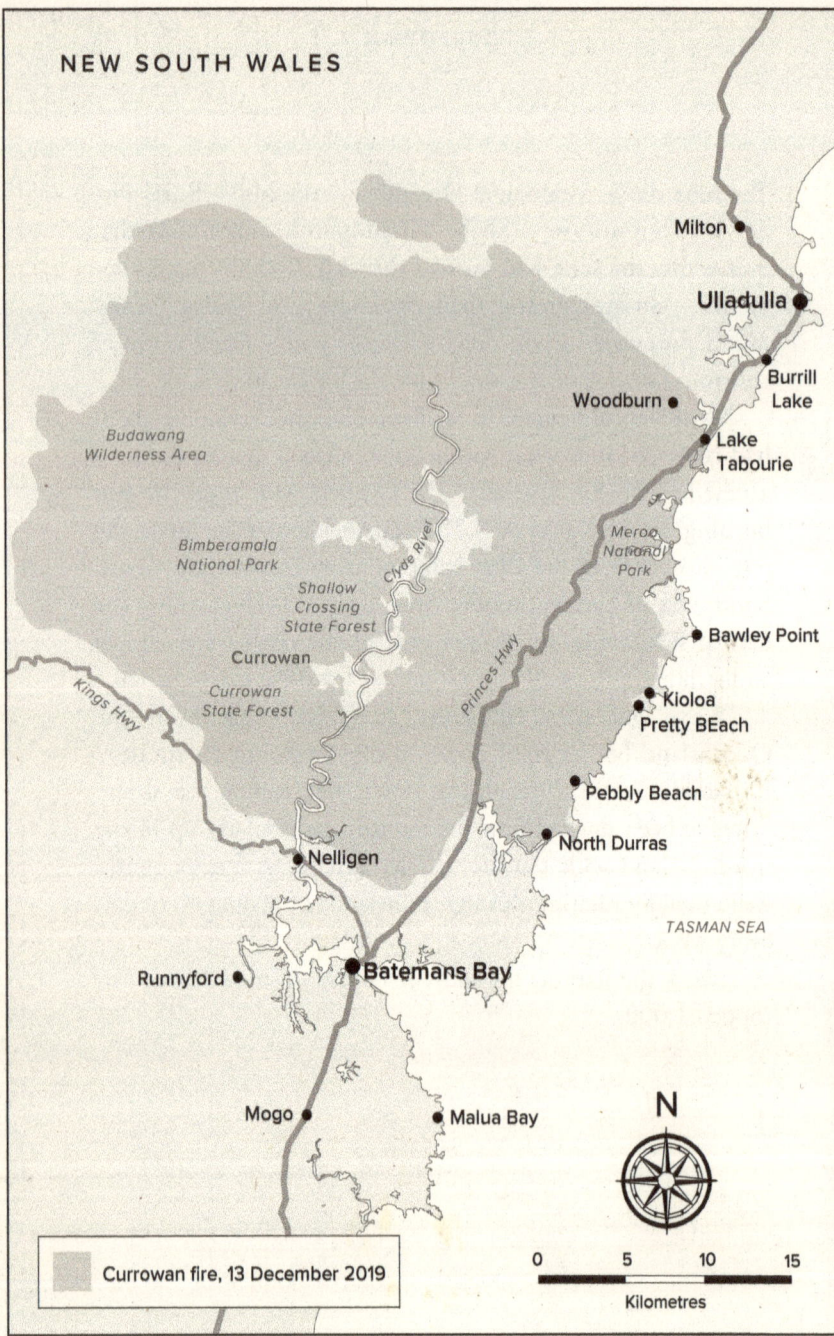

NEW SOUTH WALES

Milton

Ulladulla

Burrill Lake

Woodburn

Lake Tabourie

Budawang Wilderness Area

Meroo National Park

Bimberamala National Park

Shallow Crossing State Forest

Clyde River

Currowan

Bawley Point

Currowan State Forest

Kioloa

Pretty BEach

Princes Hwy

Kings Hwy

Pebbly Beach

North Durras

Nelligen

TASMAN SEA

Runnyford

Batemans Bay

N

Mogo

Malua Bay

Currowan fire, 13 December 2019

0   5   10   15

Kilometres

CHAPTER 5

THE BEAST

We were now entering the third week of living with the Currowan fire, and part of me felt, by rights, it was surely time to breathe again: *We made it, that's enough now.* Except I knew we had barely even started.

On Wednesday morning, 11 December, I went into Ulladulla to visit real estate agents and start the process of looking for somewhere to live. With all our power, water and waste systems destroyed, I knew it would be many months before we could move back home. Seeing the town civic centre and library had been converted into a disaster recovery centre – the sight of the new banner hanging outside the library, a haven of safe memories since I was a child, giving me a weird lurch in my guts – I wandered in.

Inside the main auditorium, I discovered the incident controller for the Currowan fire, Mark Williams, speaking before a crowd of people seated on plastic chairs. It was one of a series of community meetings he'd started holding in towns along the coast, trying to brace everyone for what lay ahead, and I sat down to listen.

The Currowan fire was now 880 square kilometres in size. Unlike normal fires that tend to move in one direction, it was burning on all points of the compass – reaching out towards multiple communities, in places distant from one another. For now, though, it was largely confining its spread to the forests and gorges of the hinterland region. With a map on a screen behind him, Williams was explaining the latest strategy to try to make sure it stayed there.

It was no longer feasible to contain it within a box – it was simply too large. Instead, the plan was to put in strategically placed containment lines to halt its spread. These lines would be established by back-burning and the use of heavy machinery to scrape lines of bare earth through the bush – fifty heavy machines were being brought in to assist. But there were no guarantees that this would work: at one of these community meetings a few days earlier, Williams cautioned that because of the dryness of the landscape, he was only putting his chances of successfully holding the fire to these lines at 'fifty-fifty'.

On this morning, he reassured the crowd that 'we are pouring every single resource we can into it' – taking into account the demands of all the other fires in the state. He said that RFS headquarters in Sydney had boosted his resources: he now had ten aircraft, and five specialists had joined the Nowra team from the northern hemisphere, bringing skills such as mapping and logistics. But his central message was to expect the worst. 'There is no direct threat now, but that could change at any time. Remain vigilant,' he said. 'This fire emergency is far, far, far from over. We still have to go through the hot part of the summer.'

Looking around, I recognised many of the faces in the room. It was an audience that skewed older – there were many grey heads – and I could see the same kind of fear I saw in the faces at Nelligen the day the Currowan fire started. Something like distress, muddied with anger, rose in my throat.

A few days earlier, I'd watched an interview on the ABC with the federal finance minister, Mathias Cormann. Despite the crisis engulfing the nation, Corman had said that no extra support for the fires was necessary. 'If and when additional support is required, then of course we would consider that. But right now, as we speak, we planned for this bushfire season,' he said. It was so at odds with what I had just witnessed, his words had stuck in my craw.

When I stood up from my seat – voice tight and breaking, not sure if I was speaking as a journalist or a private citizen – I asked Williams whether we would all be here now, in this terrible situation, if we'd had more aerial resources at the very beginning.

'We are not the only fire in the state. There is only a finite number of aviation resources and all those resources are fully stretched,' he answered. 'Did we have enough? Well, I didn't have enough fire trucks on every corner either. Could we have done more? Yes, we could have done more with more, we always can. But realistically, taking into account the weather conditions we had at the time, we would not have been able to put this fire out.'

Over the following week, the Currowan fire proved immune to attempts to stop its growth, continuing its steady advance across the landscape and over every containment line. A local woman took on the role of citizen journalist, updating locals via Facebook on sightings of what she called 'the Beast'.

The fire front was moving predominantly northward, up through the green spine of forests and mountains that run parallel to the coast, expanding on its western and eastern flanks as it travelled. Even once the front had passed through an area, it would still leave lingering pockets of active fire behind, just to keep everyone on their toes.

There were clear, blue-skied days when you could almost forget it was there, but then it would send a signal to remind everyone of its presence. One morning, people in the beachside village of Mollymook woke to black ash on their car windscreens. My neighbour, who'd moved to Mollymook after losing her home the night our area was hit by the fire, posted on social media: *Please can this be over?*

Most of those living closer to the fire, on farmland or bush properties, had little optimism this would happen anytime soon. Dave Howes was still working nearly every day with his harvester on the fire effort for the RFS – 'I felt obligated, the fire wasn't out' – but between times, he was readying his own property. 'We were just waiting for our turn,' he says. 'Everyone was going to have a turn. We just didn't know which day was going to be ours.'

Dave's son Steven started his preparation the very night the family came back in the door after their mad dash to save the harvester when the Currowan fire first started. A welder by trade, that night he got on the phone to his suppliers and started placing orders for the fittings he would need to build portable firefighting units that could be installed on utes. The memory of losing half the family farm to the Kingiman fire of 2018 was still raw, and he was determined not be caught out again.

He wasn't just working to protect his own family, though. Throughout December, along with his brother, Lachlan, Steven laboured steadily, building 'cubes' – named for the shape of the small water tank that sits on the ute tray – for the string of locals who kept ringing him up and asking for one. He went to every supplier he could, ordering fittings by the box load, pumps and the cube tanks wherever he could find them. With supplies running low, he started making his own parts. 'I was welding my own fittings, threading a bit of pipe and welding things on, just to keep people going.'

Some people in town, watching his frenzy of activity, teased him. 'They were being smart,' he says. 'Saying things like, "What are you doing, preparing for a napalm attack?" And I would say, "Don't you worry. This thing is coming to town. I bet you a carton of beer this is coming to town."'

Others shared his view. The brothers helped fit out the utes of 'twenty-odd blokes' in the local area with cubes. They made half of them, and the rest, he supplied the fittings 'and they put their own together, because they are all handy country boys and farmers'.

Together, this group of 'cubies' formed a loose alliance. They were men who'd known each other since childhood, from families connected by generations, all with a similar ethos. 'My protocol is, if there are people out there in the line of fire and they need a hand, you don't just stand there,' says Steven. 'While there is a chance and while there are people in there with a heartbeat, you don't leave them behind.'

Even on the days it didn't make the news or onto the Fires Near Me app, the Currowan fire was always having a go at someone, somewhere. Late one night, Dave and his sons raced out to help an elderly man they knew whose home in the forests was about to be swamped by the fire. Debbie stayed in town, trying unsuccessfully to get a fire truck sent out – but with their cubes the boys managed to save the house and the man's life.

Yet as the year began to draw to a close, with fires burning right down the eastern seaboard and into South Australia, Steven couldn't source a pump anywhere in Australia. 'I kept getting messages on my phone, *I got your name off such and*

such, can you make us a cube, I don't care what it costs, but there
was nothing left.'

I was fortunate; it only took a few days to find a new place we
could move into straightaway, in Bawley Point. Chris was out
so often with his brigade that our new neighbour assumed I
was a single mother; the first time she spotted a dishevelled,
dirty stranger letting himself into our house she nearly called
the police.

I'd started the laborious process of lodging an insurance
claim for our property. But with trees still coming down and
roads so regularly closing at short notice, even getting an asses-
sor onto the site was difficult. We needed to rebuild our entire
infrastructure, but with every piece of heavy machinery in the
area now co-opted into the fire effort, I was resigning myself to
the fact that nothing would begin until the summer was over.

I went up to our property on days it seemed safe to do
so. There was no sign of any wildlife, not even a single bird –
the silence so loud as to be deafening – so I became interested
when I heard about a wildlife carer from further south who,
through fundraising, was supplying food for what was left of
the animals in the fire-affected areas.

Rae Harvey came to her property at Runnyford, on the
banks of the Clyde River, from Melbourne: walking away
from a twenty-year career as a rock-band manager, selling up
her possessions and memorabilia – including an ARIA Award
– to create a wildlife sanctuary. While she still looks like she
could belong in the world of rock music, with vivid carmine-
coloured hair, sleeves of tattoos and a wardrobe of all black,
Rae's universe is now her flock of eastern grey kangaroos. They
are mostly orphans she has raised by hand since they were joeys,

pulled from the pouches of their mothers who were killed by cars or shot by farmers.

I collected some of the special pellets Rae had been distributing and started leaving them at a feeding station on our property, along with tubs of water. Each time I came back, I raced to check for scats.

I was also still working on my story about the fire season – albeit with a personal angle that wasn't there when I started writing – and so kept tracking developments beyond my own burnt backyard.

By mid-December, the Gospers Mountain fire had grown to nearly 4,000 square kilometres. Cracks were appearing in weary bushfire-affected communities across the state. In some places, RFS brigades launched appeals on social media to raise money to buy equipment, including P3 masks to protect from smoke inhalation.

The federal government had finally changed its stance on additional funds for aerial firefighting. On 12 December, the same day he first used the phrase 'national disaster' to describe what had been happening over the past three months, the prime minister announced a cash injection of $11 million to the National Aerial Firefighting Centre. It was a one-off payment, not the permanent increase requested in its 2018 business case. And when the organisation requested the lease of a fleet of CL-415 water-scooping planes from Canada a week later, it was already too late. Icy conditions in the northern hemisphere meant they would stay grounded for the season.

While all seven of the Large Air Tankers leased at the beginning of the season were now in the country, they were being stretched in ever-expanding directions. In mid-December, one had to be sent to Western Australia, to assist with serious fires in that state.

Significant political shifts were underway. The same week that the air quality index in Sydney reached eleven times higher than 'hazardous', with buildings – including RFS headquarters – evacuated as bushfire smoke triggered fire alarms, the New South Wales environment minister, Matt Kean, linked the fires to climate change, saying, 'This is not normal and doing nothing is not a solution.' The substance of his comments was not controversial – scientists had been saying similar for years – but they were rare words to hear from the conservative side of politics, which has long been drenched in climate-change denialism. Just the month before, for example, the deputy prime minister, Michael McCormack, had said only 'pure, enlightened and woke capital-city greenies' linked climate change with the current fire season.

On 16 December, I saw a crazy rumour on Twitter that Scott Morrison was in Hawaii on holiday. His office denied it, but a few days later journalist Samantha Maiden wrote a story confirming it was true.

It is the driest December ever recorded in Australia. The early wet-season rains in the northern tropics haven't arrived, so heat is building in the north of the country. Midway through the month, this mass of hot air starts travelling south, encompassing the entire continent.

The seventeenth of December is Australia's hottest day ever recorded, with a national average maximum temperature of 40.97 degrees (the previous record of 40.30 degrees was set in 2013). But this new record is smashed the following day, 18 December, when the national average reaches 41.88 degrees. When the third day, 19 December, hits a phenomenal 41.01 degrees, it is merely the second-hottest day ever recorded.

This extreme heat propels the fire season to even more dangerous heights. One hundred fires are now burning in New South Wales, seventy in Queensland. With more bad fire weather ahead, the New South Wales premier declares another seven-day state of emergency – the second for the fire season.

The Currowan fire, like other blazes, responds to this weather with enthusiasm. Already a beast, on 19 December it throws out its tentacles even further.

Brendan Cowled has been expecting the Currowan fire for weeks. From his cattle farm – a clearing of pasture nestled high in the foothills, just below the lip of the escarpment that starts rising west of the town of Milton – he's been watching its steady approach ever since it started, more than 50 kilometres to his southwest.

Even before the fire ignited, Brendan had been witnessing the drought tighten its grip and suspecting a bushfire was imminent. He has two school-aged children and normally spends his Sundays volunteering for the Nippers on the beach at Mollymook. But in November, he started leaving Sundays clear for fire preparation: bulldozing in containment lines, setting up firefighting equipment, methodically sealing every gap in the roof of the house and the sheds. Once the Currowan fire kicked off, he knew it was just a question of when it would arrive at his farm. In mid-December, his wife, Kim Wilson, rustled up the family for a surfing holiday further down the coast, but Brendan was only there for half an hour before saying, 'This isn't right, I have to go,' and heading back alone.

On 19 December, a Thursday, Brendan is joined at the property by his father, Murray, who has travelled from his home in northern New South Wales to assist his son in the anticipated firefight. Brendan has asked him to come because, at a sprightly seventy-three, Murray has a wealth of firefighting experience – including twenty years as captain of an RFS brigade in the state's west.

Both men are on high alert. While they haven't seen flame yet, they know the Currowan fire is at this moment advancing rapidly through the deep gorges of the escarpment to their southwest. Immediately to their northwest, in the same stretch of mountain ranges, a new fire has broken out near Tianjara Falls – believed to be deliberately lit – and is ripping through the heavily forested, rugged sandstone country.

Early in the afternoon a strong nor'wester springs up and an ember sails over the escarpment. They see a small pocket of fire, no bigger than the size of a car, start up in a deep forested gully north of the farm, inaccessible by road. It's not an imminent threat – to them or anyone – but both can see it's a dangerous place to let a fire take hold. Once it gets going somewhere like this, you'd never extinguish it – and to its east lie the semi-rural areas of Little Forest and Yatte Yattah, scattered with houses, and further still, the coastal hamlets around Lake Conjola.

Murray worked as an air-traffic controller when he was with the RFS. He thinks a quick dump of water would sort it out. They've already seen water-bucketing helicopters in the sky that day – the Currowan fire is making runs all over the place – so they know they're around.

Brendan calls triple zero to explain the situation. The operator, 400 kilometres away in Newcastle, sounds unsympathetic: 'Yeah, mate, choppers are all tied up at the moment.' When Brendan presses his case, the operator becomes terse, telling him, 'You've got about ten trucks in your area already.' When Brendan starts to explain, again, that this new spot fire can't be accessed by road, the operator cuts across him with a 'See ya later', sounding like he's going to hang up on him.

Murray tries next. He cites his credentials up front – 'I'm an ex-RFS captain, so I know what I'm talking about' – but he receives a similar response.

The fire is growing before their eyes. Brendan tries calling the RFS fire control centre in Nowra, where he is transferred to a media liaison officer. A couple of hours later, three Fire and Rescue NSW trucks arrive at the farm, saying they've been tasked to 'put out' the spot fire. Brendan and Murray are exasperated, explaining again that a chopper is needed.

Soon, a local RFS crew turns up. Finally, Brendan thinks, after hours 'of arguing until we are blue in the face', they have an ally. But when the captain radios in for aerial support he's told none is available because of smoke around Nowra. It's too late anyway. The spot fire has grown to a size where it's uncontainable.

Throughout the evening, Brendan watches in dismay as this new fire rampages through the bush. He knows he has many more days of danger ahead. He still has the main body of the Currowan fire burning through the escarpment behind him – it seems inevitable that it will soon join with the one in Tianjara – but he fears that all for the want of a single helicopter, this spot fire brewing in the forests below the escarpment is a time bomb for another day.

That same day, all the way over on the western edge of the same mountain ranges – the other side of the green spine – in the high, flat grazing country of the southern tablelands, Justin Parr is about to meet the Currowan fire head on.

Forty-seven-year-old Parr is captain of the RFS in Nerriga, a tiny inland village of weatherboard houses where the last census recorded the population at seventy-five. The area around the village is a mix of large working farms, smaller rural holdings and innumerable hand-hewn shacks and converted sheds hidden away in the bush; places you'd only live if you liked the isolation. The next village, another tiny one, is over 50 kilometres away.

Nerriga is here – wedged between wilderness and grazing land – due to the wild ambition of a handful of wealthy graziers in the 1840s. The men wanted to create a new trade route for their wool. Instead of the long journey north to Sydney, they envisaged a road that went due east, straight through the heart of the ranges to the coast, where they also planned to build a port. They purchased seventy convicts to construct their dream. In some small sections, the route followed the foot-worn tracks established over thousands of years by the Yuin people, an easier path, but mostly it was just brute-force blasting and cutting a way through the towering sandstone plinths and thickly forested mountain ridges. The road made it to the coast, but the graziers' business venture failed; the road too steep for bullock carts, the port not financially viable, a depression hit. For most of its backers, it proved their financial ruin. But Nerriga, the starting point of the road, persisted.

Justin Parr's first sighting of the Currowan fire came the same day as mine. Back on 26 November, he'd been in the caravan park in Nelligen with his wife, enjoying a short holiday, when they were told to evacuate. As they started the 90-kilometre drive back to Nerriga, watching the growing plume come up from the forests, he said to his wife, 'Gee, I feel sorry for the poor buggers who are going to have to fight that fire.'

But it didn't take long before it was his problem too. One of the first failures of the containment box on the Currowan fire – back when it was just days old – was on the western side, when fire escaped into the rugged Budawang Ranges, a place of steep mountainsides and deep valleys, accessible only on foot.

Mark Williams had said that while they 'pumped everything' into trying to stop it, once it was headed off into this inaccessible area he decided 'we'll have to walk away from it' – letting it burn through until it came out at the pastures on the other side of the range.

By the end of the first week of December, it had made its way through the ranges to the tablelands and started launching sorties against farms and rural properties about 50 kilometres south of Nerriga. Parr – who'd already been out fighting fires closer to Canberra nearly every day since his aborted holiday, his paid work as a rural contractor all but abandoned – started working on the defence of his home territory.

Parr grew up in Nerriga, and when he signed up as a volunteer firefighter aged eighteen, it just seemed part of the deal of living here. 'It wasn't a choice,' he says. 'If you lived in the community, you were part of the RFS. Particularly as a young male, you just joined. There weren't many of us, so you had to defend your town.'

For the past week, the Currowan fire has been sweeping up the ranges of the Morton National Park, gradually getting closer to Nerriga. Parr and his small brigade have been trying to stay one step in front, using machinery to put in containment lines ahead of its advance, so that every time it runs up the escarpment and makes a dash for the tablelands they can flank it and steer it back down into the recesses of the wilderness – shepherding it away from any farmland or houses.

He hasn't heard much from the fire control centre in Nowra. 'I have to say, we kind of felt like it was our fire, it wasn't theirs,' he says. 'We were doing our own thing the best we could with the bit of gear we had.' He hasn't been given many line scans, so most of the time the only way he knows where the fire is located is when he sees it rush out of the ranges.

On the afternoon of 19 December, Parr drives out along one of the fire trails that cuts into the ranges to see if he can spot what the Currowan fire is doing. As is not uncommon at this time of day, a sea fog is rolling in low across the mountains, coming from the coast more than 60 kilometres away. As he stands there scanning the horizon, the silence is broken by a tremendous roar. The next moment, Parr sees waves of flame erupting above the height of the fog. Straightaway, Parr knows he is in for 'a bit of strife'.

The fire is crowning and travelling at incredible speed. It dives into a deep forested gorge, following its winding path until it comes blasting out into a semi-rural area about ten kilometres south of the village – where Parr and his brigade race, plunging into an intense firefight.

By the morning of 20 December – they've been fighting all night – conditions finally ease. They've lost one home, but the incursion has been stamped out. Parr knows, though, that this is not the end: there's more of the Currowan fire out there, hiding somewhere deep in the ranges of the national park. He is expecting it will make another strike, but in 150 years fire has never reached the township of Nerriga; many of the old-timers in the area say it's impossible. Parr never, for a moment, thinks the village will be at risk.

Across a vast geographic area, so many of us are now hostage to the rhythms of the Currowan fire. That same morning, I decide it is time to take heart and start my Christmas shopping. I'd left my daughter with my parents at their home on the outskirts of Milton and have only just walked into an arcade in Ulladulla when Mum calls. 'You better come,' she says, using her best I'm-trying-not-to-sound-alarmed voice.

But because I'm her daughter, I recognise the tone and race back to my car.

As I approach their house I can see several columns of smoke coming up from below the escarpment about one kilometre away and two helicopters flying in with brimming water buckets.

Mum is already outside waiting when I pull into the driveway – she is calm, but clearly eager to hand back the responsibility of a child. I tell my daughter to get in the car – well practised by now at being bundled in and out of vehicles at short notice, she climbs in without question – but I am caught in indecision about what to do with our belongings. Even after we moved to Bawley Point, I left all our boxes of valuables from our evacuation back on 1 December at my parents' house, because it seemed somehow safer: it was my childhood home, after all. While I can see there is no imminent threat to my parents or their house, it dawns on me that perhaps their continued safety is not necessarily a sure thing.

As I scarper back to Bawley Point, car full of boxes again – only just making it through before the road closes, as another finger of fire surges in south of Ulladulla – I think, *Where's safe anymore?*

CHAPTER 6

A PYROCUMULONIMBUS UPON NERRIGA

It's 9.00 am on Saturday, 21 December, and the temperature in Nerriga is already 30 degrees. A hot nor'wester is blowing dust from bone-dry paddocks down a deserted main street: past the handful of fading white weatherboard cottages, one fronted with a rose garden in bloom and a polite sign requesting flowers not be picked; past the wooden community hall with its neat A-frame roof; past the pub and the three-bay tin shed that is home to the local RFS brigade.

Over the road, in her caravan that's parked in a paddock next to the fire shed, seventy-three-year-old Pamela Parr is starting to wonder if she's overreacting, hiding out here in a sweltering-hot van, instead of being in the comfort of her home.

She drove up here on Thursday, when the Currowan fire started its sudden advance, leaving her home three kilometres south of the village. It was just a precaution; she packed a few changes of clothes but left everything else at home. She's only still here because everyone is saying today could be even worse.

The RFS has raised the fire danger rating for the South Coast and Southern Tablelands to the highest level: *catastrophic*. The advice is to 'avoid bushfire-prone areas' and look to safe locations in 'large towns, cities and shopping centres'. 'Homes are not designed to withstand fires in catastrophic conditions,' the RFS warns. 'For your survival, leaving early is the only option.'

Throughout the morning, Pamela's been calling her partner, Terry, who stayed behind to protect the house. He keeps assuring her everything is fine. The sprinklers are on and the hoses are ready, but nothing's happening. He's inside with the air-conditioning on, watching television.

'Fernlea' has been Pamela's home for forty years. She built most of it by hand. When she arrived in Australia as a 'ten-pound Pom' – part of a post-war migration scheme to encourage British migrants by offering cheap boat passage – she settled first in western Sydney. But after she visited the piece of land in Nerriga she and her then husband had purchased as a weekender, she never wanted to leave. She began living there in a caravan; then in a house run by solar power, back when this was still a curious idea. She grew food, sewed her own clothes and raised two boys. Her eldest son, Justin, is now the captain of the Nerriga RFS. They share the same blue eyes and fair complexion.

Over years, 'Fernlea' evolved – mains power eventually arrived – and by 2019 the place is looking more brilliant than it ever has. With a small inheritance from her mother, Pamela has installed a new kitchen, air-conditioning and a sewing room. There is a greenhouse full of seedlings waiting to be planted.

It's four days till Christmas and there's things she could be doing at home. By lunchtime, the temperature in the van is 47 degrees, and when she sticks her head outside, the sky is blue and the strong nor'wester seems to have disappeared. She wonders, *Maybe I should just go home?*

Over the road, at the Nerriga Hotel – a long, single-storey wooden building painted rust-red and roofed with silver tin – publican Sarah Martin is searching for something to do. She and her husband, Phil, have already finished their fire preparation. There'll be no customers from passing traffic today – the road to the coast, popular with day-trippers, has been closed by the Tianjara fire – and Phil sent the word around to locals on Friday night that with the dangerous day ahead, they'd be limiting the sale of alcohol.

Some have already left town. On Thursday, after the Tianjara fire broke out to Nerriga's east and the Currowan fire surged in from the southwest, an RFS volunteer visited the pub and told Sarah it might be time to get her children away. Sarah's father was visiting from France, so she arranged for him to leave with four-year-old Hugo. But six-month-old Oliver was still breastfeeding, and as much as she tried, she couldn't convince him to take a bottle. She was concerned about the risk of dehydration in the hot weather if he couldn't feed without her. On Friday, when the fire danger rating for the following day was raised to *catastrophic*, Sarah and Phil sent away two French backpackers staying with them and Sarah again tried Oliver on a bottle, without success. So now baby Oliver is in her arms, teething and fretting with the heat.

When long-time local Leon Hagel comes through the door, she's glad to see him. In her seven years in Nerriga, Sarah's grown close to the small community. Before, she'd only ever lived in cities – Paris, where she grew up, and Sydney, with Phil. When they bought the pub, almost on a whim, and relocated, she couldn't believe how nice everyone was. It made her wonder: *what would we have gotten ourselves into if people hadn't been so friendly?* Once the couple announced they were pregnant with their first child, they were overwhelmed by the genuine excitement of their neighbours. When they tried to sneak Hugo's first birthday by with a small event, no one would have it – it ended up being a party at the pub for 100 people, with lamb and a pig on the spit.

Leon is tall and in his mid-sixties, ex-Navy, with a swooping handlebar moustache tipped with silver and a sleeve of tattoos. He lives on a property about a kilometre from the village – you can see it from the front verandah of the pub. He's also finished his fire preparations, so he and Sarah sit down over coffee and make a list of everyone they can think of who's decided to stay behind in Nerriga, in case it will be useful later.

Around ten kilometres south of the village, Justin Parr has been working frantically all morning helping to build a defence for Nerriga. He's managed only a handful of hours of decent sleep since his twenty-two-hour overnight firefight on Thursday, but he's not feeling fatigued. While he's known since he was a boy it was his duty to protect his community, this is the first time the threat has ever got so close.

Parr and his small brigade have just received much-needed support. Earlier that morning, a strike team with eight RFS trucks from towns closer to Canberra arrived, joining the three based in Nerriga.

The morning's strong nor'wester is not the concern – it's just blowing the Currowan fire deeper into the national park. What everyone's worried about is the forecast southerly change, expected to hit mid-afternoon.

Crews are working off fire trails deep in the forest, using heavy machinery to push and scrape wide lines of bare earth. These lines are about ten kilometres south of the village; the Currowan fire is approximately another eight kilometres south again. The hope is that once the southerly hits and pushes the fire towards town, these lines will be enough to stall or at least slow it.

When forty-eight-year-old Nick Hornbuckle, captain of the Queanbeyan RFS, turned up for his shift earlier that morning and was handed the job of leading the strike team bound for Nerriga, it was a responsibility he gladly accepted. Hornbuckle has been a volunteer firefighter for twenty years. He's a former army officer who now manages operations for a large technology firm in Canberra – he thrives on risk analysis and exercising leadership, so leading a team on a catastrophic fire day seems a good opportunity to use these skills.

By around 2.00 pm, the line he's walking between completing the defensive lines for Nerriga and exposing his crews to unacceptable risk is becoming razor-thin. Right now, his crews are working on the flank of the Currowan fire; it's moving away from them. But once the southerly hits and the fire changes direction, they'll be directly in its path. Fire scientists call this space the 'dead man zone' – because this is what can happen to firefighters if they don't get out of the way in time when the wind changes.

Hornbuckle has driven up to a vantage point. He's getting constant updates on the progress of the southerly change as it makes its way up the South Coast, and he has his eyes locked on the smoke plumes of the Currowan fire, looking for signs of change.

When he sees an enormous billowing cloud forming over one of the smoke columns, then another, he realises instantly the line has been crossed. While this is the first time he's ever directly witnessed such a thing, he knows what he is lookin' is the formation of pyrocumulonimbus clouds – also kn'

*

David Hanzl, a fire captain on board one of the fire trucks in the strike team, has also seen the pyrocumulonimbus forming, and so is already scrambling his crew to make a quick getaway when Hornbuckle's evacuation order comes over the radio. They drive hard for fifteen minutes until they're well out of the forest, pulling into a cul-de-sac that runs off the main road into Nerriga only once they're confident they've outrun the fire. The sky outside is still blue, and they've met up with a water tanker, so everyone piles out to start refilling the truck.

Hornbuckle and his truck come around the corner. Hornbuckle has also briefly managed to get ahead of the fire, but he can see the darkness closing in behind him and knows they've only got seconds left before it catches them again. When he sees Hanzl and his crew standing on the road outside their truck, he tells his driver to lean on the horn to warn them.

Before they can respond, Hanzl feels it: 'Fire everywhere, ferocious heat, smoke, embers blowing into faces, down necks, into ears.' He and his crew dive back into their truck, hauling the water-tanker driver in with them.

Being overrun by fire, called a flashover or burnover, is potentially deadly, even inside a fire truck. The men and women inside both trucks in the cul-de-sac are now using everything they have to survive: everyone dons their full personal protective equipment, including goggles and masks; external water sprays are turned on; crew members hold shields up against the windows to deflect the intense radiant heat.

Hornbuckle radios all the other trucks in his team, telling everyone to hold their position. 'Stay still, let the truck protect you, let the equipment protect you,' he says. While it may feel counterintuitive to stop fleeing, he knows the greatest risk now is a vehicle accident caused by trying to outrun the firestorm.

But he has no way of knowing if everyone has heard him or how they have reacted to his instruction. Some of the crew leaders are veterans, but others are 'fairly green'. From inside the truck he can hear the wind howling and the *tink, tink, tink* of embers against the vehicle, like hail on a tin roof. Outside, everything is red. There is no smoke, just intense burning, as though they're 'sitting in hell'.

Yet the worst thing is not knowing the fate of the rest of his team. 'I just had to trust their crew leaders had put them in a position that was survivable when it came through,' he says. 'It just happened so quickly.'

The fire front passes after about ten minutes, and Hornbuckle opens the door and steps out into a world transformed. All the foliage is gone, replaced by black sticks on bare, smouldering earth. 'It was strange,' he says. 'And the wind, it was strong and really cold, like ice.'

After conducting a welfare check on his team, ascertaining that everyone is safe, and inspecting the fire truck for damage, Hornbuckle has to quickly come up with a plan. As expected, the southerly has swung the fire towards the township, but the firestorm has delivered a level of intensity no one predicted, sending out large fingers of fire and new spot fires well ahead of the front. No dozer line is going to stop the fire hitting Nerriga now. They have to get back there, but Hornbuckle knows there are countless isolated rural properties on the way – all in the fire's path. He tells his team to adopt a leapfrog tactic. 'Go and find a property and if there is a truck there go to the next one; find another one and another one, all the way back to Nerriga.'

He knows they won't have enough trucks or time to save

everything they find, so he instructs them to 'just protect the most important things'. It's going to be triage, with difficult on-the-spot assessments: *Is there someone still inside this burning home, or are we right to leave now the house can't be saved? Is that an empty farm shed about to be hit, or does it contain someone's irreplaceable home?* 'I just had to leave it up to the crew leaders to do their thing and what they thought was right,' he says. But they have to act fast.

Justin Parr tells Hornbuckle that he won't be going with them. He's going to remain behind, deep in the fire front. 'I knew there were people staying at home trying to defend themselves,' he says. 'I knew if we pulled all the trucks back to the village and the worst happened, we wouldn't be able to get back to them.'

Parr is in his brigade's smallest vehicle, the Cat 9, a single-cab ute. One of the larger Nerriga trucks stays with him for a short while, but he soon sends it back to the village because he knows the crew on board have homes and family there in need of protection. Parr does too, but this is a sacrifice he only expects of himself.

For those in the village, memories are foggy about the exact moment it turned from a hot, blue day of interminable waiting to one of sheer terror.

Pamela Parr remembers leaving her caravan to walk over to the pub to buy a lemonade when she noticed cars pulling up outside the community hall, the designated evacuation centre. She thought, *I'd better go and see what's happening.* The next thing, smoke starts rolling in, thicker and thicker. Then she's inside the hall; more and more people are coming in; she can barely breathe.

Inside the pub, someone rings the landline. 'It's happening. It's coming straight for town and you don't have long.' The mobile phone network is down, so Sarah takes a walkie-talkie and gives one to her husband. A friend who's arrived to help defend the pub gives her an old RFS jacket to wrap around baby Oliver as she walks the few hundred metres down to the hall.

It's dark inside the old weatherboard building – the town's power has just gone out – and the room is hot and dense with smoke. There are about forty people inside, many of them elderly, all struggling to breathe. Through the windows, Sarah can see the sky is turning red and clouds of grey ash are billowing through the air.

The door flings open, and Pamela's partner, Terry, comes charging in. 'It's gone,' he says to her. 'It's all gone.' Pamela can hear herself screaming hysterically and feels a woman's arms wrap around her. Sarah crouches by her side, saying, 'Breathe, just breathe.' All Pamela is thinking is, *I don't want to breathe, I want my home*.

Everyone in the hall, most of all Sarah, is worried about Oliver, the only child in Nerriga. One of the older women, a former nurse, tells Sarah she's worried about the effect the smoke could have on his lungs. Sarah radios Phil, her husband, who's still at the pub. When her father left on Thursday, Phil asked her to go with him and take both the children, but she was the one who said no. Now, quietly weeping, she keeps telling him she's sorry, that she didn't know it would be this bad.

There's one road out of town still open and a couple is about to attempt an escape. Sarah agrees to give them Oliver, but by the time they finish fiddling around with the baby capsule it's too late and the road is no longer safe to travel.

From the hall, Sarah can see that the fire shed over the road is still empty – none of the brigade's three trucks that left earlier that morning has returned. She steps outside and walks through the thick smoke and blasting ash-filled wind to the shed, where a single volunteer is manning the radio.

'Is anyone coming?' asks Sarah.

'Yes, they'll come,' the woman replies with confidence.

Nick Hornbuckle and the strike team are nearly back to the village when he gets a radio message that there's an elderly lady trapped in her house south of town. Taking one other truck with him, he turns back, heading down a dirt road through the forest to find her. It's still daylight, but as they drive the sky suddenly darkens and huge trees start heaving onto the road. It's not fire toppling the trees, though it's getting close – he can see its glow now through the forests. It's wind and the energy of the approaching front. For the first time that day, Hornbuckle feels fear.

The sight of trees falling ahead 'was the trigger point for me', says Hornbuckle. 'I realised that something much bigger than what we can deal with is going on here. I couldn't put six people's lives in danger for that one person. It was a hard call. But I told everyone to withdraw back to Nerriga.'

When the first fire truck pulls into Nerriga around 5.00 pm, its flashing lights are the only illumination in town – the village has been plunged into darkness. There's no electricity or running water, no phone signal and the generator keeping power to the still-empty fire shed is nearly out of fuel. Those huddled in the undefended community hall are starting to panic.

The captain on the truck calls a quick meeting in the hall. He fears people are in danger of asphyxiating if they stay in this building; they need an alternative. Sarah offers up the pub as a refuge – they've got a generator, which means they can at least have light, running water and ventilation from ceiling fans. The wooden structure – built in 1862 – is hardly ideal to shelter a community from a climate-change–fuelled catastrophic fire, but it's the best they can do. When Sarah radios Phil to tell him that they are the new evacuation centre and everyone is on their way, he's willing but feels daunted by the responsibility. 'That was the lowest point because all of a sudden it was all on us. We are now looking after people, not just a building,' he says.

As the pub fills, Phil wets towels and places them under doors to try to stop the smoke getting in; two older women take Oliver into a bedroom, giving him ice to suck, trying to soothe him, while Sarah starts distributing food and water.

Then she looks out the window and sees a miraculous sight: fire truck after fire truck is rolling into the village.

When Nick Hornbuckle and his strike team pull in to Nerriga, he estimates they've got twenty minutes, maybe thirty, before the fire hits. He sets up six trucks directly in front of the pub – their only job is to defend the building.

He's thankful to see another strike team from out of the area has just arrived, and that all the heavy machinery at work in the forests earlier in the day has made it back to town. He can now put in place an offensive strategy. He knows there's no way to stop the fire, but 'I didn't want the pub to be hit at full force. So the idea was to split it.' He sets the machinery to work bulldozing lines in the paddocks in front of the pub – a physical barrier that will slow the fire and encourage it to run either side of the building. He puts the strike team in position to chase down any spot fires and help shepherd the fire around the pub.

Leon Hagel, who just hours earlier was having a quiet coffee at the pub with Sarah, can see the plumes approaching his house and thinks they look 'pretty nasty'. He's fought plenty of fires in his Navy days and always planned to stay and defend his home – a beautiful place made of pressed earth and rock, with big yellow-box beams – but at the sight of these plumes he changes his mind. He puts his two dogs in his ute, takes one last photo of the house and drives towards the pub.

On his way, he spots his mate Pedro outside his house and stops to lend a hand. Before long, it's pitch black and roaring. 'You could hear gas bottles exploding through the bush as it was hitting different properties,' he says. 'Pedro didn't want to go. I said, "Mate, we have to go. We're going to perish." I got in my car, and by the time I got to the pub it was raining fire. It was the scariest thing I had ever been in.'

Inside the pub someone is yelling, 'Everyone inside, it's coming.'

The crew of the six fire trucks are standing outside, hoses drenching the pub. Hornbuckle sees a glow, 'and then, *bang*, there was flame'. The front has arrived.

Inside, almost everyone is silent. They can hear gas bottles outside exploding like bombs, and know that each one represents someone's home. Sarah notices the landline just keeps ringing and ringing. Pamela can hear the incessant yap of a dog. She's thinking about her son Justin – his is the only fire truck still not back. Leon Hagel sticks his head out of the front door of the pub for a peek just in time to see his house explode.

No one's sure how long it takes – maybe twenty minutes, maybe more. But eventually the noise quietens. The fire has passed. And they're alive.

It's night by the time Justin Parr makes it back to Nerriga. The front has passed, but the landscape is still alive with fire. The previous hours are a blur. He'd focused on getting to the homes where he knew people were planning to stay and defend, and discovered many in unwinnable situations. Like the couple standing with a garden hose and 'a crowning fire coming at them'. Parr told them it was 'a waste of time', and after 'a fairly stern conversation' they finally agreed to leave. His message to almost everyone he found was simply, *Get out*.

Now, back in Nerriga, Parr joins the crews venturing out with heavy machinery to clear the roads of fallen trees. Incredibly, they find people alive beside their ruined homes, including the lady who'd been reported as trapped. She is fine, objecting only to the fact that those searching for her were describing her as 'old'.

As Parr heads down the road that leads to 'Fernlea' – his boyhood home – past incinerated forests and multiple remains of houses, he knows the chances are not good. 'It was completely dark when I got there, but I could see the house was gone,' he says. 'I knew Mum was at the pub, so it wasn't so bad. But to be the fire captain and lose the family home, that was tough.'

Nick Hornbuckle's strike team doesn't stop working until late in the night – there are plenty of fires to be extinguished. 'People were shattered,' he says. 'Even climbing out of the fire truck seventy or eighty times a day – it's two metres above the ground – is a lot. It was an eighteen-hour day at the end of it.'

Hornbuckle thinks that the day showed how his team's training paid off. Of himself, he acknowledges that 'on a day like this, experience only takes you so far'. He coped by 'just breaking it down in simple terms. Taking known facts. And dealing with those. Taking emotion out of it.'

The fire run of 21 December was larger and more intense than Justin Parr had ever expected. 'I knew that we would be impacted by fire, but not to the extent that we were,' he says. 'What we had, I think, over three hours was a 30-kilometre fire front.'

Almost as soon as the pyrocumulonimbus exploded that day, Parr was certain that there must have been more fire hidden in the mountain ranges than he ever realised. The sheer breadth of what came at Nerriga indicated that what he *thought* was out there, what he'd caught a glimpse of back on Thursday, 19 December, was 'just a tiny little finger' of a bigger body of fire. He wondered if RFS headquarters in Sydney knew more than him. As the fire had started barrelling towards the village that day, he looked up and saw one of the elusive RFS Large Air Tankers in the sky. Like a Hollywood star making a cameo, it dropped two lines of pink fire retardant in front of the fire and promptly disappeared. The people who sent it 'obviously knew something we didn't, because they had it ready to go', says Parr.

Many dozens of homes were destroyed that Saturday in Nerriga. For Justin Parr, though, the most important result of the day was that no one died. 'It was good luck story, because we didn't lose anyone,' he says. 'I don't know how we didn't, because there were some people in some pretty ordinary situations and they thought they would be okay and they weren't.'

the loss of their home and those living in the fear that they are 'still waiting to burn'. Mostly, though, the people of Nerriga are just feeling fortunate to be celebrating this Christmas at all. Later in the afternoon, a group of locals take to the deserted road outside the pub and dance the Macarena.

On the other side of the escarpment, Christmas Day celebrations are largely shelved for Brendan Cowled, whose property is now surrounded by fire. He's been sleeping in shifts, with friends and more family rotating in to help. The spot fire he tried in vain to get water-bombed on Thursday, 19 December, has continued to grow; it made a strike for the farm a few days ago. They saved the house and most of the fencing, but his father-in-law had only narrowly escaped when fire rushed his vehicle, and everyone is rattled. The Currowan fire is moving across the top of the escarpment behind him, passing through an old army artillery training area, with thunderous rumbles coming every ten minutes as it ignites unexploded ordnance. 'Awe-inspiring,' says Brendan – but anxiety-inducing.

Further south, in Bawley Point, I've reluctantly accepted this will be a Christmas largely absent of the usual traditions. My box of decorations was destroyed in our shipping container, and sourcing new ones – or a tree or a ham, let alone soaking fruit for a cake – seems too hard. The Currowan fire has been forcing constant road closures between Sydney and Canberra, meaning many extended family events are cancelled, so a large group of our friends gather at a beachside reserve for an orphan's Christmas. The organiser insists there should be no formality: just bring lots of food and eat what you want, when you want.

It was overcast, and we sit on the beach under low grey clouds, watching the waves deliver large swirls of burnt leaves onto the sand, pulling prawns apart with our fingers. The water is stained ash grey. An enormous tribe of children and dogs run off largely unsupervised into the bush, returning only to eat multiple serves of dessert for lunch. My kids declare it their best Christmas ever.

Around the state, 1,700 RFS volunteers are spending their Christmas on fire duty. Justin Parr is one of them – just squeezing in time for a sausage sandwich for dinner. People everywhere are exhausted. By now, the Gospers Mountain fire in the Blue Mountains has grown so large it has earned the unenviable distinction of becoming the biggest forest fire from a single ignition point in Australian history. A local man who's been living with it for nearly a month and witnessed the terrifying sight of flames climbing up a 200-metre sheer cliff describes to a journalist a sentiment common across so many communities:

> Growing up here, everyone is used to the threat of bushfires. We're used to sirens going off. But when it's on your doorstep and it's been going on for weeks, you get tired. The NSW RFS are tired and exhausted. It's been unrelenting for a month, there's been no break and they're not paid. They need more legs. A human body can only go so far.

On Boxing Day, on the other side of the world in a little village in the Andalucia region of southern Spain, an Australian fire scientist is sitting down at his computer to write a letter to the man in charge of combatting the fire emergency engulfing New South Wales: RFS commissioner Shane Fitzsimmons.

Nick Gellie specialises in fire reconstruction – like a pathologist, he carries out post-mortems, but on fire. Over the past fifteen years, working as a private consultant, he's completed more than 100 of these reconstructions, including after the 2009 Black Saturday fires in Victoria, before moving to Spain in 2017 in search of a life reset.

Since the beginning of December he's been spending every night in front of his computer, back on southern hemisphere time, using any data at his disposal – satellite images, weather observations, vegetation maps – to unpick what's been happening back home. He's concluded that the RFS is getting too many things wrong – missing opportunities to contain fires, using the wrong tactics – and wants to offer his advice on how to change course before it gets worse. Even given his level of experience, trying to school the commissioner of the RFS in fire strategy is bold. But watching fires continually consume the landscapes to which he feels a deep connection is leading him to despair.

In this letter, he tells Fitzsimmons that the firefighting community needs to accept that the rules of engagement have changed; to 'recognise that we are working in a climate-change world and adapt our firefighting policies and practices accordingly'. He can see a pattern forming in which many fires are only being fought once they emerge from the forests and threaten properties. He tells Fitzsimmons a better strategy would be to use the days of mild weather to identify these problem spots in remote areas and go in hard – target the fire when it's 'at its weakest point' with aerial water-bombing so as to 'minimise the size of a fire and the width of head fire before a blow-up day'. He tells Fitzsimmons an example 'of how not to do it' is what's just happened in Nerriga.

Gellie has seen a satellite image of the area around Nerriga taken on 21 December, just hours before the arrival of the southerly change. It shows an enormous 23-kilometre fire front, burning back deeply into the ranges. Justin Parr's suspicion that there must have been more fire lurking in the remote gorges and ranges south of the village than he realised was correct. For Gellie, this large body of fire provides a perfect explanation for why a pyrocumulonimbus occurred. A large fire like this, consuming 'bone-dry fuels', is ripe for such an event. Assuming the RFS knew it was there – which he does – he thinks that instead of ignoring it until it had formed into an unstoppable firestorm about to hit a village the weekend before Christmas, the RFS could have attacked it days earlier, mitigating its severity.

Gellie is also concerned about what he considers an over-reliance on large-scale back-burning. He knows that lighting up long lines of back-burns drains resources, chewing up hours of time that could be spent on other tasks. But he is mostly worried about the way the perilously dry landscape is reacting to fire – making what has long been a standard practice inherently riskier. 'I am also critical about some of the failed back-burning strategies that caused new fires well away from the main fire fronts,' he writes to Fitzsimmons.

The RFS has already publicly acknowledged that one of the back-burns lit this season, on the Gospers Mountain fire, escaped and destroyed more than twenty homes in the Blue Mountains. But from what Nick Gellie has seen, there have been many more escapes: a multitude of smaller ones that served to make fires bigger than they needed to be, but also one with disastrous consequences. Gellie believes a devastating fire run into the village of Balmoral, in the Southern Highlands, in mid-December, was the direct result of a back-burn. From afar, Gellie could see that this burn was lit on the eve of forecast temperatures of 40-plus degrees and strong winds, and escaped under these conditions the next day. (An RFS internal inquiry, held after the fire season, will confirm this.) This Balmoral fire destroyed more than twenty homes.

Gellie doesn't advocate abandoning back-burning, just reconsidering it in certain circumstances, like 'the day or hours before a hot and dry and windy wind change which spread the fire'.

As he finalises his letter, Gellie is not hopeful he'll be listened to. He thinks the state already failed to heed the most fundamental of warnings in the lead-up to the fire season. 'Because of the severe drought across New South Wales, the State should have been prepared for very large areas burnt this fire season,' he writes. Even before the climate started changing, Australia's largest fires have almost always come after periods of prolonged drought. 'This is not unprecedented,' he writes, 'going back in time 1.3 million ha were burnt in Victoria in 1938–39.'

Because Australia has always been a fire-prone country, there are many lessons in the past. Starting in 1937, a severe drought gripped eastern Australia. Two years later, the summer of 1938, a ferocious fire season launched along the eastern seaboard.

By the second week of January 1939, the state of Victoria was weary after more than six weeks of unrelenting bushfires. With more than 75 per cent of the state affected by fire, and nearly all the forests of the Great Dividing Range alight, it was hard to imagine how things could get worse.

But on 13 January 1939 – a day that would become known as Black Friday – extreme heat and wind fuelled several major fire runs. In a single day, six villages were destroyed and thirty-six people killed. The judge appointed to lead the royal commission into Black Friday, Leonard Stretton, wrote in his report:

Dry heat and hot, dry winds worked upon a land already dry, to suck from it the last, least drop of moisture. Men who had lived their lives in the bush went their ways in the shadow of dread expectancy. But though they felt the imminence of danger they could not tell that it was to be far greater than they could imagine. They had not lived long enough.

On 27 December 2019, the RFS starts warning New South Wales to brace for an exceptionally dangerous fire day on New Year's Eve. Temperatures, already above 30 degrees in most places, are going to climb every day until 31 December, when they will soar above 40 degrees.

This dangerous day is coming as more than eighty fires still burn across New South Wales, with serious blazes also underway in Victoria, South Australia and Western Australia. On the South Coast, Mark Williams, incident controller for the Currowan fire, has just four days to prepare for this new threat.

The scale of what he's facing is immense. The Currowan fire is still travelling through the forests that lie parallel to the coast, with the entire area of the fireground more than 2,700 square kilometres. If you were to follow the Princes Highway along the fire's north–south axis, from near Batemans Bay in the south all the way north to Nowra, you would travel a distance of nearly 120 kilometres.

The hot and dry weather that's dogged Williams all season is now turning its screws. Since Christmas, he's noticed a rapid acceleration in dieback – trees and plants dying where they stand. It's both a sign that the soil is too dry to sustain life and additional tinder in the landscape. Even the wind is behaving differently. The nor'easter – which usually blows in off the ocean, bringing moisture and humidity – seems to be coming in dry.

He also has a new fire. A week before Christmas, a blaze broke out in bushland just south of Nowra. The Comberton fire is minuscule compared to the Currowan – just a few dozen square kilometres – but it's hovering close to urban areas and burning through a swampy region layered with peat, which, once alight, can burn underground for weeks. This fire's level of danger is disproportionate to its size, and so it is sucking up his scarce resources, consistently demanding water-bombers, heavy machinery and crews.

While the head of the Currowan fire is now hovering near Nowra, it's persistently burning in many places within its guts, including areas not far from our property, where landowners have now been living with it for a month. Some of Williams' divisional commanders, who are 'getting flogged' on the northern push of the fire, grumble to him about all the resources still down that way; he has to remind them that 'no one is standing around with their thumb up their bum'. Everyone is flat out.

A new complication is that huge numbers of tourists are streaming into the fire zone. It's peak holiday season along the South Coast, when the population swells threefold or more. Numbers seem slightly down this year, but they're high enough to be concerning.

It's a predicament for the authorities. Police working from the emergency operations centre housed inside the RFS fire control centre in Nowra can see that the influx of visitors is adding to the burden on emergency services. But the local economy relies on tourism. For many small businesses, summer trade is the only way they make it through the winter. The operations centre opts for a message of gentle deterrence, telling prospective visitors, 'If you don't need to be here, then we are encouraging you to reconsider your travel plan.'

Most won't be budged from long-planned holidays. Some call ahead to ask their caravan park or Airbnb host, *How smoky it is down there? Sydney is shocking!* Mostly they're told, *Everything is fine. Please come.*

Williams is again treading the floorboards at community meetings, focusing on the villages and urban sprawl around Nowra. It's all happening fast. Just half an hour before he's due to speak at the Bomaderry Bowling Club in Nowra, the Comberton fire jumps containment lines. He's only just finished redirecting water-bombers when he walks out in front of the crowd.

Williams is speaking to an audience of the largely uninitiated – people who live in neat suburban blocks and have never had to consider the prospect of a wildfire. One elderly man asks, 'Should I clean out my gutters before I put water in?' A woman speaks with a hint of complaint: 'How long are we going to be in limbo? I've got horses.'

Williams is patient yet blunt, warning that if the forecast conditions eventuate on New Year's Eve, 'We will not be in a situation where we can stand firefighters in front of the flames and expect them to pull this thing up. We are getting additional assistance in ... but there cannot be, and there will not be, a fire appliance for every resident.' In other words, don't expect a fire truck.

As the year draws to a close, I am thinking, *Good riddance.* December 2019 has been a hideous month.

Later, though, I will come to judge this period less harshly. Yes, it was gruelling, sad, disruptive and terrifying, but even amid all this there was a tenuous sense of order to be found; a path through to normality, even if dimly lit. I will only come to this view once I am forced to compare it with what comes next. When this long-running disaster that is only tenuously being held in check descends into chaos.

PART TWO

DAY OF DISASTERS

NEW SOUTH WALES

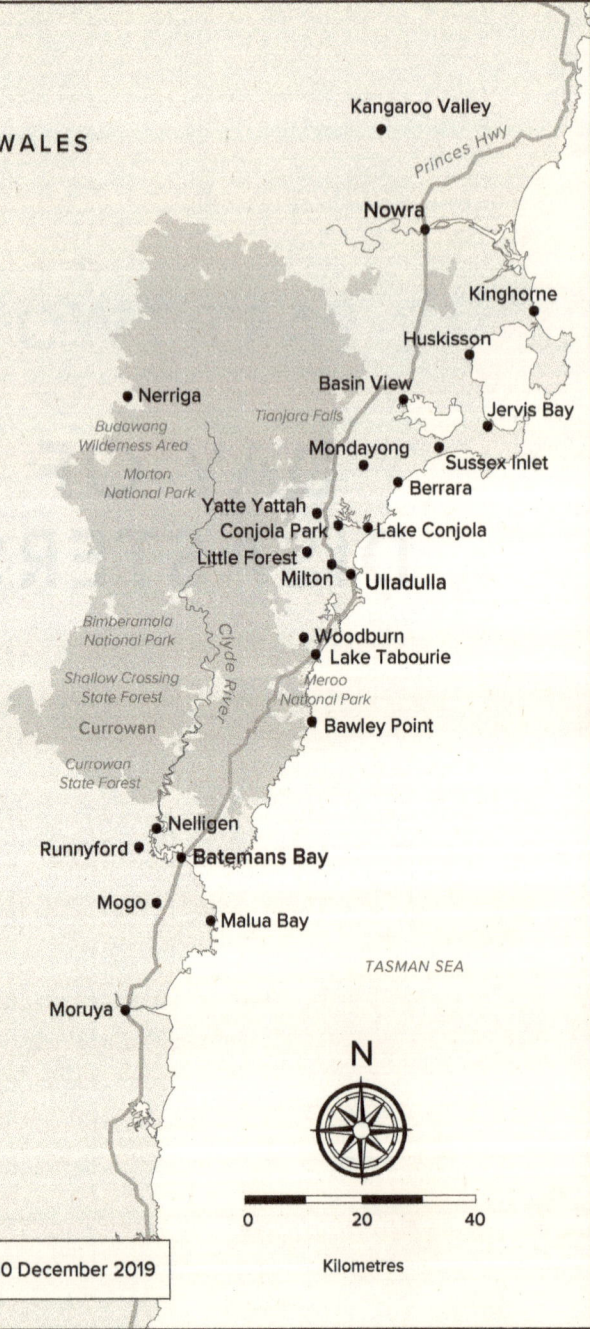

Kangaroo Valley

Princes Hwy

Nowra

Kinghorne

Huskisson

Nerriga

Budawang
Wilderness Area

Tianjara Falls

Basin View

Jervis Bay

Morton
National Park

Mondayong

Sussex Inlet

Berrara

Yatte Yattah

Conjola Park

Lake Conjola

Little Forest

Milton

Ulladulla

Bimberamola
National Park

Clyde River

Woodburn

Lake Tabourie

Shallow Crossing
State Forest

Meroo
National Park

Currowan

Bawley Point

Currowan
State Forest

Nelligen

Runnyford

Batemans Bay

Mogo

Malua Bay

TASMAN SEA

Moruya

N

0   20   40

Kilometres

Currowan fire, 30 December 2019

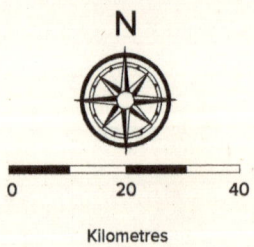

CHAPTER 8

BEST-LAID PLANS

If not for the relentless haze of bushfire smoke, on 30 December 2019 Lake Conjola – a little village of 400 people, tucked in between a coastal forest and an estuary – would have looked exactly as it always does at this time of year. On the foreshore, all four caravan parks are brimming with thousands of holidaymakers; beach towels are slung over railings of cabin verandahs, and caravans and tents are hemmed in on the grass like stamps. It's belting hot, in the high thirties, and almost everyone is making a beeline for the water. Boats are launched from the jetty as people go in search of flathead or bream. Families with children carrying buckets and shovels troop the few hundred metres along the sand to where the lake meets the ocean. Surfers paddle out towards the tiny island off the coast in search of waves.

Further up the lake, in the quiet leafy hamlet of Conjola Park, Justine Donohoe has arrived back home after spending Christmas in Sydney. It was a brief respite after an unsettled month spent watching the Currowan fire progress up the coast, and she's looking forward to unpacking and returning some normalcy to her summer.

Conjola Park is largely residential, removed from the hol-

iday hustle down at the lake's entrance. Justine loves that she
can let her boys, aged eight and twelve, roam like 'free-range
chickens' here, without worrying 'a car is going to come flying
past and knock them off their bike'. Few of the homes in her
street have fences, and there's a mix of older people and young
families like hers. 'We're all raising our kids in this wonderful
knowledge that it's a safe little street, off the beaten track, just
such a safe nest of family comfort,' she says.

When the Currowan fire hit Bawley Point back in early
December, even though Conjola Park was 40 kilometres north,
Justine immediately packed up important family documents
and placed a 'grab bucket' by the front door, filled with fire-safe
clothing and masks. She instructed the boys, 'If it comes, if it
happens, when I say it's time to put these clothes on, you must
listen to me.'

Justine's husband works on the ports in Sydney, meaning
he is away for long stretches of time, and together they had
decided on the family fire plan. 'We both work our arses off
to insure our property,' says Justine, 'so our plan was always, if
it comes anywhere near us, or if there is a warning even close,
we're out.' When the fire started passing west of Conjola Park
and Lake Conjola in the week before Christmas, she – like
many of her neighbours – followed the RFS warnings and
evacuated, taking the kids and staying overnight with a friend
in a nearby town. But today the atmosphere on the street is
more relaxed. Anxiety has eased now the fire front has moved
at least 50 kilometres to their north.

The RFS has been sending out a barrage of warnings about
the impending dangerous fire weather for days. The official
fire danger rating for the South Coast tomorrow is *extreme* –
only one lower than *catastrophic*. The RFS has released a Fire
Spread Prediction Map for New Year's Eve, showing which

communities it expects will come under threat from the Currowan fire. It identifies two areas of potential fire spread: the northern front, pushing towards Nowra; and the southern end of the fire, spreading towards the coastal town of Batemans Bay. The map shows ember attack coming from the long eastern flank of the fire, but nothing crossing over the highway towards the coast. Both Conjola Park and Lake Conjola are fire-free.

Justine still has her bucket by the door and is regularly checking the Fires Near Me app, but she's feeling good about finally 'plugging back into life'. At 5.00 pm she's meant to be meeting her neighbour for a puppy play date in the park, but it's way too hot to be outside, so they stay in, where they share a bottle of champagne and laughter, making plans to catch up again on New Year's Eve.

Down the road at his home in Lake Conjola, Peter Dunn is one of the few not settling into the seductions of this festive hot summer's day. He's edgy – perplexed at how the RFS fire-behaviour analysts who created this prediction map have come to the conclusion that Lake Conjola and surrounds will face no threat tomorrow. He's been studying the weather forecast, and from what he can see, tomorrow is going to be 'seriously dangerous for this community'.

Dunn is a former commissioner of the agency that oversees all emergency services in the Australian Capital Territory and a retired army major-general, so he knows plenty about analysing risk. He's also acutely aware of the dangers of this fire season. Earlier in the year, he was enjoying his lakeside retirement with his wife, Lindy, when he received a phone call from Greg Mullins, asking if he wanted to join Emergency Leaders for Climate Action. Dunn accepted immediately, because he believed that government assertions Australia was ready and resourced for the fire season were 'absolute rubbish', and in November he travelled to Sydney to speak at some of the group's press conferences. But now, his focus is narrowing to his own community.

There's a couple of things troubling Dunn. With strong nor'westerly winds forecast for the morning, he can't see how the eastern flank of the Currowan fire is not highly susceptible to a fire escape – one that places this coastal area directly in its path. The lack of evacuation routes is also an enormous hazard. Like many South Coast villages, there is only one way in and out of both Lake Conjola and Conjola Park – a long, narrow, tree-lined road off the highway. *If things go wrong*, he thinks, *what's the plan for the thousands of people here?*

Dunn calls a colleague, another former high-ranking emergency services leader, to get a fresh perspective. 'I said to him, "I think it's going to go pear-shaped," and he agreed. It was disconcerting.'

That afternoon, Peter and Lindy warn some of their immediate neighbours: *We don't like the look of this*. After hearing what they have to say, at least one family packs up and leaves.

The Dunns have experienced what happens when fire hits a town before. They were at home in Canberra in 2003 when fire roared into the suburbs, killing four people, injuring hundreds and destroying more than 500 homes. Peter and Lindy defended their home then, and now set about preparing to do it again.

At the fire control centre in Nowra, Mark Williams and the incident management team are preparing for what will almost certainly be the Currowan fire's most dangerous day yet. Their only measure of relief is that the scale of what they're facing has been reduced. RFS headquarters in Sydney has just carved off the southern section of the Currowan fire, the front that is threatening Batemans Bay, and handed over its responsibility to a new incident management team based further south.

Williams and the team are now left with the northern front, advancing towards the densely populated urban area south of Nowra, and the long eastern flank, hovering close to a string of coastal villages, including those around Lake Conjola. Their assessment – supported by the Fire Spread Prediction Map – is that the northern front holds the greatest threat. When they set about planning resources for the following day, they allocate the vast majority of fire trucks and firefighters to this area, at the expense of the eastern flank. For the night shift of New Year's Eve, the eastern flank is assigned no resources at all.

Part of the reason for the confidence that this eastern side of the fire will pose less risk is that crews have been working non-stop since Christmas to put in a containment line down a large part of its length – nearly 60 kilometres, built with back-burns and heavy machinery. If any fire escapes on New Year's Eve, the idea is that this line will prevent it reaching the coastal villages. It's been an ambitious undertaking. Now it's nearly finished, bar one section northwest of Conjola Park, where a planned back-burn hasn't yet been started.

By Monday, 30 December, winds are due to start picking up by evening, with humidity dropping overnight and an increased fire danger by the early hours of Tuesday morning. Williams decides that if they don't do something about this gap in their defensive line it will be a 'major flaw' in their system – akin to 'leaving a gate open' on a farm, allowing a route for the animals to escape. So the incident management team instructs crews to light up a length of back-burn five kilometres long.

When a National Parks and Wildlife crew rolls up in the semi-rural locality of Yatte Yattah late on Monday afternoon and prepares to light one of the sections, locals who see what's happening are furious. Everyone in this area is already on edge. Properties here are bordered by the hinterland that sweeps down from the escarpment – dry eucalypt forest and rainforest struggling in the drought – and the prediction map has identified them as a target for ember attack the next day.

Like most of their neighbours in Yatte Yattah, Ian and Fiona Stewart have been working solidly for weeks preparing for the Currowan fire – clearing undergrowth, setting up water pumps and fitting sprinklers to their home of thirty years. They are already uneasy about the back-burning operations they know are underway further out in the forests to their northwest. They received a text message from the RFS on Christmas Day informing them that incendiaries were being dropped from helicopters, and Fiona, perplexed as to why they were being dropped in this location and wanting to know the plan to safeguard their area, called the fire control centre several times, but felt fobbed off. 'It was like they didn't want to know about us,' she says. Since 27 December, the Stewarts have seen fire trucks turn up at a road near their property continually, with the crews on board explaining that they are waiting to assist a planned back-burn. But nothing has been lit – until now.

The Stewarts are horrified it's still going ahead, just as the weather is about to worsen.

In a paddock, some of their neighbours get into an angry confrontation with the fire crew. 'Everyone was saying, "Don't light it,"' says Fiona. 'If it was four days ago, sure, maybe, but not now.'

Yet by nightfall, the back-burn is raging; the Stewarts and their neighbours watch it climb higher and higher, up the trunks of trees, spitting out embers. When the Conjola RFS brigade turns up, tasked with mopping up this burn, volunteer Martin Lee encounters the group, who he says are 'furious, rabid'.

When Lee sees the back-burn, he thinks, *What the hell?* The wind is already up and fire is racing off into inaccessible gullies. It was preposterous to consider that a fire lit in those conditions could be extinguished. 'We didn't put it out – we couldn't put it out,' he says.

At 8.30 pm, an RFS line-scanner plane flies over the eastern flank of the Currowan fire. It captures several small glows of fire, burning just below the escarpment a few kilometres south of the back-burn. One is above a semi-rural area called Little Forest. The incident management team in Nowra note this fire down, but decide not to commit any crews to it, because of concerns over sending them in to unfamiliar fire trails in the dark.

From his farm just below the escarpment, Brendan Cowled can also see the glow of this fire above Little Forest. He knows it's his old adversary: the spot fire from 19 December that he couldn't get water-bombed. Now even more spread out around him, it's starting to stew. He can also see the other fire, just further north; it's a spillover from the escarpment of the Currowan fire. As he's found often over the previous weeks, the Fires Near Me app is not reflecting what he can see on the ground.

Brendan is at home with his wife, Kim Wilson – their children are with family elsewhere – and they agree to keep watch throughout the night, trading off in two-hour shifts.

It's late when Michelle Morales returns to her home in Conjola Park, after an evening out in a nearby town with visiting family. She discovers that while she was out she missed a drop-in from her partner, Laurie Andrew. She only knows he's come by because a neighbour tells her they spotted him watering her plants. *Typical Laurie*, Michelle thinks. Like everyone in the forested areas west of the coast, he'd be busy with preparations for the treacherous fire day tomorrow, and yet here he was, still looking out for her.

Michelle is sixty-three, with short silver hair, large dark eyes and an effusive demeanour that, as anyone who knows her will tell you, only becomes more pronounced – she becomes almost giddy – when she talks about Laurie. They've been a couple for fourteen years. Laurie, who is seventy, is something of a South Coast raconteur. He first arrived in the area nearly fifty years ago, as part of the surveying team that designed the system which delivers water from the escarpment to the whole district, and has been here virtually ever since – working, surfing, volunteering for local sporting clubs, seeking out local music. 'He just knows about so many things,' says Michelle.

They've always kept separate homes. Michelle's is by the lake; Laurie's is a bush property just a few kilometres away. Over December, she's noticed he's become increasingly preoccupied by the drought and by readying his property for the Currowan fire. Even when he's sitting on her front patio, he's still looking out at the national park across the lake and spotting dying trees. 'Look, Michelle, there's another one,' he'd say.

Michelle is not concerned for her place, but she knows Laurie is expecting tomorrow could be bad for his – so it's unlikely she'll see him again tonight, or even tomorrow. But she's not overly worried by all the disruption of the last month. They've both just retired, Michelle from teaching, Laurie from the local council; once this fire is over they'll have all the time in the world.

*

Almost 70 kilometres south of Conjola Park, the southern end of the Currowan fire is burning in mountainous forests, where it is poised directly to the northwest of the large town of Batemans Bay and dozens of smaller coastal villages. The area is home to around 6,000 residents, though like everywhere along the South Coast right now, it's heaving with many thousands of tourists. The last-minute call by RFS headquarters to hand over responsibility for this section of the fire to a newly assembled incident management team – a decision no doubt influenced by the scale of the threat – has left the new team little time to prepare for New Year's Eve.

On Sunday, 29 December, members of the new incident management team hold their first community meeting, at a function centre in Batemans Bay, to warn residents about the dire day that is coming. Hundreds of people turn up. 'Bottom line,' one says to the crowd, 'if you live close to the bush and you are not prepared to defend, we recommend you are not there after 9.00 am.'

The Currowan fire is here, at this new doorstep, because of failed attempts to contain it. Initially, it only moved slowly south. By mid-December, it was being held at the Kings Highway, the main route between the South Coast and Canberra. Holding it there was crucial: once it got over into the wild terrain on the other side of the highway, a whole new slew of coastal communities, including Batemans Bay, would become exposed. Within days, though, it escaped in several places. One escape came from a back-burn. Another, a spot-fire that ignited in the remote reaches of the Monga National Park, where ever since it's been burning uncontrolled through temperate rainforests and deep valleys of eucalypts.

The RFS team tell the community meeting that this fire in Monga looks to be dangerous – signs of pyrocumulonimbus storms have been spotted. But as yet they don't really know what it's doing. Smoke is hampering opportunities to get line scans, and because the fire is in an area inaccessible to fire-fighters, even figuring out exactly where it is involves 'a bit of a guesstimation', one says.

They set out their strategy. Heavy machinery has been working for days, constructing lines between the forests and the urban areas – a buffer to try to halt any fire before it reaches the villages. Unlike their colleagues managing the eastern flank of the Currowan fire, they won't be back-burning. 'Ahead of the weather conditions over the next couple of days, it is not safe to introduce any more fire,' one of the team says.

The weather outlook for New Year's Eve is so grim they warn that once the fire starts running, retreat will be the only option – they will 'watch the fire as it spreads' and pull back to focus on 'the protection of life and property'.

The Currowan fire is not the only one on their watch. Another four fires have recently started along the far South Coast. One, the Badja Forest Road fire, ignited a few nights earlier from a single strike of lightning and is burning uncontained in remote national park west of the farming village of Cobargo, about 100 kilometres south of Batemans Bay. 'It is currently up in extremely remote country,' one of the team tells the community meeting. 'We are just sitting and watching that one at the moment. It's not affecting anybody, it's not threatening any property at the moment. And we will deal with that one once we can. But our priority at the moment is addressing the fire among the community of the Batemans Bay region.'

The next day, Monday, 30 December, is only this new incident management team's first full day of operations. They are setting up, still gathering staff, at the RFS fire control centre in the country town of Moruya, about 20 kilometres south of Batemans Bay. Even though they are now less than twenty-four hours away from what looks to be the most dangerous day of the entire fire season, with several out-of-control fires lurking to the west of many thousands of homes, they still don't know the contours of what they are facing. At 8.00 am, when they issue their first Incident Action Plan – a document meant to guide operations for the next twenty-four hours – both the area and the perimeter of the fires they are responsible for are marked as 'TBC' (to be confirmed). The plan notes that they are still requesting access to an RFS line scanner plan to map the fires.

It's late in the afternoon on 30 December when the captain of the Malua Bay RFS, Ian Barnes, sits down at his computer to write an email to all his brigade members. He knows trepidation is growing about the coming day, and a couple of have asked for his assessment of what they could be facing.

Malua Bay is one of the little villages in the area of tightly packed coastal development around Batemans Bay. The RFS's Fire Spread Prediction Map for New Year's Eve shows the southern front of the Currowan fire surging through the forests, and visiting a vast spray of ember attacks upon Batemans Bay and surrounds – including the fringes of Malua Bay.

Being the captain of a Rural Fire Service brigade is always a heavy responsibility – especially considering it's a volunteer position – but at this moment the weight is especially pressing. While Barnes and his crew have been venturing all over the South Coast fighting the Currowan fire nearly every day for the past five weeks, he knows that tomorrow there is a strong chance it will be coming to them.

It is exactly the terrifying scenario Barnes envisaged back in November with his training workshop, 'Fire from the west' – an out-of-control blaze barrelling out of the forests and into the urban areas.

Barnes takes stock. His brigade's area of responsibility around Malua Bay covers nearly 1,500 homes. He has two large fire trucks and a LandCruiser ute, and around twelve volunteers he expects will turn up ready to fight. As always, his priority is making sure every one of his volunteers returns 'alive and well'. He knows his members are dedicated, but they're weary. As is not unusual for brigades in what he calls 'the retirement dormitories' along the coast, the average age is 'well over sixty, nudging seventy' – himself included. There's even an eighty-year-old. The best he can do now, he thinks, is to make sure they are all well informed of the risks, and organised.

Barnes scrutinises topographic maps, satellite images and the RFS Fire Spread Prediction Map to give his members the most accurate picture possible. In his email, he tells them that they're facing 'the worst scenario' he's seen in more than fifty years. He identifies three fires as potential threats. One is a small new blaze in a place called Deua River Valley. The other two are sections of the Currowan fire: an area burning near Nelligen, and the blaze that's been brewing in the Monga National Park for the past eleven days, which he calls 'a child of the Currowan fire'. (The RFS has now given the southern section of the Currowan fire a new name – but it is the same fire.)

He writes that under the forecast hot westerly winds, all three of these fires will almost certainly make a run towards the coast. Exactly when, and how far they will reach, he has no way of knowing. He says he thinks it unlikely, though not impossible, that fire will enter the urban area of Malua Bay, but he warns his members they should expect to be defending homes on the outskirts of town.

He tells everyone to assemble at the Malua Bay fire shed at 8.00 am to be on standby. The usual practice for assembling a crew is that the fire control centre pages volunteers once a fire emergency has been identified. But given the danger of the day, Barnes believes it's wiser to be proactive. If all hands are at the station by 8.00 am, he'll be better placed to organise them to respond to whatever the day brings.

In the meantime, he writes, they should all keep their phones and pagers on them in case anything changes.

That night he goes to bed – pager beside him – uneasy about the morning, but confident he has a plan in place.

Barnes has no way of knowing that he is missing two crucial pieces of information the incident management team in Moruya has received but not passed on to him – even though it is Barnes and his crew who will be the ones standing in front of the flames. One is a new line scan, taken around 8.00 pm that evening, showing the Currowan fire already on the move, heading for the coast. The other is another Fire Spread Prediction Map – different from the one that was released to the public – that a fire-behaviour analyst has prepared specifically for the RFS team in Moruya. This map is more detailed, tracking the path of the fire in three-hourly intervals. Not only does it show the fire advancing much further than in the public map, engulfing the whole of Malua Bay, right down to the water's edge, but it shows it arriving in the urban area sometime between 9.00 am and midday.

If this prediction is right, not only will the day be much worse than Barnes expects, but 8.00 am is going to be way too late to assemble his crews.

CHAPTER 9

COLLISION COURSE

Everything starts veering off-course while Ian Barnes is sleeping.

Early in the night of Monday, 30 December, not long after he sends his email, one of his crews heads off in a fire truck for a regular overnight shift. They're tasked with helping to contain the Deua River Valley fire. It's not expected to be an eventful shift. Fires don't usually run hard during the night – cooler temperatures and higher humidity, which feeds moisture into the vegetation, are usually enough to still or at least slow a blaze. It's a time when firefighters typically have the upper hand against even the most ferocious fire.

But when they arrive around 8.00 pm, the Deua River Valley fire has already broken through containment lines and is bolting into mountainous, rugged country. It is completely unstoppable, so the crew is sent back to the station.

Soon they are called out again; triple-zero calls are coming in from a semi-rural area just west of the village of Nelligen. The Currowan fire is now also awake.

When they arrive at the site at midnight, a hot westerly is blowing, with spot fires lighting up in paddocks all over the place. The crew immediately set about defending homes and lives. In the dark, smoky night, they trundle up the unfamiliar and narrow tree-lined driveways in Malua Bay 1, a 13-tonne truck, staying alert for safe places to turn around. As they pull into one property, fire suddenly roars in and the driver has to quickly pull in behind a shed for shelter.

Most residents they encounter are up and fighting, but some need waking. At one property, they find an elderly couple trying to beat back the flames with a stick. The pair refuse to leave their home, and eventually the team must move on. Another man, blind drunk, is more easily convinced.

At 3.00 am, one of the crew yells, 'What's that noise?'

Malua Bay 1 is being led by Graham Skelton, a sixty-seven-year-old retiree, and for the first time in three hours he pauses. He can hear it too – it sounds like a freight train, and it's coming from the other side of the valley, where beyond the black outline of the ridge he can see flashes of light bursting into the night sky.

Skelton immediately understands what's going on. This is the 'child of the Currowan fire' Barnes warned them about – the one brewing in Monga National Park. Not only is it on the move, but it's already crowning and travelling at great speed.

Skelton gets one of the crew to radio the fire control centre in Moruya, to tell them what they're witnessing. He and his crew know this fire run is not coming for them at Nelligen; instead it's barrelling towards the coast, in the direction of thousands of homes where people – including their own families – are sleeping. But there is no time to dwell on this – they must return to fighting the fire in front of them.

The last day of the year is only three hours old, and already all three fires that Ian Barnes had identified as potential risks are on the move.

*

Outside the RFS fire control centre, on a wide residential street in the country town of Moruya, the night is still. Dim street-lights cast shadows over the double-storey blonde-brick build-ing and the empty playing field beside it. The row of weath-erboard homes opposite is dark, and the only sound is the occasional lowing of a cow, floating in from the surrounding farmland. But inside the building, a handful of overnight staff are being bombarded with reports of simultaneous life-threat-ening fire emergencies.

It's not just the Currowan fire that is making a night-time run. One hundred kilometres further south, the Badja Forest Road fire – the one the incident management team decided thirty-six hours earlier to just monitor because 'it's not affect-ing anybody' – has also exploded out of the forests and is right now racing across farmland and towards the far South Coast villages of Quaama, population 280, and Cobargo, 800.

This is freakish fire behaviour. The weather conditions are far exceeding any of the forecasts. At 1.00 am, a weather station located on a private property near the Badja fire records the temperature at 34 degrees, with wind gusts up to 75 kilometres per hour and humidity dropping as low as 9 per cent – a com-bination that translates to a fire danger rating of *severe*. Before it is overrun by fire, another weather station just further north records values equating to *catastrophic*, *extreme* and *severe* – all before dawn.

Aggressive fire behaviour at night is a new phenomenon being witnessed in wildfire-prone countries around the globe. Scientists say it is the latest symptom of a warming world. Alarm bells are ringing in California, where recent analysis shows night-time temperatures are increasing faster than daytime temperatures. Scientists suspect that heatwaves – like the ones Australia has just experienced over December – are also driving night-time fires. Prolonged periods of heat during the day reduce overnight humidity, meaning vegetation misses out on an injection of moisture. Heatwaves also limit the formation of the atmospheric blankets that usually descend close to Earth's surface at night, cooling and stilling winds – meaning the night becomes more exposed to strong and gusty squalls.

Australia is not equipped to tackle this upending of the natural order, of the night no longer being safe. Adaptions had been considered – back during the 2016–17 fire season, the RFS conducted a trial of night-time aerial firefighting operations. Aircraft were upgraded, pilots trained and night-vision devices purchased for the trial. But the RFS did not document the results and nothing was implemented.

Now, all the incident management team in Moruya can do is try to get people out of the way. At 1.30 am they send out the first emergency alert for the night – to the mobile phones and landlines of people in the path of the rapidly moving Badja Forest Road fire. At his farmhouse near Quaama, my brother receives one of these text messages. It's what has him and his family out of the house and onto the road, racing towards a coastal headland, when I make contact with him at 3.00 am – after I've jolted from sleep in Bawley Point and seen the Fires Near Me app, which has been updated to show this night-time fire run.

RFS emergency alerts never reach all their targets, though. The strike rate for successful delivery is between 70 and 80 per cent. Mobile phones can be switched off; people sleep through a ringing landline; other times there's no explanation at all. So, by 4.12 am, when the Badja fire has covered more than 20 kilometres and is roaring into the little village of Quaama, and by 5.10 am, when it's hitting the town of Cobargo, many people are waking for the first time only to discover flames on their doorsteps.

The resulting chaos is what I am listening to on the scanner from my kitchen in Bawley Point: firefighters panicking because residents are trying to escape Cobargo but are driving directly into the path of the fire; reports of the family in need of rescue, whose children's bare feet are burning as they flee from their home.

The first big hit from the running Currowan fire comes without warning. At 4.14 am, in the little riverside settlement of Runnyford – about five kilometres upstream of Batemans Bay – Rae Harvey is roused by banging on her bedroom window. She's only been asleep for a few hours, having stayed up late to make last-minute preparations for the high-risk fire day ahead. Now she can hear her neighbour, Simon, screaming, 'It's here. Get up. Get ready!'

Rae stumbles outside. The first thing she notices is that the kangaroos are gone. Rae is a wildlife carer – she's the person who's spent the last month supplying food for wildlife feeding stations on properties further north already hit by the Currowan fire, including my own. Usually at this time in the morning she'd have thirty to forty eastern grey kangaroos on the grass in front of her house – animals she loves like a mother loves her child.

The team in Moruya issued an emergency alert for Runnyford at 3.58 am – most likely due, at least partly, to the intelligence Graham Skelton and the crew of Malua Bay 1 radioed in. But the Deua River Valley fire has already burned through a nearby telecommunications tower, knocking out most mobile-phone and internet connection, so no one on the scattering of properties here receives it. Either way, Runnyford is tucked between bush and river – the only way out is via dirt roads through the forest – so by the time the alert is sent it's far too late to leave anyway.

Through the smoke and roaring wind, Rae spots Lily and Holly and another kangaroo she can't quite identify. She tries to coax them inside her house – it's sturdy brick and should be safe – but they're terrified and take off.

Rae has a volunteer from the United States staying with her, and for the next few hours they wet down the house and its surrounds. Rae waters the grass that leads to the mangroves in case any kangaroos appear and need a safe passage. When it's clear the property is about to be overrun, she grabs her cat and they sprint down to the river, flames at their back, and jump in. But it's deep. Rae knows she can't hold the cat and stay afloat for long, but she won't let the animal go. With her free hand she gets her phone and takes a photo of a marker post on a nearby oyster lease so at least it will be known where she died.

Then, out on the water, a silver tinnie comes motoring through the smoke and roaring noise towards them. It's Simon, the neighbour, back to get them. As they pull away from the bank, the dawn river – normally a clear glass plate – is slate grey and choppy, like the ocean; the sky above them is a deep orange streaked with black. About 100 metres from shore they look back, and both Rae and Simon see their homes explode into flames.

By dawn, the reach of the Currowan fire running from Nelligen has merged with that coming from Monga, and the Deua River Valley fire is running alongside. Together they form a 30-kilometre-wide fire wall that is racing at speed out of the forests, towards the coast. It is now inevitable that the fire will soon start charging into villages both inland and along a vast portion of the coastal strip, from Batemans Bay down to Malua Bay and beyond.

At RFS headquarters in Sydney, planes and strike teams are being scrambled to assist with the simultaneous catastrophes now unfolding along the far South Coast.

At 5.30 am in Nowra, Mark Williams gets on the phone with his counterpart at the fire control centre in Moruya. 'He was shell-shocked,' says Williams. 'He just got absolutely pummelled, he was on that red phone doing emergency alerts all night'.

'He was certainly very, very professional and did an outstanding job, but he was very overloaded with the amount of work that was still coming in,' says Williams. He decides that he needs to go and help. Leaving his post in Nowra, Williams drives down the highway, past the eastern flank of the Currowan fire, towards the exploding southern front.

The fire is moving so fast that Williams nearly doesn't make it to Moruya. When he's 17 kilometres north, just about to enter the inland village of Mogo, he encounters a bend where fire is sweeping across both sides of the highway. He's in a command vehicle, not a fire truck, and conditions are on the cusp of being too dangerous to continue. But he pushes through, reaching Mogo, where 320 just-awake residents are spilling out of their homes and into thick smoke. Mogo is home to a large Aboriginal community, and Yuin Elders are being bundled into cars to escape, while others are pulling out garden hoses. On the main street, which is lined with heritage wooden buildings, shop owners are frantically wetting down their stores. Williams spots a couple of fire trucks and warns them about what's coming down the highway before pushing on again.

When he pulls into the fire control centre, he discovers the incident management team still trying to figure out exactly what's happening. 'Fire was just going on everywhere,' says Williams, 'so it was a matter of trying to find exactly where the fire had got to overnight. They were trying to get their situational awareness back up to speed.'

Williams starts helping to prepare for what he knows is going to be an 'Armageddon-type day'. The town has no dedicated emergency operations centre, where emergency services such as police and paramedics base themselves during a fire emergency, so a makeshift operation has been set up in the little red-brick RSL hall a few streets away from the fire control centre, with trestle tables from Bunnings hauled in. Williams works to 'get communications up to speed' between the two buildings. Moruya itself is not immune to the encroaching fires, so in the back of his mind he's thinking, *Okay, what are we going to do if we have to pack up?* There is absolutely no prospect of stopping or even directing this fire – the strategy for the day is just to survive it.

When Ian Barnes pulls up at the Malua Bay fire shed just before 8.00 am, he has no idea what's going on. Inexplicably, he hasn't received a page or a phone call from the fire control centre in Moruya. He also didn't receive the emergency alert that was sent out to the phones of residents in the Malua Bay area around 6.00 am. All he knows is that there is fire 'to the west of us, and big fire, because there was smoke everywhere'.

Even worse, both his fire trucks and most of his members are AWOL. Graham Skelton and the crew aboard Malua Bay 1 still haven't returned from their night shift, and he can't raise them on the radio. The only clue he has about the other missing truck, Malua Bay 7, is a message scrawled in chalk on the shed door: *Dave and Peter, Dog Trap Road, Cat 7, 6.30 am.*

Barnes is shocked the fire has come so early. He feels a flash of anger that he hasn't been paged when he is clearly needed, but quickly shakes this off. He has five volunteers in front of him now and the brigade's LandCruiser ute, Malua Bay 9: he needs to make a new plan for the day.

It's dawn outside Milton, and Brendan Cowled and Kim Wilson have been awake for hours. While they'd agreed to spend the night taking turns sleeping and keeping watch, the arrival of a hot wind in the early hours of the morning made them both too anxious to sleep, so at 3.30 am they got up and started filling gutters with water and getting the pumps and hoses ready.

Further along the eastern flank, fire crews working the overnight shift had also noticed a change after 3.00 am. They've started sending reports to the incident management team in Nowra that the weather conditions are 'deteriorating' and a 'significant escalation in fire activity' is being observed. By daybreak, the eastern flank of the Currowan fire is undoubtedly starting to simmer.

Brendan and Kim are standing in their front paddock, looking out across the bush below them, when they witness the first breakout of the eastern flank. It erupts out of the gully to their north like an explosion, sending a mushroom cloud of smoke billowing into the sky. Within minutes, they see flames shooting high above the canopies. It's coming from the place the RFS line scan captured glowing at 8.30 pm the night before – the one the incident management team decided not to commit any resources to. It is a reactivation of the spot fire that's been taunting Brendan ever since 19 December.

With the strong nor'wester behind it, they watch as it starts galloping away from them and straight towards the farmland and dozens of homes in Little Forest.

Kim calls triple zero. She tells the operator exactly where the fire is and where it's heading. 'There are houses down there and they might not know about it,' she says. It's 6.28 am. By now, the state's fire service is inundated with triple-zero calls coming in from the fire runs underway further down the South Coast, in places such as Cobargo, Mogo and Nelligen. (It will become a record-breaking day for the fire season, with more than 3,300 emergency calls for help.)

The operator replies, 'I can't promise what is going to go on here, but I will note it down and we will do what we can.'

After she hangs up, Kim climbs into her children's treehouse. From her vantage point she can see the fire gathering pace. 'It was igniting ahead of itself, four or five spots every minute,' she says. 'A whole new spot would come up several hundred metres ahead of it and then, *kaboom*, you would hear trees explode.' She phones those she knows down in the farmland, to warn them what's coming, but trusts that her triple-zero call will take care of the rest.

More fire begins to erupt from other sections of the eastern flank around 8.30 am. By just after 9.00 am, spot fires are landing west of the highway in semi-rural properties around Yatte Yattah and landholders are fighting back flames and calling triple zero. The direction the fire is coming from leads some to believe it's the back-burn that's escaped, and they tell emergency operators that the firefighters need to come and fix what they started. Soon, local fire trucks are responding to numerous individual callouts across the locality.

In Nowra, the incident management team knows fire is running from a number of places across the eastern flank, but there's confusion about exactly where it has broken from and how far it has travelled. The incident controller, Mark Williams, is still down in Moruya dealing with that crisis, but is on the phone to his deputy when he can. The team is still waiting on a line-scan plane to fly overhead so they can get an accurate picture of what's happening.

By 10.00 am, with three major bodies of fire blasting out of the eastern flank, no RFS emergency alerts have been issued and many thousands of people remain oblivious.

In Conjola Park, Justine Donohoe has just put on a load of washing – marvelling that the smoke haze has finally cleared for the first time in days and it's a blue-sky morning. She's deciding whether she will make a quick trip into Milton. She has a skin therapy business in town and a single client booked in; her husband is away working in Sydney, but she thinks, *Maybe I should just duck in and leave the boys home alone? I won't be long.*

The washing is still in the machine when she steps outside and notices smoke starting to gather in the distance. Then she spots a water-bombing helicopter, scooping from the lake and flying off to the northwest, only to see it return not long afterwards for more. 'I thought, *That's weird, it's not going very far.*' She's confused, because nothing is showing on the app, but decides she'll cancel the appointment and take the boys into town for the day, just to be safe.

It's only a few minutes' drive to the highway, but when she gets there, the way out is blocked by two utes. She doesn't know who the men are – they're not wearing any uniform – but they say, 'No, love, you can't get out, fire is already coming across the highway.' Justine is so panicked by this news that she can't even remember driving back home. Next thing she knows, she's standing in her kitchen, thinking, *What do I do now?*

A couple of kilometres away, forty-nine-year-old David

Bland is pulling out of his driveway in Little Forest to travel into town and get some horse feed. His elderly mother, Joan, is beside him. It's now been nearly four hours since Kim Wilson's triple-zero call warning that a fire run is headed for his area – something he knows nothing about. As he puts his foot on the accelerator he glances in the rear-view mirror, noticing a haze of smoke that looks somehow different. 'I can't remember if it was the smell or the look of it, but something had changed,' he says. He wasn't overly concerned; he'd checked the Fires Near Me app just before he got in the car and the Currowan fire was still at *advice* level, which means there is no threat to lives or property. But still, he decided to turn around. 'I said to Mum, I just want to go back and check on everything.'

While he's a plumber by trade, David has spent most of the past decade as a carer for his mother. They live together on a ten-hectare farm, in the house that David's now-deceased father built thirty-five years ago. He's been following the Currowan fire vigilantly ever since it started – 'I was checking the maps not once a day, I was checking them once an hour' – concerned for his own property, but also for the destruction of the landscapes he's traipsed through and felt a deep connection with ever since he was a boy. This area below the escarpment has fragmented remnants of both sub-tropical and dry rainforest – much of it critically endangered – and in recent years he's worked as a volunteer to preserve it. Aside from Charlie, his white sulphur-crested cockatoo, which he's raised from an abandoned chick, his most valued possessions are the botanical specimens he's gathered over the years – including a vast collection of rare rainforest seeds he's keeping for the restoration projects.

Joan goes inside to watch television and David checks the app again. Nothing has changed, so he wanders over the road.

His elderly neighbour is dragging out some hoses, so David stops to give him a hand. Then he looks down the paddock.

Out of nowhere, the crown of a tree explodes in flames.

Sprinting back to his house in a panic, he's aware of something – almost a presence – following behind him. He can also hear a growing roar, as though he's being chased by helicopters. But it's not until he's back in his home paddock that he stops and looks over his shoulder. A 'vortex thing' that resembles a tornado, spiralling furiously, is rising up over him. 'I thought for a second I might take my phone out and take a photo,' he says, 'and then I remember consciously thinking, *No, I don't want to remember that.*'

There's no sign of any flames – it's more like a wild windstorm. But he runs into the house and says, 'Mum, there is a fire.'

'What do I do?' she says.

'Call triple zero.'

David races back into the drought-parched paddock. He sees a single burned leaf flutter down in front of him and bends down to touch it to see if it's warm. 'And then I heard a noise like frying bacon. I turned around and a patch of grass behind me about six metres round was on fire.' He grabs his hat and starts beating out the flames. 'I got it out. And I thought, *I've done it!*' But by the time he stands upright, exhausted, 'everything, just everything, is on fire'.

'It just started raining fire. Snowballs of fire. They were making a sound when they hit the ground. Not one or two. The ground was littered with burned debris. That vortex thing had sucked everything up off the ground and lit it up and thrown it all the way from here to Milton.'

Their water tanks are nearly dry, but he's got a water pump set up in the swimming pool. He's given the cord just two quick pulls when 'the vegetation along the fence and the paling fence just erupted'.

At the same moment, seventy-nine-year-old Joan walks outside, phone in hand, saying, 'They won't answer, they won't answer.' David says, 'Put the phone down, Mum, we gotta go.' And without even going back into the house, they get in the car and drive away.

They're a kilometre down the road when David remembers he's left Charlie behind in her cage. He's completely distraught. They've pulled over along with others who have just fled Little Forest and he has to be physically restrained from turning back into the path of the fire.

What some of those who have spilled out of Little Forest see when they reach the highway is convoys of fire trucks coming south – a vast line of them. Many are relieved because they think help is on the way; a few even try to flag them down. But these are strike teams from Sydney destined for the other unfolding emergency – the southern front of the Currowan fire, which is right now tearing into Batemans Bay and Malua Bay. It is only over the coming hours that people on this eastern flank will discover that no such cavalcade is coming for them.

CHAPTER 10

MALUA BAY: FIRE FROM THE WEST

By just after 8.00 am, Ian Barnes has made a new plan. He and a driver will take the only fire vehicle left, Malua Bay 9, the single-cab ute, and the other four volunteers will follow in convoy, travelling in a private vehicle. Their first mission will be to find the fire truck on Dog Trap Road so they can team up and get everyone in a proper firefighting vehicle.

But they're only on the road for minutes before they run into fire. A house on an acreage, on the outskirts of Malua Bay, is being rained upon by embers – the owner and another two Cat 9s from elsewhere are trying desperately to save it. Barnes and his crew join in, rounding up the spot fires that are rapidly dotting the grounds. But suddenly, according to Barnes, 'It just goes crazy.'

In forty years of firefighting he's never seen a fire behave anything like this. Spot fires the size of a small dinghy are turning into the size of a house in an instant; turbulent winds are roaring in from all directions; embers are pouring from the sky like rain. Barnes can feel waves of radiant heat pushing towards him. They're all nearly out of water – a Cat 9 only holds 600 litres – so Barnes runs up to the house and says to the owner, 'It's time to go. You can't save it.'

It's a tough call to make – the owner is one of his brigade members, a man he knows well. But Barnes has to get his crew, who are unprotected in the private vehicle, out of danger, and he knows there's nothing they can do anyway.

Barnes directs his volunteers in the car to go back into the village, away from the fire, to start setting up standpipes (attachments fitted into the underground water mains so fire trucks can be refilled rapidly). He gives them a series of pre-arranged times to meet back at the fire shed; the mobile phone network has gone down and he doesn't want to lose track of anyone else.

Then Barnes and his driver set out along the ring roads that separate the rural residential parts of Malua Bay from the densely populated urban area. Blast of embers are coming down and fingers of fire appearing out of nowhere, but he's still hopeful the fire won't venture into the heart of the village. Yet around 10.00 am, he sees a body of fire on the wrong side of the road and knows that hope is gone: that 'embers are about to start dropping into backyards'.

No firefighter ever wants to turn their back on anyone in need, but Barnes has no choice. He tells his driver, 'We have to forget about the rural residential area, they're on their own. We have to start preparations to defend the urban area.' They swing their vehicle around, heading for town.

When Susan Magnay and her husband, Philip Bull, woke at 6.00 am in their townhouse on Sylvan Street, Malua Bay, to an automated phone message from the RFS warning that they were at risk and should head to the beach, she was 'concerned, not alarmed'.

Part of the reason the couple had chosen Malua Bay when they were looking to downsize from their acreage further south was that the town would be safe from bushfire. Retired, and with Philip not in great health, they wanted easier, trouble-free living, and had found it in this neat two-level – one of twelve in the row – just 500 metres from the beach.

Still, Susan thought it better to be cautious, so they packed a few changes of clothing, photos, documents and medication. 'We had a coffee,' says Susan, 'but we didn't have breakfast. We packed a few bananas but no water. We had a very short-term view of what was happening.' When they walked outside the sky was a strange red – *a terrible colour*, thought Philip, who remarked to his wife, 'This ain't right.'

By 10.00 am, they've been crammed alongside hundreds of others in the small brick surf club on the reserve next to the beach for nearly four hours. Susan is looking out the windows at the ocean, watching the colour of the sky changing like a kaleido-scope: moving between hues of red and orange, yellow and grey, and, increasingly, black. The power has gone out, so there's no air-conditioning or running water for drinking or flushing toilets. Smoke is coming in, and asthmatics and some older people are starting to wheeze. The temperature is 38 degrees and climbing.

The surf club is not an official evacuation centre, but the volunteer lifesavers have taken over the organisation of the growing crowd, which, including those gathered on the beach and grass reserve, now numbers around 1,500. Lifesavers are marshalling cars, finding spare Ventolin, bringing in food and hauling buckets of seawater up to the toilet block. There are no police, ambulance or firefighters in sight, and no one has mobile phone reception.

Inside the surf club, when Susan hears one of the lifesavers tell the crowd that everyone has to leave the building now and go to the beach, she feels 'numb'. She isn't frightened, because she can't take in what is happening.

As the crowd starts moving to the water's edge, Robyn Butcher is hovering close to her six elderly friends, four of whom have walking sticks, helping them as they navigate the uneven terrain over the low sand dunes towards the ocean. A brisk woman in her late sixties, Robyn is president of the Malua Bay Ladies Bowling Club, one of the most popular sporting clubs in town, and she had started corralling her 'bowlers' and their husbands earlier that day. Two slept through the early-morning RFS warning because they had their hearing aids off – they'd been oblivious to what was happening until she finally got through on the phone. They're all struggling to breathe in the intense smoke. One of the lifesavers had handed everyone in the group a wet Chux as they left the surf club, and Robyn has one pressed over her face and another over the nose of her Jack Russell, Beau, who's tucked under her arm.

It's only once they get safely to the water's edge that Robyn turns and looks back. From the beach, there is a panoramic view of the entire village, now shrouded in smoke. Homes start just over the road from the grass reserve, spreading up the gently sloping hills and wrapping around both headlands. She can see straight up Sylvan Street, where the Malua Bay Bowling Club is – also the site of weekly bingo sessions and Raymond's Chinese Restaurant – and to the street that runs behind it, where she's lived for more than twenty years.

No one knows what to expect. 'Everyone was quiet, we were stunned,' says Robyn. Then the silence is broken by the piercing ring of 'hundreds and hundreds' of household smoke alarms.

The bowling club is one of the first buildings to ignite. An elderly man who is slow to evacuate witnesses it happen. He hears a whistle and sees what looks like a missile of fire come from the sky, landing on the hedge next to the bowling green. The hedge explodes into flames and sends out another bomb that lands on the building.

When Ian Barnes drives into Sylvan Street around 10.30 am, he's confronted by 'an apocalyptic vision'. The roof of the bowling club is already collapsing, and multiple homes are on fire. 'I thought, *This is not good. This is going to be big time, and I have no resources,*' he says. 'Houses were on fire everywhere, cars still streaming down to the beach, people on foot carrying cats and dogs, a woman leading a horse.'

After operating alone most of the morning, Barnes has just managed to team up with another fire truck. It's not from the Malua Bay brigade – he still doesn't know where his trucks are. It belongs to RFS State Mitigation and happened to be parked at someone's home overnight, so has been commandeered by a volunteer. It's a bigger vehicle than Barnes' ute, but it's crippled – the water pump is broken and they're out of water. Barnes helps rig up a portable water pump so they can refill – not to the same capacity, but it'll do.

Barnes knows that when fire hits an urban area, it often spreads through house-to-house ignition – a domino effect, with each burning house lighting up the one next door – so along with the other truck they focus on pouring water on those homes not yet fully alight, trying to break the chain. But fire is appearing everywhere – all the hedges and gardens are catching alight – and they don't have much water. Barnes empties his tank on the flames under the deck of one house, but still it burns down.

On the beach, Robyn Butcher can see her beloved bowling club going up. She can't tell if her home is too. So many houses are burning that she loses count. 'It was like, *Oh, there's another one. Another one. Another one.*' The sound of gas bottles exploding across the village is coming in a steady rhythm. She sees a gas barbecue that's sitting on the verandah of a home across the road from the beach explode. The house is not on fire, so she thinks it's probably from the heat.

Flames are leaping through the treetops in a gully behind the surf club, and a lifesaver is standing on the roof with a hose. One tree on the southern headland of the beach catches alight, and within minutes the whole headland is on fire. On the other side of the headland, out of sight, is the little tree-fringed hamlet of North Rosedale. Whatever maelstrom is going on in there is so intense, it momentarily seems to suck in all the smoke haze that's layering the beach.

Robyn is terrified, thinking she could die. 'It was coming at us from all directions. We were trapped. The only place we could go was in the water,' she says. By midday, the only sign of help she's seen is a single police car. *We're on our own here*, she thinks.

Susan Magnay has watched the fire come rushing down her street and she can only guess if her townhouse is one of the many homes burning. She's sitting quietly, trying to endure it all. 'It was just a matter of holding your breath and getting through it,' she says.

Some people on the beach refuse to watch, instead hunching under beach towels with their back to the fire, looking out to sea. There's a menagerie of animals on the sand – horses, dogs and cats, birds and rabbits in cages – and a few micro dramas play out. Two dogs fight; a young boy starts crying when a thirsty dog laps out of a bucket that holds his pet turtle. But mostly the crowd is silent, waiting.

It is perhaps fortunate that no one on the ground can see what a satellite orbiting 786 kilometres above Earth is capturing at that moment. At around 11.00 am, a vast swathe of land, from the forests west of Nelligen all the way to the Pacific Ocean, is glowing orange. More than half a dozen small villages and towns, an area with a combined population of around 13,000, is quite literally being encompassed by fire. Where the land meets the sea, along the densely populated coastal strip, enormous white smoke plumes that look like churned ice-cream are reaching skyward – the breath of burning homes.

When Ian Barnes drives up to the hill to the fire shed to rendezvous with his volunteers, he comes upon a new disaster: fire has swept through here too.

The fire shed is still standing, but electricity lines are sagging, and the cars belonging to many of the volunteers are either smouldering or incinerated. Even the cables that climb up the Telstra tower behind the shed are burning.

Barnes extinguishes flames on a couple of cars and races into the shed to try to figure out what's going wrong with his radio network. He still can't raise anyone, including the fire control centre in Moruya. But he soon decides, *I can't waste time on all of that*, and heads back into the burning village. Gnawing at him is that he still doesn't know the whereabouts of the night-shift crew aboard Malua Bay 1, or the two volunteers on Malua Bay 7 who headed out to Dog Trap Road earlier that morning then disappeared.

Graham Skelton, who left for his night shift on board Malua Bay 1 back on 30 December, doesn't remember the sun coming up on New Year's Day. The firefight they embarked on at midnight at Nelligen is still underway by daybreak.

By early morning, he and his crew are feeling 'pretty chuffed': they haven't lost a single house at Nelligen. But they are exhausted, so they radio in to the fire control centre in Moruya, asking for relief. No one answers, so they keep working. Fourteen hours into their shift, they try again. This time they are told, 'No, we can't relieve you, everyone's in the same boat.'

Skelton knows snippets of what's been going on elsewhere – he'd heard over the truck radio his fellow volunteers down in Cobargo screaming for help when they were hit by the Badja Forest Road fire before dawn. But now he hears a voice coming through that he recognises. It's a firefighter from a neighbouring brigade, 'sheer panic in his voice', saying he needs more trucks because he's losing houses in Catalina – a little hamlet between Batemans Bay and Malua Bay. By now, mid-morning, they've been out for nearly fifteen hours and are almost out of fuel anyway, so Skelton makes the call – 'I said, that's it, we have to go back.'

It's not until they crest the hill above Batemans Bay that he understands the enormity of the situation. 'Jesus Christ,' says Skelton. Red flames and smoke and 'super-heated air and gas and dust' are rolling over the town. A long line of cars is backed up along the narrow road that runs between the shopping strip and the bay, with people desperately trying to get to the Batemans Bay evacuation centre.

Skelton tells his eighty-year-old driver, 'Just go.' With lights and sirens blaring, 'We're going on the wrong side of the road, jumping over gutters, just tear-arsing right into it.' In Batemans Bay they stop to fill up with water; no one has eaten or stopped moving since 6.00 pm the day before, so when they see a wave of fire wash over the ambulance station right in front of them, Skelton says, 'We were that knackered, we were just standing there watching it, going, "Wow." We were numb.'

Once they get back to Malua Bay, into Sea Breeze Estate, the first three houses they see are on fire. They get to work again.

In Batemans Bay, where fire is encroaching into the town, local brigades are radioing in from all over the place asking for backup. Crew leaders are hanging on for the arrival of the strike teams coming down the highway from Sydney.

In the industrial area, the captain of the Batemans Bay RFS, who's been working since the night before, comes across a tow-truck driver trying to put out a burning building with a garden hose. Nearby, Betta Electrical, Furniture One and an auto wrecker are all in flames, beyond salvation, and several fire trucks are pouring water onto the cavernous Bunnings to try to stop it going the same way.

A few streets away, inside 'The Glen', a residential aged-care home, staff looking out the windows can see fire approaching on two sides of the building. There has been no time to evacuate the elderly residents, so everyone has been moved to the middle floor of the three-level building – deemed the safest place. Family members of some residents had raced to 'The Glen' when they heard the fire was coming, so they too are sheltering inside. The power is out, the air-conditioning down, and staff are running outside and putting out spot fires in the grounds. The arrival of several fire trucks from a coastal RFS brigade and a water-bombing helicopter save the building and all inside.

On the water, where the Clyde River meets the ocean at Batemans Bay, wildlife carer Rae Harvey is still in the tinny with Simon and her houseguest from the United States, look-

ing for somewhere safe to come ashore. After being chased out
of Runnyford at dawn, they'd motored downriver, sheltering
for a while on the northern side of the bay, but now burning
leaves are falling into the boat and they're being buffeted by
roaring winds and waves of smoke and heat.

They dock near the shopping strip, planning to go to the
evacuation centre, which is in a function centre closer to the
ocean front. But when they arrive, there are already thousands
of others trying to get in and Rae thinks it looks way too
crowded. Then, she looks up and sees a large plane dropping a
line of the 'pink stuff' behind the evacuation centre. It's one of
the RFS's Large Air Tankers, laying down fire retardant – but
rather than giving her comfort, she thinks, *There must be fire
coming there. No way am I going there.*

Instead, still clutching her cat, she and her American friend
venture back through the deserted town; past the shuttered-up
surf shop, the fish-and-chips takeaway and the ice-creamery, and
into the large shopping complex that houses the Woolworths.
Everything in here is closed too, but they decide to set up camp,
on the grotty white tiles amid abandoned shopping trolleys.
They meet a couple from Mogo who've also fled after losing
their home. When a young worker collecting supermarket trolleys sees them, he leaves and comes back with food and water.

Before lunchtime, convoys of fire trucks from Sydney start rolling into town – fifteen trucks and nearly 100 firefighters from
the Sutherland Shire alone, with many more from the Northern Beaches. *Thank god*, the Batemans Bay fire captain thinks
when he sees them coming in.

The fire trucks fan out across the burning district. On board
one of them is Greg Mullins, the former commissioner of Fire

and Rescue NSW and the man who set up Emergency Leaders for Climate Action – here now as a volunteer for his local RFS in Sydney. Over his forty years as a professional firefighter, Mullins has seen plenty of what the worst Australian bushfires can offer up, but he's still taken aback by the carnage he encounters on the South Coast. 'I've seen a lot of houses burnt down, I've seen a lot of dead bodies,' he says. 'But what undid me that day was I saw some things moving by the side of the highway just south of Batemans Bay. I walked up to see what it was, and it was a mob of kangaroos. They'd all jumped out of the bush on fire and were just dying on the side of the road in agony.'

At 4.00 pm, for the first time all day, Ian Barnes manages to make radio contact with the fire control centre in Moruya. By now, he's heard that Graham Skelton and Malua Bay 1 have been sighted back in town, but no one has seen Malua Bay 7 all day, so Barnes asks the fire control centre to do a welfare check on them. They try twice but can't raise them.

Barnes has some inkling they are alive. One of the two men on board is volunteer David Beare. While the phone network is down, occasional text messages are getting through, and Barnes has received a text from David's wife's number. 'It said, "It is a shit fight out here." And the language was enough to tell me it was Dave and not his wife.'

In this disjointed day, with an uncountable number of different fronts simultaneously underway, David Beare and his fellow crew member on board Malua Bay 7 have been engaged in a solo epic battle.

The two were the first to arrive at the Malua Bay fire shed that morning – nearly two hours ahead of schedule, because both received the 6.00 am RFS emergency warning on their home phones and knew something was happening. Beare, a tall, silver-haired man, ex-Navy, a keen lawn bowler at the Malua Bay Bowling Club, immediately radioed the fire control centre in Moruya, telling them to page the rest of the Malua Bay volunteers.

'The only reply was to go out to Dog Trap Road,' he says. He was in two minds. There were two of them – normally they'd only go out with four or five, and he knew Barnes was expecting them to be there at 8.00 am. 'But we were told to go,' he says, so he scrawled his message in chalk on the shed door and left.

After arriving at the fire on Dog Trap Road, on the outskirts of Malua Bay, they were told to move on – another brigade was on site – and diverted to the village of Mogo. When they got there, joining a handful of other fire trucks, the town was under heavy smoke – clearly about to be hit. They drove through the residential area, yelling at people to get out, before heading back to Mogo's main street – a popular tourist strip, lined with heritage timber buildings converted to cafés, and shops selling local arts and crafts – and setting up their hoses at the northern end.

At 8.00 am, the sky turned pitch black. 'For a brief moment I thought there were tankers flying overhead because I could hear what sounded like a jet engine,' says Beare. As fire roared in, a voice came down the radio telling all units to withdraw to the southern end of town: around twenty residents were sheltering in the Mogo fire shed and the building needed protection.

By this stage, Beare was pretty sure they were trapped – fire was coming towards them, but it was also behind them, so he wasn't confident they could retreat south to the fire shed even if they wanted to. But because he could see a group of young men over the road preparing to defend a building, he decided, 'I couldn't leave them.'

They were now the only two firefighters, standing with their hoses out, in the middle of Mogo's main street, wind, fire and smoke howling in their faces. 'We couldn't put water north; it just blew back in our faces. You could only put water at a right angle, or behind you,' says Beare. 'We were retreating back and back. I was screaming at the young people.' When he finally saw them turn and sprint south down the street, he felt immense relief.

The battle to save what they could of Mogo's shopping district lasted for five hours. A line of four shops went up like 'matchboxes' before they could do anything; so too did the 120-year-old heritage-listed church, home to a local pottery business. They thought they'd saved the Local Aboriginal Land Council building, which was hit by a massive ember attack that started a fire under the eaves, but when they moved to start on another building, it too dissolved into flames. It was like 'chasing your tail', says Beare. 'It was too wild. There was just a futility to what we were trying to do.' But they persisted, saving numerous businesses and the local preschool.

When the southerly change finally came in, the fire was turned back on itself. Everything was still burning, yet it 'died down from a bun fight to a normal catastrophic day', says Beare. 'But if that southerly didn't happen, we would have lost the whole place.'

With the brief respite, standing alone in the middle of a still-burning village, buildings gutted and smoking either side of them, yellow uniforms blackened with soot, Beare tried the UHF radio to see if there were any other fire crews nearby: 'Anyone in the Mogo area?' Silence. Then he tried the fire control centre. More radio silence.

'We had no information about what was happening elsewhere,' Beare says. He thought briefly of his own home, on the outskirts of Malua Bay. 'It backs onto bush, so I expected it would be gone, but I just had to put it out of my mind.'

Right across the far South Coast, RFS crews confronting the raging fires were blighted by poor radio communications. At the height of the firestorm in Cobargo, local crews lost contact with the incident management team in Moruya after a transmitter burned down. For the rest of the day they could only make contact with a fire control centre much further south, in Bega, where the one staff member on duty was also unable to reach the team in Moruya. It wasn't just destroyed infrastructure that was the problem; there were simply too many messages coming in from the multiple catastrophes for staff to deal with them all.

Later in the day, though, some in the Malua Bay brigade discovered a more prosaic reason for their communications problems – the channel to call in to the incident management team had been switched, but in the chaos, no one had told them.

The southerly change plunged the temperature on the beach at Malua Bay, leaving many who'd evacuated in the heat of the morning shivering. For the surf lifesavers still running the impromptu evacuation centre, the next battle was to feed 1,500 people.

Robyn Butcher says 'it was like loaves and fishes' – except with sausages. 'They would cook a sausage and cut it into four.' People were on the hunt for food everywhere. 'You'd see someone with an apple and you'd be like, "Where'd you get that apple?"' Robyn's husband is diabetic, and by evening all she'd manage to scrounge for him was a jam sandwich.

As night fell, Robyn put her husband in the car and took herself and two of her elderly bowlers to a half-built hotel on the foreshore. Still a worksite, it was little more than a concrete shell. 'I dived into the dumpster at the back of the building and got sheets of cardboard for us to sleep on,' she says. 'But none of us really slept.'

In the middle of the night, she was walking through the reserve to the toilet block when she spotted someone barbe-quing pork ribs and handing them out. Robyn swooped, deliv-ering them with excitement to her husband in the car.

Susan Magnay and her husband were swept up by strang-ers and offered a night in their spare room. No one had been allowed back up to the still-smoking Sylvan Street, but before they left the beach Susan saw her neighbours from their town-house complex who 'were in tears, incredibly distressed', telling the couple that the building was gone.

Ian Barnes worked well into the night, traversing the streets now littered with burned-out homes. Nearly 85 per cent of Malua Bay had been affected by the fire, with about ninety homes destroyed. In and around Mogo, the tally was about fifty homes and another 100 buildings. In North Rosedale, the next coastal hamlet south of Malua Bay, eighty-four homes were gone – nearly three-quar-ters of the entire village. 'I went down to North Rosedale and it was a mess, hardly a house left, powerlines down everywhere,' he says. 'There was this bloke standing there still trying to save his home and we gave him a hand, emptied our tank.'

It wasn't until late in the evening that Barnes finally com-pleted his most important task of the day – ascertaining that every member of his brigade was alive. But after an instant of shared relief, it was back to business. 'We arranged for a 6.00 am start the next morning,' he says, 'and that was our routine for the next three weeks.'

After saving an uncountable number of homes belonging to other people, the volunteers from Malua Bay RFS saw out the year by going to discover the fate of their own.

Graham Skelton first went in search of his wife, knowing she'd be worried. The absence of telecommunications meant the partners and families of the Malua Bay crews had spent the entire day without knowing if their loved ones were safe. Skelton found her sheltering in the half-built hotel at the beach. Then he went to check their home – discovering it unscathed. He was reeling from the day's events. 'There just weren't enough resources on the ground,' he says. 'We were just a bunch of old people trying to save their community.'

When David Beare left Mogo, just before 10.00 pm, he returned to his home to discover fire had burned right up to his back fence, but no further. His neighbours had put the flames out.

One of the very last to knock off was fifty-two-year-old carpenter Steve Hillyar. He was the youngest volunteer on board Malua Bay 1 with Graham Skelton, in the firefight that started at midnight in Nelligen and accelerated all the way through until nearly midnight on New Year's Eve. When Hillyar finally got back to the fire shed late that night, he discovered the back of his ute had been burned. 'It squeaked a bit, but I managed to get it going,' he says.

He started the drive towards his home, in a semi-rural area on the outskirts of Malua Bay. 'Trees and power lines were down, monstrous trees, one I went around was still on fire, but I kept snaking my way up,' he says.

As he began driving up his street, he saw lots of houses were gone and he thought, *It's not looking good.* But as he got closer, 'I see the house on the left is good, but the one behind is gone, so I'm thinking, *Okay, I am in with half a chance.* And then I get to the crest of the hill and I see it. It was just a roof on top of footings.'

There was nothing to be done. He took a photo, grabbed the chickens, had a quick beer with a neighbour whose house was still standing and went in search of his wife to deliver the bad news.

CHAPTER 11

CONJOLA: BLINDSIDED

When a line-scan plane finally flies over the eastern flank of the Currowan fire just before 10.00 am on New Year's Eve – the first aerial view in thirteen hours – the incident management team in Nowra realises that not only is the containment line not going to hold this fire off the coast, but it's now too late for anyone in Conjola Park or Lake Conjola to get away.

Three waves of fire are about to cross the highway, and if several thousand people all take to the road now to escape, it will undoubtedly result in gridlock – sitting ducks right in the firepath. So the first emergency alert of the day for this area, sent out just before 10.30 am to landlines and mobiles in Conjola, tells people to 'seek shelter … it is too late to leave'.

It may be sound logic. But because the warning has come so late, thousands of people are caught off-guard; many are in positions where they have no choice but to flee.

Justine Donohoe is still standing in her kitchen in Conjola Park, having just returned from being turned away at the highway, when her mobile pings with the RFS text message. She's starting to panic, but 'I was just like, "Right, seek shelter, that's what we have to do."' She grabs water bottles from the fridge and throws them into the bucket by the door, yelling at the boys to grab their devices and the dog and get in the car.

Yet when she gets out of her driveway and onto her street, she doesn't know where to go. Plumes of thick smoke are rising from the lake a few hundred metres away. It seems the whole neighbourhood has spilled onto the road. Some people are climbing onto roofs with hoses; others are standing by their cars in shock; a woman clutching a wailing baby with one hand is trying to shove a pram into a car boot with the other, screaming at her husband to come. 'No one knew what was going on, everyone was confused, like, "What the fuck is going on?"' she says. 'The wind was just roaring, it was circling all around us and there was this glow coming up in front and behind us.'

Justine calls her husband in Sydney, and he tells her to drive to the lake – into it, if she has to. 'I can't, I can't get to the lake,' she replies, because now flames are leaping through the trees along the foreshore in front of her, blocking access to the water. The orange glow from behind the hill is getting bigger.

Two fire runs are rapidly closing on Conjola Park, squeezing in towards Justine's street like a vice.

Not everyone is trying to flee the approaching fire. Many people who are away from their homes in Conjola are now desperately trying to return. The instruction to shelter in place means nothing if you're separated from someone you love.

Grant Goozee, a former policeman and keen surfer who lives in Lake Conjola with his wife, Nikki, is at a petrol station in Milton, filling up his car with fuel, when he looks north and sees an enormous plume of smoke rising up from the direction of his home. *Shit*, he thinks. *Nikki's home by herself.*

Nikki has a progressive neurological disorder called Charcot-Marie-Tooth disease. She's confined to a wheelchair and needs a ventilator to help her breathe. Grant had left her at home while he ducked into town to grab a coffee and to see if he could get their sixteen-month-old grandson, who they were babysitting, to have a nap in the car. Now he swings the car around and heads north, back up the highway.

But before he reaches the turn-off into Conjola, he's halted on the highway by a long line of stationary cars. Others are also trying to head north to get back home, but a roadblock has been set up to stop people entering the fire zone. Grant sits in the traffic for ten minutes and then thinks, *Stuff this*, pulling out. He drives up the highway on the wrong side of the road, swerves around the roadblock at the entrance of the road that leads into Conjola Park and Lake Conjola, and races down the path towards home.

Jen Dudman-Chopping is sitting in the same line of traffic. She was at work at an aged-care home in Milton when she got the RFS text message. Her husband and twenty-one-year-old son are home, but her husband's Parkinson's disease has affected his cognitive ability and he's liable to falls – her main worry is he'll start getting up on a ladder to fill the gutters. 'There's so much to do in a crisis situation that I knew the two of them wouldn't cope together.' When she realises she won't be getting home by road, she turns around to try the backup plan she's had in mind all summer.

Standing on the rocks at the mouth of a coastal inlet that flows to the sea about eight kilometres south of Conjola, Jen starts pulling off her shoes. She's just grabbed a wet bag from a friend's house and she puts her phone and shoes inside. She's going to swim across the inlet, then hike up the beach – a long strip of narrow sand fringed by bushland on one side and ocean on the other. Looking north, she can just make out the little island off Lake Conjola that marks her destination.

The mouth of the inlet is wide and deep, known for its treachery on the outgoing tide. But the current is still flowing in. She dives and starts swimming.

When Grant arrives home in Lake Conjola, he and Nikki decide the quickest way to get to the caravan park down at the lake's entrance – where she'll shelter while he defends the house – is for Nikki to travel the one kilometre in her four-wheel drive motorised wheelchair, while Grant takes the baby in the car and meets her there. Nikki grabs the spare batteries for her ventilator, and because there are no footpaths, motors off down the road.

As soon as she pulls out of her street, Nikki finds herself in the middle of a 'mass exodus of crazy, frantic people'. The road is clogged with cars – many pulling boats and caravans – either heading down to where the entrance meets the sea at Lake Conjola or back towards the highway for their escape. *I feel like I'm on the set of a Hollywood blockbuster*, Nikki thinks, as she manoeuvres her wheelchair through traffic. One lady pulls up beside her, paralysed by fear. 'She was just screaming. She was losing her mind,' says Nikki. The woman is holding up the traffic, so Nikki tells her, 'Just go.'

At the lake's entrance, thousands of people are scattered along the foreshore, watching the billowing orange and grey plumes and intermittent leaps of flame coming from the bush further up the lake. Boats have clustered together in the middle of the lake like ducklings; cars are being driven onto the sand. Some people go as far east as possible, walking over the dunes and into the ocean, standing knee-deep in the choppy waves. Others appear to still be in holiday mode, in board shorts and thongs, beer in one hand and phone in the other, filming the show.

Nikki wheels into the caravan park manager's office. Grant has gone back to their home and she's got the baby. As someone who is used to relying on her sharp intellect to navigate through tough situations, Nikki now feels utterly defenceless. 'I was thinking, *Oh my God, this is horrible. I've got this precious little baby – Grant has always looked after him and now Grant is telling me I have to look after him.*'

Further up the reaches of the lake, in Conjola Park, Justine Donohoe can now feel waves of radiant heat pushing in. With a neighbour, she leaves her car in the street and runs back towards her house to scope out the laundry as a possible sheltering place. 'We were so confused about what to do,' she says. But then an ember falls onto the road in front of her, burning a hole in the tar, and suddenly people are screaming 'Get out, get out' and everyone is piling back into their cars. Moments after she drives away, the last neighbour to leave the street sees Justine's home implode – later telling her 'it just squished in and then the roof blew off the top'.

In her car, Justine joins a convoy that's making a dash down the narrow, tree-lined road towards Lake Conjola. Things are burning everywhere, and the road is bedlam. The boys are in the back seat, tears rolling down their cheeks, asking, 'Mum, are we going to die?'

Before they can reach the coast, fire comes over the road in front of them and their escape is blocked. Justine turns the car around, deciding to try to get out at the highway again.

When she arrives at the exit onto the highway, she faces a choice. Fire has apparently crossed over it both to the north and the south, but an RFS volunteer is saying he's going to lead a band of cars out – whoever is willing – on an escape attempt north up the highway. She can risk staying inside this rapidly closing vice of fire, or take a chance on the road out.

Justine decides to go, taking her place at the back of a convoy of about ten cars that pulls onto the highway. The driving is intense. Fire is burning in the forests along both sides of the road. The smoke is so black and disorientating she can hardly see where she's going, and more than once she nearly crashes into the car ahead. Glancing in the rear-view mirror, she can see her boys are quiet. *They're paralysed by fear*, she thinks. She's had her husband on FaceTime ever since she left the house, so he's hearing and watching the whole journey.

After driving with deep concentration for who knows how many kilometres, she suddenly emerges from the smoke into a surreal moonscape of blackened tree stumps and white ash. Shocked, she stops the car. The highway is deserted – the other vehicles have disappeared – and there's complete silence. It's such an otherworldly scene she thinks, *My God, I've died.*

By around 11.30 am, anyone left in Conjola Park, which is taking the brunt of the bursting eastern flank of the Currowan fire, is fighting to save their homes and lives.

Scott Brennan, an off-duty firefighter for Fire and Rescue NSW, has never witnessed anything like this. The behaviour of the fire he can see racing down the hill towards his home is 'ridiculous': it's going down the hill and across the wind. *It is not supposed to do that*, he thinks.

Like everyone, Scott and his wife, Kris, have been blind-sided, and Scott's only had time to half-throw on his firefighting gear. They're outside hosing down their house. The wind is blowing away from them, so they're not getting any embers, just blasts of radiant heat. 'You could feel everything drying out,' says Kris. 'It's like the air was just sucking up every bit of moisture.'

Even before the fire arrives, trees in their yard start exploding into flames. Scott notices the heat is starting to melt the laminate coating on his professional firefighting goggles. When the flimsy bucket hat he'd thrown on at the last minute blows off his head and ignites on the grass in front of him, he screams at Kris, 'Get out of here!'

Parts of the foreshore are already on fire, but Kris drives a few hundred metres to a jetty. The first boat she tries to flag down doesn't stop, but the second – a dinghy with a terrified family from Sydney – motors over and she clambers in.

As Scott keeps trying to fight off the fire, he can see the row of homes in the street above him are starting to ignite, toppling like dominoes. Then, along with everyone else in the surrounding streets, he makes a horrifying discovery – the taps are running dry. Even though Conjola Park's water system is built to New South Wales standards, it can't cope with the demands of nearly everyone in the village turning on all their taps at once – extreme events are not factored into the system design.

Scott knows it's time to leave. 'I had no water, I wasn't dressed properly, all the grass in front of me was alight, and I thought, *I won't have a chance unless I get out of here.*' He runs across his lawn, dodging flames on the ground, to where his ute is parked on the street. The two vehicles either side are on fire, but his is still intact, so he gets in and tears up the road looking for somewhere to shelter.

A few streets over from the Brennans, embers are dropping into Michelle Morales' backyard, but all she's worried about is what's happening at her partner Laurie's place, a bush-fringed home a few kilometres west. When they last spoke, at 10.30 am, he was turning on his sprinklers and getting ready to fight. She knows he'll be in the midst of it now and is resisting the urge to call him again.

Standing on the road outside her house, she starts to film a jerky video of the orange smoke coming from the direction of his property, and a water-bombing helicopter hovering overhead. She's breathing rapidly, almost whimpering. 'That's Laurie's place for sure I wanna ring him.'

Embers are lighting up everything they touch – trees, lawns, verandahs, houses. Anyone who thought to fill a bathtub in the minutes before the fire hit is now hauling buckets of water outside. The homes without water or someone to defend them don't stand a chance. Michelle hears rumbling emanating from black smoke that is pulsing down the road towards her. 'Why is the garbage truck coming now?' she asks a neighbour, momentarily confused. Her neighbour tells her it's time to go, leading her into a brick bunker under their house.

In the minutes before the fire hit, one of the strike teams coming down the highway from Sydney was diverted to Conjola Park. The four Fire and Rescue NSW trucks have arrived in an unfamiliar village, on fire, with no running water. The team eventually locates a fire hydrant, but it takes them ten minutes each to fill a tank. There are flames in virtually every street. At 12.42 pm, the leader of the strike team films houses combusting before him and says, with despair in his voice, 'There's nothing we can do. I apologise to the landowners. It's heartbreaking for us.'

The community doesn't even have access to its own RFS trucks. One of Conjola RFS brigade's trucks was seconded elsewhere earlier in the fire season – no one's seen it for weeks – and the other truck is shared with another coastal hamlet, where it's now parked in a shed, cut off by fire.

By now, Scott Brennan is sheltering with a group of residents on the foreshore – he estimates there is one hectare of safe ground left in Conjola Park. There was just 'bewilderment', he says. 'Thousand-yard stares. Eyes like big plates. There were tears, people were distraught. It was like, *What happened? What's going on?*

With such a rapid onslaught, lives hang on split-second decisions. On a hill about a kilometre south of Conjola Park, eighty-year-old Frank Condello is standing at the top of his drive, water pump ready and fire hoses laid out, watching the fire roll over the hamlet. Suddenly, a ball of fire lands on his front gate, followed by wave after wave of fire. 'It was like the breakers you see on the ocean but fire – great big monsters rolling down on us, right up to the tops of trees,' he says.

In the face of such force, water from his hoses just blows away on the wind. Frank's wife and a friend yell at him from the house, 'Get inside, you're going to get yourself killed!' He turns and runs down the driveway – past the retail nursery he operates, filled with native shrubs and trees, a fernery and a collection of rare native orchids and bonsai trees, a quarter of a century of his life's work – and tries to fling open the sliding door to the house. It's too hot to touch.

He gets inside through a side entrance. Exhausted, he throws himself into his reclining armchair, tilts his head back and sees that the ceiling is on fire. 'I said, "For Christ's sake, get out and get out now."' All three pile into a small Toyota sedan. Frank screams for his two border collies. Georgie comes, but there's no sign of Ryder.

Casting around for somewhere safe, he spots a smouldering paddock that the fire has already ripped through and accelerates into the middle of it. When they pull up, Ryder comes racing through the flames and they haul him in.

Huddled in the vehicle, they have a crowning forest fire on one side, and their burning home, nursery and sheds on the other. It takes fifty minutes for the fire front to pass. 'If the air conditioner had stopped working, we would have suffocated for sure,' he says.

About ten kilometres south of Conjola, in Milton, the RFS has set up a temporary command post in a van parked at the local showground. Working inside is seventy-eight-year-old volunteer John Ashton, divisional commander for the day. Based on what he's hearing from crews on the ground, it sounds as though it's some kind of wild windstorm, with gusts over 100 kilometres an hour and temperatures above 40 degrees, that has blown out the eastern flank of the Currowan fire.

Ashton has been volunteering for the RFS for more than half his life – he's a highly regarded figure among the firefighting community on the South Coast. This is undoubtedly the worst day of his career. He's in charge of moving the resources he's been allocated around this section of the fireground, but when it comes to Conjola Park, 'I had nothing to give them. Nothing to help any people there. And that's my job. It was pretty hard.'

With most of the firefighting vehicles already allocated to the northern front of the Currowan fire, and the extra strike teams from Sydney needed in Batemans Bay, Ashton doesn't have enough trucks to deal with an emergency unfolding across a vast area. 'When that containment line blew, it didn't just blow in one spot, it blew the whole length of the line. It was burning from Sussex Inlet all the way through down to bloody Milton.' That's a distance of 23 kilometres.

A number of his resources are either unusable or unsuitable. Trucks from some coastal brigades are trapped in their villages by fire or needed by their own community. He's got a fleet of Fire and Rescue NSW trucks, but they can't go off road so there's a limit to where he can send them. And after five weeks of continually battling the Currowan fire, several trucks belonging to South Coast brigades are broken down, awaiting repair. The RFS radio communications system is overwhelmed by the volume of requests for help. Inside the van, Ashton has a radio operator sitting beside him trying to log every call, but there's so many coming in 'we probably only got a quarter of the messages'. Once telecommunications drop out, 'There was no bloody phone service. It was just a kerfuffle. I had no trucks, nothing left on the shelf and I had people screaming on the radio for help.' He gets so desperate he starts sending volunteers in RFS Personnel Carriers – vehicles without any firefighting capability – out to someone who is just about to 'be overrun by a fire', telling them to go and see what they can do.

Fire is also approaching Milton, running up a hill towards a primary school less than a kilometre from where Ashton is working. The wind is blowing a gale, and inside the van everything is quite literally going out the window. 'Most of our paperwork was blown up and was stuck on the fence around the blooming showgrounds,' he says.

Across a vast swathe of burning farmland, men in utes with firefighting cubes on the trays are plunging into the breach. The 'cubies' are responding to calls for help coming in on their two-way radios or just following their noses to places that look like they are in trouble. Steven Howes is among them – 'just hooking in and getting it done'.

Steven left the family farm earlier that morning in his ute, with his cube set up ready to go, to drive into town for supplies. 'I knew it was blowing up pretty bad and we'd be fighting fires for a couple of days,' he says, 'so I thought I'd go and get a couple of slabs of beer and milk for Mum.' It's been five weeks now that the Howes family's lives have been entwined with the Currowan fire – starting from when Steven's father, Dave, was chased out of the forests the day it ignited – and they all knew this was going to be one of the worst days. But before Steven even got to the shops, he received a call over his two-way radio from a mate about the fire coming up to the school at Milton, and he immediately changed route.

He helps extinguish the fire at the school – halting it at the playground – before beginning the drive north out of town. As he crests the hill, he is greeted with a vision that looks like 'something you would see in a zombie movie'. Bursting through the smoke on the highway are 'people on Harleys with no helmets coming up, people in vintage cars, people in the backs of utes, four-wheelers coming down the road, everyone trying to get their valuables out'.

His first stop is a dairy just outside of Milton. When he gets there, flames are licking at fences and embers are flying, while inside the dairy shed a herd of Holsteins are midway through their milking. A handful of other cubies are also there, and because the power is out and the generator isn't pumping any water into the depleted troughs, they're all hurtling down the hill in their utes to a creek, where they refill the cubes with brackish water. As they fight the fire around the shed, the dairy hand keeps running out and yelling, 'You got it, boys? You got it? Do I have to get out?'

Steven goes to see what's happening up in Little Forest, discovering a house mid-burn. The original homestead is unscathed, but a newly built wing is in flames, and the owners are trying to put it out with hoses before it ignites the rest of the house. Seeing this is futile, Steven pulls out his chainsaw. 'It is pretty much a no-no to cut through nails and things,' he says, 'but I was just chainsawing through the house, cutting in half, like an amputation.' The sacrifice is a success; the homestead is saved. Grateful, one of the owners runs inside and returns with slices of watermelon – pretty much the only food Steven will eat all day.

At their farm, Brendan Cowled and Kim Wilson are feeling a small measure of relief; even though they are encircled by fire, and have been on-guard all day, it seems they are escaping the worst of the fires racing across the district. Yet as they watch the blaze they reported at 6.30 that morning sweep through Little Forest, making its way towards the area around Conjola and then out to the coast, joined by new rushes of fire roaring over the escarpment, Kim feels ill. Looking down across the burning pastures of Little Forest and Yatte Yattah and at the black plumes consuming Conjola Park, she wonders, *Are we watching people die?*

In Yatte Yattah, Ian and Fiona Stewart, who are fighting off a fire they suspect emanates from the previous evening's back-burn, are facing the possibility of losing a life.

After waking at 4.00 am to embers flying over their house from the direction of the back-burn, around 9.00 am they retreated to a neighbour's house on clearer ground, about 300 metres as the crow flies from their place. Their adult son James stayed to defend the family home. Both households soon have fire descending, and Fiona is fighting off 'a constant arc of firestorm' coming for her neighbour's home, while staying in phone contact with James.

At first, James is telling her that while the fire is extreme at home, everything is going to plan; the sprinklers are on and both fire pumps are operating. The Stewarts' house is built with fire-resistant concrete blocks, they've got plenty of water and James has a background as a professional firefighter, so everyone's feeling confident.

But then things turn. James is telling Fiona that the shed containing one of the water pumps has just caught alight when he pauses and says, 'Holy hell, there's a cyclone on the dam,' describing as he watches the second water pump being destroyed. Now without any water, James is inside the house, telling his mother that he can see ash dropping on the kitchen floor. 'Our conversation was calm,' says Fiona. 'I said, "Well, you and I both know, James, that's it, the house is gone." He said, "I know." Then I said, "But have a go, see what you can do."'

With Fiona still on the line, James walks upstairs with a Super Soaker. Before she left, Fiona filled garbage bins and the bath with water and left out towels and water pistols in case they lost water supply.

James tells her he can see that the inside of the roof is on fire, but he can't get to it.

'James, be careful, you don't want the house to collapse on you,' Fiona says.

They both know he needs to get out of the house quickly. But the firestorm outside is too intense. Fiona has already called triple zero twice, requesting help for James, and now Ian tries, telling the operator his son is trapped in a burning house; his 'life is at risk' and 'there is no fire support here despite the fact the fire was started by the firies'. The operator – who deflects this last claim by saying 'that's an issue for another day' – tells Ian, 'Well, there's a lot of people in the same boat, but we'll do our best.'

James is telling Fiona he can see the Oregon beam in their cathedral ceiling burning.

'James, you have to get out,' she says. 'You can't stay in there.'

'I can't get out, it's too dangerous. The firestorm is still on me,' he replies.

No one is sure how much later – perhaps half an hour – a helicopter arrives, likely responding to their calls for help. It flies overhead and drops a load of water on the shed, but it makes no difference to the house.

By now, Fiona and Ian are beside themselves. Ian tries triple zero again, repeating that his son is in a life-threatening situation, and is told, 'He's not the only one. I'm sorry, but this is an ongoing fire and there's a lot of this going on.'

Ian and Fiona are still fighting back the fire that's burning towards their neighbour's house. There are dozens of others spread out along the road also battling flames, and Ian spots a man in the distance who looks to be wearing a uniform and runs over to him. He's an off-duty professional firefighter, here helping a friend. Now Ian makes his third call to triple zero, and this time hands the phone over to the off-duty firefighter, hoping he can be more persuasive. But the response from the operator – who sounds stressed by what he has to say – is even blunter: 'We have nothing out there, matey. Everything is taken up.'

Fiona is back on the phone with James, pleading with him to get out of the burning house.

'I'm cooked. I can't get out,' he keeps repeating.

The off-duty firefighter offers to go in his own vehicle to try to rescue James. But the firestorm in the forests around the house is too intense to get close. They all know a strong southerly change is forecast to hit any minute, and the man tells the Stewarts that from what he's just seen of the fire, once it arrives, James will almost certainly die.

Desperate, Ian asks the man if *he* can talk to James, handing over the phone. In a quick conversation, the off-duty firefighter tells James what will happen if he doesn't try to leave now, and suggests an escape route out through a trail at the back of the property, where the fire is slightly less intense.

Fiona is not sure how long they wait after hanging up – 'time is immeasurable in these situations' – but soon she sees James in his car, hurtling out of the forests and up the road towards them. Not much later, they see explosions coming from the direction of their house and hear the sound of their roof falling in.

The southerly change that sweeps up the coast after lunch spreads the fire further across the landscape – some properties that were hit from the northwest by the first fire runs of the morning now get hit again by more waves coming from the south.

The southerly also launches the northern front of the Currowan fire, south of Nowra – the front the RFS incident management team always believed would be the biggest danger of the day. A pyrocumulonimbus forms and the skies over the fire control centre on the edge of Nowra go black. In the firestorm that follows, two fire trucks travelling south of the town get caught in a powerful burnover, with both vehicles almost instantly incapacitated – one starts to melt, while the other catches alight. The eight crew on board don breathing apparatus and – somehow – walk out through the fire unscathed. Homes in the semi-rural area on the outskirts of Nowra are lost, but the blaze stops short of the urban area.

While it was wreaking havoc elsewhere, the southerly change more than likely saved Jen Dudman-Chopping's life.

After swimming across the inlet, she'd started her hike along the beach for home. For the first four or five kilometres, it was uneventful. All alone on a long sweep of sand, nothing but bush to one side and ocean stretching to the horizon on the other – it almost felt like an adventure.

But then it started to become smoky, and the strangest thing happened. Three towering waterspouts appeared over the ocean – tall, spinning columns of water moving like tornadoes, so powerful that one sucked a baby wattlebird from the sky and spat it at her feet. It was disconcerting, but Jen just scooped up the shocked bird, put it in her wet bag and kept walking.

Exactly three minutes later, fireballs started flying out of the bush towards her. 'They say to watch out for the embers. Well, these were fireballs shooting at me. And I'm like, *Geez, this is getting a bit scary.*' She could see flames coming over the sand dunes, and the air became so thick with smoke she could hardly breathe. By the time she pulled out a towel to wrap around her face and waded knee-deep into the ocean, it was as black as night.

'I couldn't see anything, I couldn't breathe, I'm in the water up to my knees and I'm thinking, *This is really not good,*' she says. 'I was panicking because I thought, *I'm going to die and no one's going to know where I am.*' She called triple zero, but all the operator could advise was that she stay in the water and get as low as she could. She then called her son, telling him, 'I'm in serious trouble. I'm suffocating. I need help.'

Jen waded out deeper, up to her thighs. Then, all of a sudden, a kangaroo with its tail on fire came flying out of the black and dived headlong into the ocean beside her. Soon there were numerous burning kangaroos plunging into the water alongside her and tumbling in the waves. *My god, if I stay here I'm going to get taken out by a kangaroo*, she thought.

Then something switched inside her head – she understood that none of the people she'd called for help could do anything for her. 'I just knew that it was *me* that was going to get me out of here, nothing else, purely me. And I was just determined to get home.'

Jen wet the towel and wrapped it tightly around her head and upper body – her work uniform from the aged-care home was made of nylon and she was worried one of the flying fireballs would melt it on her skin. But it was the smoke that felt deadliest. 'Your natural reaction is to take a big breath, but there was no air there. It was just purely smoke. I did that a couple of times and nearly choked on it.' Once she was out of the water, she put her head down, eyes marking a line in the soft sand – *not in the water, not in the dry sand* – and started 'powering' along the beach.

She's not sure how long she'd been walking when something made her glance up. 'I saw that bright light at the end of the tunnel. And honestly, it was so bright I remember letting go of the towel and putting my hands up over my face,' she says. 'And I just went, *Oh my god, that's it. I've died. End of life.* And then I went, *Oh, hang on a sec, no I haven't.*'

It was the southerly change – taking the fire and smoke that was bearing down upon her and turning it away to her north. In an instant, she could breathe and see again. Adrenaline pumping, she started walking faster, and soon she could see the crowds of people who had fled the fire standing on the beach at Lake Conjola.

When she saw her son emerge from the crowd and run towards her, she started running too. 'And he gets to me and says, "Mum!" and gives me a big kiss. And he says, "Do you want me to carry you?"'

'Oh no, I don't think you'll be able to,' she replies.

*

By mid-afternoon, fire is still burning in the bushland all around Lake Conjola and the reservoir that supplies water to the village is empty. It can't be refilled because there's no power to the pumping station – or anywhere else. Local authorities know an emergency generator is needed, but with the road access cut there is no way of bringing one in. Helicopters are water-bombing the perimeter of the village and a handful of Conjola RFS volunteers are working out of a private car.

Nikki Goozee is still sitting inside the office at the caravan park – watching squalls of embers outside, waiting for everything around her to burn down. Joining the evacuation onto the beach will be her very last resort; even inside, her lungs are barely coping with the smoke. The batteries for her ventilator still have charge, but she doesn't know how long she's going to be trapped here without electricity. Used to being independent in her own home, having to rely on others to assist her with things like going to the toilet – even when it's done with kindness – makes her feel she has 'lost all dignity'.

Among the crowd of thousands at the caravan park is Major General Peter Dunn. He and his wife, Lindy, started to defend their home, as they had always planned, but 'we got to the point where it was so hot, so smoky and frankly so dangerous that I said to Lindy, "We're out of here. It can have it." We both said, "We would like to see our kids again."'

When he first arrived at the caravan park, he found 'chaos'. With no proper evacuation plan, there were 'kids everywhere, people in tents, fire everywhere, cars everywhere'. Some friends of the Dunns, including a former policewoman, volunteered to take charge of traffic management, and he says, 'If they hadn't have done that, there would have been panicking drivers going through the caravan park.'

Once the mobile phone network goes down completely at 3.00 pm, no one has any idea what is happening elsewhere. Similar failures are occurring right along the coast. By nightfall, there will be no telecommunications, including landlines, mobile phones and internet, anywhere along the 170-kilometre stretch between Nowra and Moruya – an information blackout for everyone in the fire zone, including hospitals.

As one of the members of Emergency Leaders for Climate Action, what Dunn is seeing unfold before him now is a horrifying confirmation of his worst fears. 'There was no one sitting back and going, "Okay, what are we really dealing with here?"'

In Bawley Point, where we've been hearing snippets all afternoon about what's going on to our north around Conjola, I'm watching as Chris and some of his fellow volunteers become increasingly agitated. The brigade has a full cohort eager to go and help, but there are no trucks. One has been seconded elsewhere, with little warning, and the other has a broken gearbox and is laid up at a mechanic's workshop in town.

After being told by the fire control centre in Nowra that there are no spare trucks available, the Bawley RFS captain, Charlie Magnuson, starts calling around stations. He discovers a Cat 7 sitting idle in a neighbouring village. It is an excellent result, but as they roll out of the village to head north, I can't help feeling uneasy about the situation they're heading into.

When Charlie steps inside the RFS command van at Milton Showground, he's shocked to see that the divisional commander, John Ashton – 'a firefighting legend in our neck of the woods' – has tears running down his face.

Ashton is at breaking point. He's already had to ring the fire control centre in Nowra to tell them he can't accept any more triple-zero calls because he has no assets left – something that makes him feel 'shithouse'. But then he received a radio call from a colleague, an off-duty RFS member, saying that both he and his wife were trapped on their property north of Conjola and have sustained horrendous burns to large parts of their body. 'He was calling in saying he couldn't hang onto his radio because the skin had fallen off his hands,' says Ashton. 'His daughter was there with him, and he was telling her to drag them and put them in the swimming pool and she was on the radio saying, "I can't, they're too heavy."'

But the unexpected arrival of the Bawley crew means Ashton now has a fire truck. He asks Charlie to go and see if he can help.

When Charlie arrives at the road into the property, the forests on either side of the narrow dirt road are in flames and he thinks, *Here we go again*. After driving in for Chris in similar circumstances at the beginning of the Currowan fire, Charlie had promised his wife, Linda, he would never take such a risk again. But, he says, 'It had to be done. Injured people needed our help if they were to survive.'

At the homestead, it's clearly a life-or-death situation; both adults have serious burns to more than 50 per cent of their bodies. The crew apply first aid on the lounge-room floor – the couple are wildlife carers, and Charlie notices baby wombats toddling around him as he works – and once the skin is wrapped in Glad Wrap, the crew carefully load them into the truck and begin a slow, steady-as-possible journey back out through the forests and to a sportsground by the coast, to wait for a medivac by helicopter.

Charlie nurses the woman, who is enduring indescribable pain, and it feels like the longest hour of his life.

*

In the town of Ulladulla, the civic centre has been made into an evacuation centre, and upwards of 1,000 people have arrived – a mix of holidaymakers who've fled from coastal caravan parks and now have nowhere to sleep, and soot- and sweat-covered locals who've just barely made it out of their homes alive. But here too is plunged into darkness when the power goes out early in the evening.

There is no emergency generator onsite, and just as the centre manager is wondering how she's going to safely shelter this many people, she notices an inflatable jumping castle coming to life on the lawns outside, where a carnival funfair is – curiously – deciding the show must go on. *They must have power*, she thinks, and races outside. The funfair can't help, but they suggest she tries the Stardust Circus, set up in the paddock next door.

Soon a circus truck pulls up behind the civic centre, with a generator loaded onto the back and a team of circus folk ready to help. They figure out they can't power the centre's own system – the wiring is not set up – so they bring in the circus lights, stringing them through the building's interior. Meanwhile, someone has tracked down the owner of the local camping shop, and they open their store so camping lights can be collected to finish lighting the centre.

In Conjola Park, when Michelle Morales emerges from the bunker beneath her neighbour's house, she finds her home still standing and two young men putting out the flames in her backyard. One is a local who's already lost his home; the other tells her, 'I just came in for a surf and couldn't get out.'

By late afternoon, she still hasn't heard anything from her partner, Laurie, and she's getting worried. She wants to go and find him, but a neighbour says he'll go instead. He returns a short while later, grim-faced, telling Michelle that he thinks Laurie hasn't made it.

Michelle says, 'Take me there.'

The driveway to Laurie's house is blocked by fallen trees and an RFS volunteer is standing guard in a truck. Michelle goes up to him and says she's heard her partner is dead. 'He said to me, "It's not true, that's just a rumour." But I could tell by his face he wasn't telling the truth.'

Along with Laurie Andrew, two other local men died on this day. John Butler was a seventy-five-year-old 'bushman' who lived in a farm cottage next door to Frank Condello. Like Condello, Butler fled the fire in his car – but he was overrun. A little further north, Michael Campbell was also caught in his car trying to escape.

In Conjola Park, eighty-nine homes are gone, nearly a third of the village, with many dozens more properties lost around Little Forest and Yatte Yattah. The community was about to wake into a new year with their lives irrevocably altered.

PART THREE

A NEW, WORSE YEAR

CHAPTER 12

WRECKAGE

E arly on the morning of 1 January 2020, Prime Minister Scott Morrison releases a New Year's message to the nation. In the short video, filmed in the gardens of Kirribilli House in Sydney, he says:

> I know it's been a tough past twelve months, especially with the terrible bushfires that have claimed the lives of so many Australians. There's also been the drought that continues and, of course, the floods earlier last year. But the one thing we can always celebrate in Australia is that we live in the most amazing country on Earth and the wonderful Aussie spirit that means that we will always overcome whatever challenges we face ... There's no better place to raise kids anywhere on the planet.

Yet all over that day's news and on social media, images are starting to appear of children up and down the coast, huddling on smoke-filled beaches. One of the most widely shared is from Mallacoota, a small town at the mouth of an inlet in Victoria's East Gippsland region. It's a photo of a long-haired boy in a boat, his small hand on the tiller as he flees a fire that has trapped thousands at the water's edge. His eyes are just visible above a face mask, the air around him an apocalyptic orange.

On the first night of 2020, I gathered with friends in Bawley Point for another communal meal. The faux buoyancy with which we'd managed to carry off the previous evening's dinner – our impromptu New Year's Eve gathering, held while everything around us burned – was fast dissipating. Anxiety was no longer confined to just what was happening with the fires. All the basics we were so used to relying on – electricity, running water, flushing toilets, access to food and safe roads, phone and internet coverage – had disappeared. It made things logistically difficult, but at a deeper level, it felt disconcerting to see everything so broken.

Dinner was being cooked under dim torchlight in the kitchen: the last limp pieces of salad assembled; meat, now pushing two days without refrigeration, eyed suspiciously (*let's just leave it to cook a little longer*). Outside, children were being directed to a tap attached to a water tank to wash their hands. It was a lucky find – most houses in the village had their tanks connected only to household plumbing, and no electricity to start the water pump meant no water.

We'd all been checking our phones regularly for signs of service, desperate for news of when the roads would reopen and any updates on the fire. So when I heard the sound of a text message coming through – and my friend who received it yelling excitedly, 'I've got range!' – I looked up from what I was doing in the kitchen and called out a cheer in response. The next moment I heard the most terrible wailing sound coming from my friend, and everyone dropped what they were doing – racing either to comfort her or to usher all the children away.

Later, when I was cycling home from dinner with my two kids through the dark streets, they asked me what had happened. I had to tell them: we'd just found out that Mrs Morales' partner had died in the fire. Michelle Morales is a popular teacher at their school and a close colleague of my friend. The children were quiet, riding the rest of the way home in silence.

It was hard to know how my kids – or anyone's – were processing this long, difficult summer. Earlier that day, I'd come home to find Charlie Magnuson sitting at our kitchen bench talking to Chris and crying quietly. I knew enough of what had happened the day before – the rescue and nursing of the burns victims – to understand why he'd be feeling this way, and automatically started to usher the kids from the room. But then I changed my mind. My son in particular looked up to Charlie, who'd always let him hang around the fire shed and been unwaveringly kind, and I thought perhaps it wouldn't hurt for him to see that even brave grown-ups were finding this hard.

Chris was still trying to come to terms with his experience of the day. Because the Bawley Point RFS had only managed to find one fire truck and there were more than enough volunteers, while Charlie had gone off with a crew to attempt the rescue, Chris and a few others had taken a personnel carrier and gone into Conjola to see what they could do. When they arrived, late in the afternoon, Conjola Park was already in ruins – with some telling them 'you're a bit late' – and he was finding this more traumatic than facing down any fire.

*

As it entered a new year, the nation looked almost unrecognisable. The Currowan fire wasn't the only blaze to have wreaked havoc on New Year's Eve – across three states, well over a dozen fires had burned simultaneously at an emergency level. In New South Wales alone, more than 450 homes had been lost and seven people killed.

By 1 January, there were only a few intervals of green space left on a 260-kilometre stretch of New South Wales coastline – fires were burning from Nowra nearly down to Bega. The tens of thousands who had spent the previous day sheltering on beaches still had no safe place to return to and were camping out in overcrowded sports halls and community clubs, or sleeping in their cars. Villages – like Cobargo and Mogo – now had large bites taken out of their main shopping streets. Inland, fires were marching into the ranges of the Snowy Mountains.

From Sydney Harbour, a Navy supply ship designed to deal with humanitarian crises was being despatched to Mallacoota, where 5,000 people were trapped by fire. While they waited for HMAS *Choules*, people were being advised to boil their drinking water because East Gippsland Water couldn't guarantee the supply was safe, and police were bringing in emergency food supplies by boat. More than 7,000 homes in the area were without power, most without phone coverage.

On 2 January, the funeral for volunteer firefighter Geoffrey Keaton was held in Sydney. Thirty-two-year-old Keaton had died alongside another volunteer in mid-December when, on his way to a fire southwest of Sydney, their truck was hit by a falling tree and rolled. At the service, Rural Fire Service commissioner Shane Fitzsimmons pinned a posthumous bravery medal onto the little chest of Keaton's nineteen-month-old son. A few days before the funeral, another volunteer was killed near the New South Wales–Victoria border, when what was described as a fire tornado – likely a pyrocumulonimbus – picked up his ten-tonne fire truck and flipped it on its roof. Twenty-eight-year-old Samuel McPaul was five months away from becoming a father for the first time.

In the nation's capital, the bushfire smoke was so bad it was rated as having the worst air quality of any major city in the world. An elderly woman died after stepping off a plane at Canberra airport into the haze, and Australia Post suspended deliveries to the city.

In Cobargo, where seventy homes and nearly 200 buildings had been destroyed on New Year's Eve, a twenty-one-year-old woman – six months pregnant, with a toddler in tow, having just lost everything she owned – displayed her fury with the situation by refusing to raise her hand when the prime minister, who'd flown in for a tour of the fireground, tried to shake it.

In Conjola Park, the days after the fire were brutal. Scott and Kris Brennan's house was one of only a handful in their street to survive. In the place of the familiar homes of their neighbourhood there were now piles of rubble covered by metal roofing, skeletal two-storey brick homes with their empty insides on full display, and charred lawns where neat concrete pavers now led down to nothing but a pile of debris. The streets were clogged with burnt-out cars and fallen trees, and treated-pine retaining walls and garden sheds kept sending noxious coloured smoke into the air.

It was a 'horrific emergency situation', says Scott. Locals were endangering themselves clearing trees and putting out lingering fires, people were suffering from smoke inhalation and cuts and burns, and none of the dinner-plate eyes he'd seen on New Year's Eve were going away – if anything, the mental trauma was getting worse. But there was no sign of the large-scale, coordinated emergency response he expected after such a disaster. Like many residents, he felt that the authorities had offered 'no protection' during the fires, then 'left us to rot. Threw us on the scrap heap.'

For the first few days, the only emergency services many locals saw were police, who arrived to set up a roadblock where the Conjola road meets the highway. Similar road-blocks were set up at the entrance to other burned localities. The rationale for prohibiting any movement into these haz-ardous landscapes seemed clear – trees and powerlines were down, buildings still smouldering. Yet locals who wanted to buy essential supplies were being met by bureaucratic enforcement; police said that if residents passed through the roadblock, they would not be allowed to return. People were furious. Many needed groceries, fuel for generators, parts for broken fire pumps; parents wanted to deliver children to safer environments, or just go to work. But no one wanted to be locked out – especially those whose homes had made it this far. Scott Brennan wasn't the only one compelled to drive dangerous back roads through the still-burning bush into town, just so he could buy some fuel for his fire pump, to be ready for when the fire came again.

While locals were not free to come and go, members of the media – wearing crisp, pristine yellow RFS jackets – were allowed through the roadblock. 'Instead of medical personnel and trauma counsellors,' says Scott, 'the community were faced with microphones and cameras.' The Brennans had the mis-fortune of being in a particularly photogenic location. Out-side their house was a car that had melted into rivulets along the road. A powerful image of the intensity of the fire, it drew media like a magnet, making Kris feel as though she were 'an animal in a zoo'. On New Year's morning, she was standing on her street, still so deeply traumatised she barely had words, when 'this journo walked straight up to me and said, "Did you lose your home?" And when I said, "No," he just turned his back on me and walked off to find someone else.'

Another local, who'd been awake for twenty-four hours defending her home and had still not managed to get in contact with her family because phone coverage was down, gave a long interview to a television reporter who arrived on her doorstep. While she wasn't forced into speaking – and many who heard her words were touched by the moving account – she says, 'I really only did it so my children and family could hear my voice and know I was alive.'

In Yatte Yattah, Ian and Fiona Stewart were feeling similarly abandoned. After losing their home and nearly their son, they slept the night in a neighbour's home, waking to see their area looking like 'a war zone'. 'It was like the Battle of the Somme,' says Fiona. Locals with their own machines cleared the roads of fallen trees, and 'no one came to see if we were alright'.

The immediate needs of survivors were being overshadowed by another looming crisis. On 2 January, the New South Wales premier declared a seven-day state of emergency – the third for the season – because more dangerous fire weather was coming. Fire authorities warned that conditions on Saturday, 4 January, could be 'some of the worst the nation has ever faced'. Compounding the danger along the South Coast was the presence of tens of thousands of tourists, whose safety couldn't be guaranteed. The government declared that from Nowra down to the Victorian border – a 14,000-square-kilometre area, where visitor numbers at this time of year are upwards of 50,000 –

was now a 'tourist leave zone'. It was going to require the 'largest mass relocation of people out of the region that we've ever seen', said a state government minister. The RFS called it 'a race against the clock'.

Virtually no visitors needed convincing. Thousands had been left with nowhere to stay, with coastal caravan parks and entire villages either inaccessible or no longer habitable; and few who'd caught even a glimpse of the fires on New Year's Eve had any wish to repeat the experience. But with fire still blocking nearly all major roads, long lines of departing vehicles stretching many kilometres, both north and south, soon ground to a standstill.

For those trying to get out, access to fuel became a problem. With hundreds of powerlines down and substations burned, many petrol stations were non-operational. The few with generators were able to get petrol pumps flowing, but because telecommunications were also down, EFTPOS machines were not working. Not everyone is prepared for a cash-only world, and there were as many stories of people generously paying for others' fuel as there were of cars driving off without paying.

Fuel supply dwindled quickly. Tankers from Sydney could not get through because of fire over the highway. A special convoy was arranged to get a tanker to a service station in Batemans Bay. When word got around it had arrived, at 2.00 am on 2 January, hundreds of cars immediately started to queue. Vehicles with interstate numberplates, presumed to be travellers needing to drive home, were divided into a separate line to be given a larger allocation of fuel.

At the Ulladulla civic centre, still lit by circus lights, the centre manager was once again having to adapt. While the building was always a designated evacuation centre, providing accommodation was never part of the protocol – the plan was always to outsource to motels or caravan parks. But this was no longer viable, and hundreds of visitors, waiting for their chance to escape, were sleeping inside on every centimetre of floor space, on bedding donated by the local community. A call had also gone out for billets, and a steady stream of locals were turning up to take in a stranger for the night.

New waves of people kept arriving. Convoys of cars came up the highway from Batemans Bay, only to be stranded when the road further north was closed by fire again, so more people arrived on the civic centre doorstep needing somewhere to sleep. Everyone also needed to be fed, and with no delivery trucks getting through, the supermarket shelves were becoming bare. One evacuation centre in a coastal village further north became so overwhelmed by the influx of visitors that locals needing help were told to go home.

It was a stressful experience for travellers, some of whom spent a night sleeping in their car in the traffic queue, unwilling to give up their spot and chance to leave. But the demands of the evacuation left many local communities short on food and fuel, as those trying to leave filled their petrol tanks and shopping trolleys in preparation for the journey.

By 2 January, with the highway north to Sydney only periodically open, incident controller for the Currowan fire Mark Williams was coming under major pressure to get things moving faster: time was running out. He'd been working with around thirty police vehicles, which were leading small groups of cars – twenty to fifty at a time – through what was still an active fire zone. But it was a stop-start operation, as fire and smoke kept encroaching upon the road.

'People were getting antsy because we told them to get out, they were ready to get out, and then all of a sudden it's, "Oh, hang on, just stop for a minute,"' he says. Queue-jumping was starting and people were getting angry. Radio stations and social media were lighting up with stories of scared and frustrated people stuck on the South Coast, and Williams was hearing about it from RFS headquarters. 'We had ten-thousand-plus people sitting out there, nowhere to go. There were a lot of phone calls between myself and numerous people in our head office saying the pressure was on,' he says.

Williams identified the main obstacle – an eight-kilometre stretch of highway lined by active fire, but also by pockets of unburned bushland. He knew that as long as there was still fuel to burn, fire would keep striking the highway – slowing the pace of the evacuation and endangering anyone who travelled on it.

He came up with a plan to block the highway altogether and put in an eight-kilometre back-burn. It was a gamble: no one, especially at headquarters, was going to be happy to hear that the evacuation had been halted, and he didn't really have the resources to put in a back-burn of this length – plus the wind was wrong. But he decided, 'You know what, we've got no choice it. Light it up.' He told his crews, 'Get in the truck with the drip torches either side of the highway and just light it up.'

It took six hours, but Mark Williams' plan was a success. With little more than a day to spare, traffic started streaming freely out of the South Coast.

It was late on 2 January by the time Tayanah O'Donnell and her family finally got on the road home to Canberra. They'd been staying in their holiday house, south of Malua Bay, and she spent New Year's Eve sheltering on a beach with her children. With no phone reception, she hadn't really understood the scale of what had happened – until she went to the local supermarket the next day. 'Everyone was panicking, people were panic buying – buying anything, buying things in bulk – and arguing with each other,' she says. 'You couldn't get cash out, so we scraped together fourteen dollars in change from the car and just bought toilet paper and pasta.' She'd been chasing fuel and trying to get out ever since, and was now heading home via a circuitous route, which would take them down the far South Coast and over the Snowy Mountain ranges before turning north to Canberra.

As they came through Cobargo, the village was deserted. Shops in the main street were still smouldering, and on the outskirts, the sides of the road were littered with hundreds of dead animals – sheep, cows, kangaroos, an echidna.

In a way, Tayanah thought perhaps she shouldn't be so shocked. She's a lawyer and academic who works in the field of climate change adaptation – looking at how governments and communities can adapt and plan for changing environmental conditions. 'So you think I would have been better prepared,' she says. 'I do all this work with governments around scenario-planning, but there's no scenario that I'm aware of that predicts what happens when you drive through a blackened field littered with dead animals and your kids are in the car.'

Adaptation, or building resilience as it's sometimes called, is one of the most pressing issues Australia faces. We are one of the most climate-exposed countries in the world – recent research suggests that more than 380,000 existing homes are at high risk of exposure to extreme weather, be it bushfires, flood or coastal inundation. Figuring out how best to prepare ourselves, our homes, our infrastructure is challenging, in part because there is no stable baseline to plan from. With the climate changing, and the frequency and severity of that change evolving, you're having to 'forward plan for something that is almost beyond the imagination of the everyday person', says Tayanah.

But even taking that into account, she thinks Australia is doing poorly. The 'scale of the system breakdown' along the South Coast is more evidence that we are not adapting in time. 'We're not. We are absolutely not, in any sense of the word – politically, socially, economically, built environments, none of it. None of it.'

Tayanah's speciality has always been coastal policy – trying to grapple with the clash between rising sea levels and the Australian predilection for building on coastal plains and ocean fronts. Yet driving home through burned-out villages, she saw the scale of the challenge – the need for urgent and smart adaptation – expand before her eyes.

As she pulled into Canberra, it was hard not to feel bleak. 'You know, there are places where we're just not going to be able to live anymore. And the way we live is going to change. I don't know what it's going to mean for people who can't pack up and move.'

Kangaroo Valley is vast and sprawling, sinking into the northernmost end of the mountain ranges that run up the spine of the South Coast. Its one small village is peppered with the centuries-old sandstone buildings dating from the time of its settlement, and from here the land spreads into gently sloping green pastures – some dairy country – and then into the forested foothills and steep mountains, where hundreds of homes are tucked into nooks and crannies.

The valley is 120 kilometres north of where the Currowan fire first began. Mike Gorman, a local electrician who's lived in the valley for decades and is deputy captain of the Kangaroo Valley RFS, had been travelling down the coast with his brigade to fight the fire ever since it started. But by Friday, 3 January, with the head of the fire now hovering north of Nowra, on the edge of the Shoalhaven River, and a strong southerly wind forecast for the next day, he knows there is no way the valley will see out Saturday unscathed.

Gorman has been sharpening his preparations for the valley's defence for the past week, though plans have been underway here for well over a year.

It started with a conversation back in 2018 between Gorman and a local policeman. Signs of the drought were starting to appear in the valley, and the policeman was thinking back to 2009, when he was seconded to the Victorian town of Marysville in the immediate aftermath of the Black Saturday fires – part of a team sent in to recover the bodies of the thirty-four people who died when nearly the entire town was destroyed. The geography of Kangaroo Valley is not dissimilar to Marysville, in that there are no easy escapes to the coast. The policeman asked Gorman, 'How ready is our community for fire?'

Gorman had already been pondering how the RFS could build better bridges between itself and the community. It was thinking sparked by a traumatic experience he had the year before, when he volunteered on a strike team sent out to a fire in western New South Wales. The Sir Ivan fire burned during the worst fire-weather conditions the state had ever seen. But it wasn't the blaze that disturbed Gorman. The fireground was plagued by conflict and distrust between local farmers and the RFS. Under dire conditions, the fire control centre ordered its trucks to withdraw – a decision poorly communicated to farmers, who were furious that they battled alone while the RFS looked on.

Gorman had a lady banging on the window of his truck, asking, 'Why aren't you helping us?' On the bus on the way home to the valley, he commented to a fellow volunteer, 'If we treated our farmers in the valley like we just treated those people, we'd never be able to walk down the street or go to the pub again.' (A coronial inquest later heard evidence that farmers felt isolated and disengaged from the RFS even before the fire, and recommended better collaboration and 'shared responsibility' between the public and the RFS.) Later, Gorman started reading the 2009 Victorian Bushfires Royal Commission report into Black Saturday, noting they'd recommended more community-based bushfire planning. 'I thought, *We don't do that*,' he says.

With the local policeman, Gorman called a community meeting to discuss fire preparedness, and around 150 people showed up – a huge turnout for a small community not currently in a fire crisis. They discovered a willingness among locals to get involved in preparing both themselves and the valley for fire, and after several more public meetings, the Kangaroo Valley Community Bushfire Committee was formed, with the intent to develop a community bushfire plan.

Gorman had invited RFS staff from Nowra along to one of the meetings, hoping to get them on board. But when the committee presented the Nowra office with a written proposal for a community bushfire plan in early 2019, the concept was dismissed as not useful. One reason given was that a community plan 'may be a distraction', with people focusing on that instead of preparing their individual bushfire survival plans (a staple of RFS communications). A more useful approach, the Nowra RFS office said, would be for the committee to assist people 'to access the existing information regarding bushfire preparedness'. It seemed they didn't relish the idea of anyone working outside of their oversight.

After the Black Saturday royal commission recommended more community involvement in fire planning, the Rural Fire Service had set up a mechanism for community protection plans to be developed for individual communities. But when Gorman looked into it, he discovered only a small number of communities in the state actually had these plans in place, and Kangaroo Valley wasn't even on the waiting list. Besides, in his view, it was a 'top-down' process led by the RFS. His vision was to start from the grassroots – getting people to understand the risks and plan for their own survival.

The Kangaroo Valley Community Bushfire Committee ploughed ahead, with members researching and disseminating information about the growing bushfire threat and how to safeguard homes. Under its umbrella, a multitude of smaller neighbourhood groups formed in the valley – often just a set of residents on a single road, sharing basic information such as one another's names and contact details.

But disapproval from the RFS in Nowra about what Mike Gorman was doing started to create tensions within the brigade. There was a sense from some that Gorman was rocking the boat. To defuse tensions, Gorman stepped down as captain, becoming deputy.

As 2019 drew to a close, with the arrival of the Currowan fire inevitable, Mike Gorman had accelerated his community work – travelling around the valley, meeting with the small neighbourhood groups and with individuals, to ensure everyone was prepared.

On the last weekend in December, Mark Williams also arrived in Kangaroo Valley, for an RFS community meeting. It was well attended, with people spilling out of the weatherboard hall to hear Williams warn that if anyone was planning on staying and defending the following Saturday, it would be a 'harrowing event' for which they must be physically and mentally prepared. 'If you are questioning yourself, your best option is to leave, and leave early,' he said.

That same weekend – and all the way up to 3 January – Mike Gorman continued his own, smaller meetings, taking off his RFS jacket so it was clear he was not speaking on behalf of the RFS. Most of the people he spoke with had also attended the RFS meeting, and he wasn't undercutting Williams' message – 'I told people you are likely to get burnt this Saturday,' he says, warning them they should not expect to see a fire truck. But what he did differently was pass on granular information about fire protection. 'I said, "Even if you are leaving early, these are things you can do to prepare your house. But if you're going to stay, this is what you need to do and what you'll be facing."'

Gorman went into detail about what it looks like to be prepared and laid out the dire consequences of getting it wrong. 'These were real conversations, not constrained by fear of litigation or wrong advice,' he says. While he wasn't aiming to convince anyone to leave, the information he passed on led several to decide they were not as ready as they thought and, after hearing him, they began to make preparations to evacuate.

Alison Baker, in her fifties, lives with her husband on a property at the far reaches of the valley. At the end of a one-way road, surrounded on all sides by forest, they operate five holiday cottages and a large olive grove. Alison had been vacillating over whether to stay if the fire came. When she first spoke with Mike Gorman, at a small neighbourhood meeting just before New Year, she told him she'd probably leave and her husband would stay and defend. But he told her this was a bad idea. 'He said it was not safe or effective for one person to defend,' she recalls. Alison knew she needed to make her choice, understanding that if she wasn't up for the fight, they both needed to prepare to leave. A few days later she came back to him with a new plan: the couple would prepare the house and cottages together and then retreat to a neighbour's wine cellar once the fire arrived. But again, Mike said this was no good – he checked the cellar and said it didn't have the right kind of opening to serve as a safe fire bunker.

For Paul Reynolds, on his property even further into the reaches of the ranges at the northern end of the valley, there was never any question around his fire plan for Saturday. His professional background is in sustainable building – including research into sprinkler systems – and he had been gradually preparing his house and property for bushfire for twenty years, working 'solidly nonstop' for the past four weeks.

He and his partner have focused on making the house ember-proof: nylon flyscreens have been replaced by stainless-steel mesh; they've installed metal shutters on windows, stapled fireproof blankets to the internal sides of window frames and plugged every single gap in the house bigger than two millimetres with steel mesh, glass fibre or putty. Outside, all above-ground plastic water pipes and fittings have been replaced by galvanised steel, and a purpose-designed fire bunker is buried in the ground ten metres from the house.

By early in the new year, lists of jobs to do during a fire have been stuck on walls, and they've been through three dress rehearsals, where they donned their full personal protective equipment and role-played everything – from the sequence of switching on the fire pumps, to how the house would be patrolled and who would operate which hoses. 'We tried to imagine what it would be like,' he says.

Paul has been an active member of the Kangaroo Valley Community Bushfire Committee since it started and is also part of his own smaller neighbourhood group. He's drawn up maps of his immediate area and handed them on to his local coordinator. On Friday, 3 January, this information, along with a list of who is intending to leave and who's staying, is passed on to Mike Gorman.

Gorman has similar lists from all the other neighbourhood groups in the valley. While he will be working as deputy captain of the Kangaroo Valley RFS tomorrow, he'll keep this information with him as intelligence should the worst come for them.

CHAPTER 13

SATURDAY'S SOUTHERLY BUSTER

By Saturday, 4 January, I've been living alongside the Currowan fire for forty days, and there is no safe place left to go.

The fire danger rating for the day is *extreme*, and the RFS Fire Spread Prediction Map is showing nearly the entire South Coast, from Kangaroo Valley all the way down towards Bega, exposed to either fire or ember attack – including the area where our property is, and Bawley Point, where we're now living.

No longer willing to believe the worst can't happen, I've spent much of the days leading up to it on the phone to friends and family, borderline bossy: *Make a plan – what's your quickest route to the ocean? Just get out, go to the coast for the day.*

That morning, I drive up to our property. I'm worried that even after all this time we could still lose our house, and I want to get some water flowing to fill the gutters and wet down the decks. Our concrete water tank that cracked under the heat of the fire back in early December has gradually leaked dry, but I've managed to get a delivery of water to top it up. Yet after several hours labouring in 40-degree sun with a friend – somehow getting a half-melted pump to start and transferring a small amount of water into the base of a melted header tank, an apparent miracle – the taps still only splutter out trickles of water. Exhausted, angry and half-weeping at the defeat, I go into the house for a quick look around, throwing another haphazard collection of things into a box and driving away.

I've offered our house in Bawley Point as a temporary refuge for the day to friends who live in places more exposed to the bush. We are just metres to the beach and around the corner from a wide, flat headland of rock. When I get home, one friend has arrived with her three children and dog. Equipped like a prepper, she is unloading flagons of water and boxes of food, setting up a gas stove and camping lights on the kitchen bench. Even though the power has only been restored for two days, official warnings are that it will probably go out again.

By late morning nothing seems to be happening, so we go down to the beach. I haven't been in the ocean all summer, so while the kids play on the sand we swim out through the wash of burned leaves, beyond the breakers. Unlike the intense heat up at our property, the air here is pleasant – a gentle nor'easter blowing – and as I float on my back in the deep green water, I am overwhelmed by relief, thinking, *I must have overreacted! Perhaps the forecast was wrong? It's not going to be bad after all.*

But as we are drying off on the beach, we look north and see it: a huge grey plume of smoke.

Quickly packing up, we walk to the headland, where we can see the plume moving towards Lake Tabourie, the next village north. Soon, people I recognise as Tabourie locals start arriving at the headland. It's a confused picture; over the phone, someone on a roof in Tabourie says they can see flames coming in towards the west side of the village; others just see smoke. I'm texting friends I know are still there, warning them that something's happening.

A friend from Tabourie calls me. She is in her car outside her house, her two small children strapped in the back. 'What should I do?' she asks.

I don't know. All I can say is that if it seems safe she should leave and come here, but if not, get to the beach now.

Before long, I have three families of escapees with me in our little house in Bawley. Like a rerun of New Year's Eve, the power goes out and phone and internet coverage starts flicking on and off. There's nothing to do but wait for something – and hopefully nothing – to happen, so we take our chairs outside to the front lawn, leaving the house and backyard to the rampaging children and dogs.

Chris is with the Bawley Point RFS in a small village just north of Conjola. Under strong northwest winds, the eastern flank of the Currowan fire is once again roaring out into places along the coast. He rarely phones when he's on a shift, but he's called several times, and from what he's said I know this is the worst firefight he's been in – they're not sure they can keep it at bay from the village much longer. I've got the RFS radio channel playing over my phone whenever the internet is working, and I overhear his crew asking for aerial support and being told they'll have to wait because everything is tied up. It's the same old story, and I'm so fed up with this whole show.

Mid-afternoon, Chris calls again for a few seconds, just to make sure I know how he feels about me and the kids. It's not explicitly a farewell message, but I understand the function of his communication.

Everyone is nervously waiting the arrival of the day's greatest danger. A powerful southerly buster – an abrupt, severe wind change – is due to start sweeping up the coast late in the afternoon, undoubtedly intensifying the fire. Just as I notice the branches on the trees in the street beginning to bend, and feel a coolness coming in at the back of my neck, I hear an order come down the RFS radio, telling all crews working on the flank of the fire to immediately withdraw because it's coming. I try to phone Chris, but the call won't connect.

I receive an RFS emergency alert text message, telling everyone from Nowra south – including us – to 'seek shelter as fire approaches'. My friend quietly suggests it might be time for me to put all my boxes of valuables in the car – the ones still stacked inside from the day we evacuated back on 1 December.

But I can't do it, physically or mentally. In a twisted Faustian bargain, I'm thinking, *I don't care, let them burn, let my house burn, as long as it means this is over.*

We are not the only ones trying to get through another bad fire day. Elsewhere, another 150 fires are burning across New South Wales, and fifty-three in Victoria. Entire towns have been told by fire authorities they 'will not be defendable'. The village of Batlow in the Snowy Mountains, known for its apple orchards, is sitting near deserted right now as a fire is bearing down.

While it's no use for anyone today, the prime minister finally announces he's agreed to permanently increase annual funding for Australia's aerial firefighting capability – nearly two years since the business case was first put forward. He also announces he's offering an extra $20 million to immediately lease four additional firefighting aircraft for the remainder of this fire season and is issuing a compulsory call-up to 3,000 Australian Defence Force reservists to help bushfire-affected communities. All of this is spruiked in a Liberal Party promotional video, complete with a jaunty jingle, released at the same time. On Twitter, an advertising executive says, 'It's like being "sold to" at a funeral.'

At Woodburn, a heavily forested locality about 20 kilometres north of Bawley Point, Scott McFarlane is inside his house, shirt and shoes off, having a beer. He's been monitoring the progress of the fire all day and knows the southerly is close, so he's taking a breather before it arrives.

Like everyone in Woodburn, he's been in the trenches for nearly a month. The Currowan fire first started encroaching into this area, with its many dozens of properties etched out in forest clearings, back in the second week of December. It's the stubborn guts of the fire, which rests at times but never goes away. Scott's had many sleepless nights; his wife and kids have evacuated five times now, and he hasn't been able to leave the property to go to work as an electrician. Often, it's been the constant roadblocks that have stopped him leaving – he can't afford the risk of not being allowed back in.

His family are nervous about his decision to stay, especially his parents in Sydney, but as Scott told his dad, 'Mate, I remember you doing it back in the eighties, on the roof with a hose in your stubbies and thongs.' Scott's feeling reasonably confident because his house is at the bottom of a small cleared valley. Following the logic that says fires run fast uphill but slow downhill, he's pretty sure that any fire runs that result from the southerly will blast past him, and what he's more likely to face is an ember attack, which he's ready for.

He's still inside the house when he hears what sounds like a helicopter landing in his paddock, so he opens the door and sticks his head outside. It's a cyclonic wind, roaring up a gully towards his house. He quickly throws on his boots and a shirt and runs outside to the fire pump. He's going to wait until the last second to start it, because he only has 8,000 litres of water left – he tried to buy more, but the local water carriers told him that after the mass exodus following New Year's Eve, they were running low on diesel and couldn't get to his place. The pump is hooked up to a sturdy fire hose that a mate dropped around only that morning, concerned Scott's garden hoses were not up to the job.

He leans over and reefs the cord on the pump just as the sky fills with embers and burning pieces of bush. Then a fire-ball comes out of the gully and jumps over his empty dam, and 'everything just erupts into flames'. A 'whirlwind of air pressure' is coming from all directions, taking an old cheese tree that stands 20 metres high in the paddock, twisting it and snapping it in half.

The collision of the southerly buster with the hot nor'west-erly fire has unleashed something he never expected. 'It didn't even come from the south, it came from the northeast,' he says. 'It just got funnelled around and spat through the gully.

'I was prepared for an ember attack, I was not prepared for this,' he says. 'I had no mask. Just a fireproof shirt, hunting pants and work boots. All I could think of was, *I'm not going to make this, I'm not going to see my children. What am I doing?* I jumped on my dirt bike to get away and then I looked at the driveway and snapped out of that freakout. *You're an idiot, you can't get out.* And then I dropped the bike, grabbed the hose and went into work mode. Just deep focus.'

Standing in front of his house, hose trained on the building, was like 'standing in a fire, it was so intense', he says. 'I don't remember much, but I do remember standing there and all of a sudden a wall of red-hot embers comes and hits me from the back and I could see a silhouette of myself in front of me, where my body was stopping the embers. I remember kanga-roos running through the paddocks and bursting into flames.'

It takes about twenty-five minutes for the firestorm to pass, and when it does, Scott and his house are unscathed. He can only attribute it to divine intervention. 'I really think God intervened and helped me out. I am not a legend. I am not some bloke who knew exactly what he was doing. My mind just snapped into gear and I focused.'

Once it tears through Scott's valley, the fire run keeps moving north, skipping across the landscape like flat stones over still water. Properties in Woodburn that have already had fire come through the scrubby understories over previous weeks now have it coming at them again through the canopies. Dozens of homes and buildings are quickly obliterated.

When Dave Howes steps outside his house, north of Wood-burn, and sees a plume of smoke coming his way, he knows that after a summer spent predicting that the Currowan fire would come for everyone eventually, it's now his turn. *This is it*, he thinks.

But the Howes family are ready. They've been preparing for the past five weeks, putting in place the lessons they learned from that strange winter fire back in 2018. 'The Kingiman fire might have taken half our farm,' says Dave, 'but it did us more good than harm. It put us in the right frame of mind.'

Sprinklers are ready, the house is wired up to a generator for when the power goes off, water pipes are buried and the boys, Steven and Lachlan, have their cubes filled and ready to go on the back of their utes when embers start dropping in the paddocks.

The only part of the plan that goes wrong is when ten cars turn up at their house from neighbouring properties and Debbie finds herself with 'all these people with cats and dogs and kids screaming "we don't want to burn" in my lounge room'. The Howes had anticipated that the fire would run in a different direction, and in the previous days offered their farm as an escape route for their neighbours, thinking they could cut through their paddocks to a laneway into town. But that exit is now impassable.

Debbie says to one of her sons, 'I can't get them out.'

He takes off in his ute to check the road and comes back to report that the neighbours can make it through – just.

So Debbie tells them, 'Put your hazards on and don't stop, just go, go, go. Get to Milton and then go to the ocean.'

On the country road that comes out of Woodburn, a mad cavalcade of vehicles is racing for town, fire blasting at their backs. A van catches alight and the driver stumbles out, continuing his escape on foot. A man in a ute with a firefighting cube on the back is accelerating as fast as he can, while his mate in the passenger seat leans out the window, water pump still going, hosing down the vehicle as they drive.

At the same moment, back in Bawley Point, I've just wandered up to the headland to see if I can find any mobile phone reception to get an update. The southerly change has passed us now, leaving the air still and cool. My phone rings. It's a man I know as unflappable, laconic, but he's speaking really fast and telling me this wild story about how he's just been chased out of Woodburn with a whole lot of other cars by some kind of firestorm.

It's a crazy tale – I'm stunned – but just as I'm starting to wonder why he is telling *me* this story, he gets to his point: 'Where are your mum and dad?'

Silently begging the few bars of connectivity on my phone screen to stay strong, I immediately hit their number. Dad answers, sounding tense, telling me they've just pulled into the showground at Milton. He tells me that, minutes before, they'd been watching television at home when everything outside suddenly went black and they heard a pinging sound on the tin roof. It was raining embers. By the time they ran to their car and got out the driveway, their yard and gateposts were already on fire.

He tells me they're okay – they're with about 100 others and they're surrounded by fire trucks.

'No, Dad, go further, go to the harbour,' I say.

It may be overcautious, but by now I'm hard-wired for the worst.

By early evening in Kangaroo Valley, Mike Gorman has parked his fire truck at a vantage point on the escarpment and is watching for signs of the southerly change. In the fading light, he can see out over the vast expanse of shadowy gorges and khaki-coloured mountainsides to his south, to where the plumes of the Currowan fire are rising. The front has already crossed the Shoalhaven River, so there will be nothing stopping it once the wind changes.

Gorman knows he's standing in the dead man's zone, on the flank of the fire, so as soon as he sees a shift in the plumes he says to his crew, 'We better get going.' Towering smoke columns are funnelling higher and higher into the sky, and he recognises that a pyrocumulonimbus is forming. Just before they drive off, he films a quick video and sends it through to the main contact person for the string of neighbourhood groups spread across the valley.

The road out is several kilometres through dense forest. Mike's crew and a second Kangaroo Valley RFS truck make it out, but unbeknown to them, a National Parks vehicle a few minutes behind gets overtaken by the firestorm that's erupted with phenomenal speed – the two men on board are forced to flee their burning vehicle and dive into a dam to survive.

By the time the two Kangaroo Valley trucks arrive back at the fire shed in the village, night has fallen prematurely. The brigade start setting up a generator (hired in case the power goes down), portable pumps and a water supply. There are only two RFS trucks in the village, and they want the fire shed and ambulance station next door to be defendable on their own in case the trucks need to move around town.

No one knows if the fire will hit the village, but the trucks will stay here in case it does. There are hundreds of other homes outside the village, spread over the valley, but after his community outreach work Gorman is confident the vast majority of people in these outlying areas have either left or are staying and defending on the understanding they must be ready to do it alone.

Alison Baker, who runs the holiday cottages and olive grove, has settled on a plan: she will stay with her husband to prepare the property, and both will retreat to a nearby neighbour's place – a fortress-like concrete house set up with a powerful firefighting system and a group of people well equipped to fight – once it's time. As soon as she sees the 'chimneys of fire and smoke' in Gorman's video, now being distributed through the neighbourhood networks, she decides, *We're out of here*.

Standing on the roof of his house, Paul Reynolds sees the pyrocumulonimus forming. The way plumes of hot air flow inside buildings has always been a source of scientific fascination for Paul – as part of his professional research, he's even conducted experiments in order to visualise it. So to see these columns of hot air and the 'extraordinary amount of energy' the fire is pouring into a thunderhead that reaches ten kilometres high is 'both a thing of beauty and at the same time very, very intimidating': 'That was when my heart rate went up.'

It's been 47 degrees most of the afternoon, and Paul, in his late sixties, 'can't deal with that without respite', so he's been taking regular breaks inside under the air-conditioning. But now he and his partner begin enacting their well-rehearsed plan.

About twenty minutes after he sees the smoke column form, the southerly hits and cuts it in half. 'One minute we had bright sunlight and the next minute it was gone,' he says. They turn on their head torches and the LED lights they've positioned around the house.

It arrives gently at first. Bits of burning bark and cabbage tree fronds floating in through the ink-black sky at an almost vertical angle. 'It was the most beautiful thing,' he says. But soon they hear a rumble and see a glow of fire coming up the ridge behind them. Then a fire run comes in from another direction, exploding the pine trees around their neighbour's place 200 metres away. Paul knows they're home, but can't tell if their house has gone up. 'Then our shed ignited. We had paint pots and mowers and things with petrol in them, so there were explosions going off,' he says. Both Paul and his partner are on a hose, actively firefighting.

But now a third reach is coming up the hill through the forest towards them and they must judge if it's time to retreat to their fire bunker. Too soon and they could leave their home unnecessarily vulnerable; too late and they could get hit by radiant heat as they travel the ten metres between the house and the bunker.

They decide it's time. Paul makes the last adjustment on the list: turning a valve so a gravity-fed tank can feed into the sprinklers. They climb into the bunker, pulling the trapdoor down.

*

By around 9.00 pm, Mike Gorman is confident the firestorm is not going to hit the village. Strike teams of fire trucks from outside the valley have started arriving, and as part of their briefing he hands over copies of the maps prepared by the neighbourhood groups. It gives the outsiders, who've arrived at night into an unfamiliar place, the location of all the static water supplies where their trucks can refill, and the locations of houses where they can expect to find those who chose to stay and defend – enabling them to prioritise checking on people's welfare over empty buildings.

Around 10.30 pm, a neighbour helps Alison Baker and her husband chainsaw their way back into their property. 'Our house must have exploded,' she says. 'It was just timber all over the ground.' Four of the five holiday cottages are still standing, but their timber uprights are burning. Although all the water tanks are flattened, because they've filled up empty olive oil containers with water and left them inside the cottages, they're able to put out the flames and save the cottages.

When Paul Reynolds opens the hatch on the fire bunker and sees his home is still there, 'it was the biggest sense of relief I have ever felt in my life'. There is still plenty of fire in the bush around the house, but when a fire truck turns up to check on them at midnight, while he appreciates they're 'checking that people like us are safe', they didn't need any assistance. 'We had no expectation of having outside help. We knew we needed to be totally independent, and I think most people in Kangaroo Valley understood that.'

More than sixty homes and another fifty buildings across the valley have been destroyed, but there are no fatalities – a significant feat for a far-flung community facing a pyrocumulonimbus event with only limited firefighting resources from the state. Mike Gorman believes the work of the Kangaroo Valley Community Bushfire Committee and smaller neighbourhood groups played a vital role in mitigating the damage of the day by fostering awareness of the risk, well-considered fire plans and cooperation among neighbours. 'It raised the awareness to the point where people were able to take informed decisions,' he says.

When I first meet Alison Baker, more than eight months after the fire, she is not only one of the most positive bushfire survivors I have ever met, she's the furthest down the road to rebuilding her home. She tells me that things have gone well with the reconstruction largely because the holiday cottages survived – which only happened because of their well-placed buckets of water. This meant they were able to keep living on the site, which has sped things up, and they've been able to have some kind of income.

Her losses have been immense: her home and everything in it and the olive grove were torched. But she's been able to find some measure of peace by feeling satisfied with her decisions on the day. 'As it was, we probably would have survived if we'd gone into one of the cottages,' she says. 'But to be frank, I wouldn't have wanted to see my house explode. I think in terms of recovery and getting on with our lives, it was better to have not seen that. I think we were in the very best place we could be, and I put that all down, really, to the work through the bushfire community groups.'

Before I go to sleep on the night of Saturday, 4 January, I lie in bed mentally ticking off the whereabouts of my family.

Chris is back. Arriving home late in the evening covered in soot, either unable or unwilling to speak a single word about what had happened in his day, he quickly passed out in sleep. My parents are in their caravan, on a road by the edge of the harbour in Ulladulla – I know there's no way they'll be sleeping, not knowing if their home has survived – and my older brother is in his car parked beside them, having evacuated from his home near Lake Tabourie earlier in the day. Much further down the South Coast, my younger brother and his family, who have been bouncing around between coastal evacuation centres since leaving their farm near Cobargo on New Year's Eve – pursued by fire all this time – have found a temporary safe haven for the night in Bega. None of us is in our own bed – but knowing that we are all somewhere safe allows me to sleep.

I didn't know it then – I could only hope – but this Saturday was to be my last direct brush with the Currowan fire.

CHAPTER 14

EXTINGUISHED

Over the following weeks of January, Chris took his first break from going out on the fire trucks, so he could look after the kids while I sat down to finish writing the article I'd started back in November. There was no space or quiet at our cottage in Bawley Point, so every day I packed food and water, a fully charged laptop, and a head torch if I thought I'd be working late, and headed up to our property.

The Currowan fire hadn't finished with its torment of other communities. Further south, it continued taking runs at the town of Moruya, one day coming within metres of the local hospital and just a few streets from the fire control centre. Eventually it merged with the Badja Forest Road fire – which itself had already joined numerous other ones – creating a band of fire that ran nearly continuously all the way to the Victorian border.

But I was hoping – needing – it to be done with me, both for my sanity and because with an approaching deadline I no longer had time for another event to be added to my already epic fire saga.

Home was now a brutal environment to be in. Writing from our kitchen table, the house still dank with lingering smoke, I looked down upon the piles of rubble littering our property – wondering how we'd ever get things cleared up and working again – and out at the sweep of charred, skeletal forests. Each time I heard another tree fall, I flinched; I ran outside to check for smoke every time the wind blew. By mid-January, any of the canopies left in the eucalypts were turning a russet orange. 'Just imagine you're in Canada in autumn,' a neighbour said with black humour.

Everyone in the neighbourhood was edgy – sightings of smoke starting off strings of panicked phone calls and text messages. For a few days, a wave of rumours about looters in the area did the rounds. It was impossible to know how much of it was true; there were clearly plenty of gawkers about, but someone I knew who lived further out in the bush had men in a car pull into his property claiming to be undercover police, only to quickly drive away when asked for identification. Coincidentally, the same morning an improbable rumour went around that thieves were in cars with fake police decals, I happened to pass a police car on the isolated road into our property. The two officers told me they were checking to see everyone in the area was accounted for after the fires, but when they drove away I was suddenly gripped with doubt and swung around to start stealthily tailing their car from a distance. It took me some minutes to rein in my paranoia.

Further south in Malua Bay, Robyn Butcher, who'd sheltered on the beach alongside her elderly bowlers on New Year's Eve, was also finding herself in a radically transformed world. When she and her husband were finally able to get back into the village, four days after the fires, they discovered that although twelve homes had burned down in their street, theirs wasn't one of them. They stayed a couple more days in a motel, but because they were worried about looters they decided to move back in – without electricity – and 'camp out' in their house. Even though it had been shut tightly, when Robyn opened the front door stagnant smoke billowed out. There was soot everywhere, inside and out, and 'the backyard was six inches deep in ash'.

Robyn and her husband had been getting their meals – a diet heavy in sausage sandwiches – at the evacuation centre. When Robyn told the volunteers there that they were going home, she was handed a box of dry food supplies to take with her. 'It was really surreal,' she says, 'because in the Ladies Bowling Club, that is what *we* do. Even just before Christmas we were filling up shoeboxes of toiletries and luxuries to send to drought-affected farmers' wives to make them feel better, and all of a sudden, *I'm* receiving a box of groceries. I've never been given anything before, I've never been in a situation where I needed.' She was grateful for it, though – supermarket shelves would remain scantily stocked for weeks.

Robyn and her husband were the only ones back living on their street, and they had no power for the whole of January. They heated up tins of baked beans and spaghetti on the gas barbeque for meals; Robyn fought unwinnable battles against the soot. 'It was impossible to get rid of it,' she says. 'Every time you opened the door, more would come in.' When she couldn't shake the persistent dry cough that started after the day after the fire, she went to the doctor, who told her she had the oesophagus of a heavy smoker.

Most days, when Robyn peered out through her curtains, she'd see cars slowly cruising her street. 'Six o'clock in the morning it would start,' she says, 'constant cars, people driving around, just looking, looking. The police were good, they did patrols. They told us people were just curious, but we were taking numberplates.'

The only patch of colour left in the village was the bowling green. Somehow it survived – a verdant square now bordered by black hedges and the crumpled remains of the Malua Bay Bowling Club. Eager to restore at least one point of normalcy to the community, the club expedited the construction of temporary fencing to cordon off the rubble. By mid-January, Robyn and her bowlers were back on the green.

In Conjola Park, Kris Brennan – whose home was also one of few to survive on her road – went from living in a leafy street where she'd hear the neighbours laughing on their balconies at night and wake to birdsong in the morning to living in an eerily quiet place that looked – depending on her outlook that day – like a war zone or a rubbish tip.

The steady procession of onlookers – curious strangers, sometimes more media – also frayed her nerves and made her feel protective. 'I didn't want strangers to see my friends' and neighbours' homes in ashes,' she says. Before the fire, Kris saw herself as a calm person – she works in palliative care, volunteers with children and practises yoga – but now she was storming out of the house to yell 'Are you *right*?' at people, and standing on the street, hands on hips, giving death stares to slow-moving vehicles. She spoke to a counsellor, who explained that 'everyone's home is usually their safe spot, their haven, but my home isn't that anymore. It's been shaken up. It has scars from the fire and it has police and strangers constantly driving past. I feel exposed to any danger that is passing by, so that's why I react.'

Down the road in Lake Conjola, Peter Dunn and his wife, Lindy, were throwing themselves into the massive community-run relief effort – sourcing generators, finding people places to live, sorting through the mountains of donations that were pouring in from all over the country. It was a focus on the minutiae of rebuilding hundreds of shattered lives – a long way from the high-level lobbying of his work throughout 2019 with Emergency Leaders for Climate Action.

It prompted something of a personal crisis for Dunn, who wondered if this is where he should have been all along. 'I'll be honest, I had to go and get counselling about it,' he says. 'I felt that our alert [as Emergency Leaders for Climate Action] to government, our attempts to get government and the prime minister to listen, fell on such deaf ears. I felt that I wasted so much of my time on the politicians and [was] really guilty that I hadn't spent more time warning my community. I would have been far better off knocking on doors, saying, "The weather conditions are so bad, it's so extreme that we are facing a disaster, and we all need to prepare much more carefully than we've ever done before."'

Justine Donohoe returned to her street for a brief visit in early January – the first time she'd been back since accelerating away in a panic, kids in the back seat, moments before her house imploded. Unlike many of those who lost their homes, who sorted through the rubble with shovels, hunting for any remnants of their former life – a broken piece of crockery, the metal leg off a favourite old dresser – she stood back, looking at what was left of her house from the kerb. She already knew she wouldn't be returning to live here; they would move elsewhere. The experience of that single day had irrevocably broken more than bricks and mortar; her sense of this being a safe nest for her family was gone.

*

As well as the Currowan fire, many other blazes burned across the southern part of the country right through January. A ski resort was destroyed, and two fires that had been straddling the New South Wales and Victorian border merged to create a 6,000-square-kilometre megafire burning across the High Country of the Snowy Mountains. On 23 January, one of the Large Air Tankers on lease from the northern hemisphere crashed while on a water-bombing mission, killing all three American crew on board.

In the Snowy Mountains foothills, near Batlow, fire-scorched livestock carcasses lined the road. In Cobargo, wildlife carers were euthanising animals they'd spent years raising and rehabilitating with no more than a sedative and a blunt instrument. On Kangaroo Island, off the coast of South Australia, soldiers were loading the charred remains of hundreds of koalas, kangaroos, wallabies and birds into a truck, to be dumped in a trench.

In mid-January, it was revealed that two of the four big water-bombing aircraft promised by the prime minister back on 4 January still hadn't arrived – delayed by tornadoes in the United States and an erupting volcano in the Philippines.

Smoke from the Australian fires visibly darkened mountaintop snow in New Zealand and changed the colour of the skies as far away as South America. A satellite belonging to NASA, the American space agency, tracked a smoke plume coming from Australia punching its way through the stratosphere 25 kilometres above Earth's surface – the greatest height ever recorded. By midway through the month, this plume had completed a full lap around the globe.

By now, a key phrase from the report into climate change

commissioned by the Australian government back in 2008 had been rediscovered:

> Fire seasons will start earlier, end slightly later and generally be more intense. This effect increases over time, but should be directly observable by 2020.

As this phrase was widely circulated by journalists and on social media, many labelled it – almost with a sense of awe – as 'prophetic'. But as its author told a journalist in a January 2020 radio interview, there was nothing mysterious about either his forecast or the outcomes. 'If you ignore the science when you build a bridge, the bridge falls down,' said economist Professor Ross Garnaut. 'If you ignore the science when you build a plane, the plane crashes.'

The Currowan fire was only officially extinguished on 8 February 2020, after torrential rain brought widespread flooding to the east coast of New South Wales, including to Lake Conjola. In the granny flat that eighty-year-old Frank Condello had moved into with his wife, after losing his home and nursery on New Year's Eve, water came halfway up the walls. By the time the Currowan fire was done, it had consumed nearly 5,000 square kilometres of land.

Australia-wide, 186,000 square kilometres burned in the 2019–20 fire season – an area nearly three times the size of Tasmania.

Across this vast landscape of fire, more than 3,500 homes were destroyed. Around 65,000 Australians were displaced during the fires, with more than 8,000 facing long-term displacement. In New South Wales, over half the Gondwana rainforests and 80 per cent of the World Heritage–listed Blue Mountains were fire-affected. Estimates of the number of animals either killed or displaced sit around three billion. Thirty-three people died as a direct result of the fire, with at least another 400 killed by smoke pollution.

In one calculation of the monetary costs of the fire season, which included the direct costs, such as losses of infrastructure, and the indirect costs, such as disaster recovery expenditure and healthcare – including mental health – one eminent economist estimated losses to the country of over $100 billion.

As I wrote from the ruins of our property, I kept wanting to draw an analogy between bushfire and war. After an initial resistance – it seemed too easy – I gave in; it seemed the simplest way of making sense of it all. Besides, it *did* feel like we were under attack, and were now living in something like a post-war landscape.

What happened was that we were outgunned – by an enemy the likes of which we'd never seen before, one we were not equipped to match, despite a multitude of warnings it was coming. Not only did we run short of artillery from the very beginning, but many of the weapons and techniques we'd used successfully in the past no longer worked in this new, unfamiliar battleground. We urgently needed to open our eyes to this new world.

CHAPTER 15

ACCOUNTING

Before the final flames were even out, in late January 2020, the premier of New South Wales called an independent inquiry into the bushfire season. The prime minister followed three weeks later, announcing a royal commission. Both leaders insisted on speed, giving reporting deadlines of just six months.

Such short timeframes were almost unheard of for such an enormous task. The 2009 Victorian Bushfires Royal Commission into Black Saturday, the examination of a single day, lasted eighteen months. The rationale for this urgency was that both governments wanted final reports quickly so that practical action could be taken before the next bushfire season arrived. But beating the next fire season in any meaningful way was an impossible task. As one of the very first witnesses to appear before the royal commission – a scientist from the Bureau of Meteorology – explained, fire seasons in eastern Australia run for four months longer than they did in the 1950s, now beginning towards the end of winter. Even the quickest of actions would have us chasing our tails.

To expedite the NSW Bushfire Inquiry, Premier Gladys Berejiklian declared it necessary to hold it behind closed doors.

'If you were to hold public hearings, that could be in the thousands of people who want to speak,' she said. True, perhaps; but what a dreadful state to find ourselves in – too many victims to be heard.

Not that anyone was in any doubt, but the final reports of both inquiries confirmed that what had happened was entirely beyond the realm of anything seen before. 'The 2019–20 bushfire season was extreme, and extremely unusual,' found the New South Wales inquiry. 'It showed us bushfires through forested regions on a scale that we have not seen in Australia in recorded history, and fire behaviour that took even experienced firefighters by surprise.'

Fire disregarded all the rulebooks: spreading quickly at night, advancing into the wind, spawning spot fires up to eight kilometres ahead of the fire front. The royal commission heard evidence that there were more fire-generated thunderstorms this season – the pyrocumulonimbus events – than the total number recorded over the past three decades. Fire ecologist Professor David Bowman told the hearings this was 'truly extraordinary, because what we would call statistically a black swan event, we saw a flock of black swans. That just shouldn't have happened.'

Both inquiries concluded that a combination of factors laid the groundwork for this extreme season. The year 2019 was Australia's hottest and driest year on record; the eastern seaboard was already in drought, coming off several decades of rainfall deficiencies; the positive Indian Ocean Dipole and negative Southern Annular Mode events supercharged the heat and drought; and there were frequent and consecutive days of record-breaking extreme fire weather – December was the most dangerous month for fire since records began in the 1950s.

Both inquiries also accepted unequivocally that these conditions are linked to a changing climate, caused by an increase in greenhouse-gas emissions. This 'clearly played a role in the conditions that led up to the fires and in the unrelenting conditions that supported the fires to spread', found the NSW Bushfire Inquiry. While climate change doesn't explain everything, it stated, the conditions being seen over southeast Australia 'are consistent with what climate change projections have been saying will happen'.

The royal commission – which examined all kinds of natural disasters, not only bushfires – found that 'extreme weather has already become more frequent and intense because of climate change', and this trend will continue. Not only will we see more extreme natural disasters more often, the royal commission said, but the nature of these events will become more complex and harder to predict, with different types of disasters potentially occurring at the same time. 'Compound disasters may be caused by multiple disasters happening simultaneously, or one after another. Some may involve multiple hazards – fires, floods and storms. Some have cascading effects – threatening not only lives and homes, but also the nation's economy, critical infrastructure and essential services, such as our electricity, telecommunications and water supply, and our roads, railways and airports.'

As profoundly shocking as the fire season of 2019–20 was, we are likely to see much worse.

Neither inquiry pursued accountability for decisions made by government and firefighting agencies in the lead-up to the fires or while they were underway. The royal commission's final report said, 'We took a deliberate decision not to find fault, "point fingers" or attribute blame.' Both reports were instead framed as *lessons learned for next time*.

The NSW Bushfire Inquiry did address the question – widely asked by terrified Australians as the fires raged – of whether we prepared adequately for this season, including whether we had enough resources. In its findings it absolved decision-makers of any failures in planning. 'The Inquiry found that NSW was well prepared for a "normal" fire season, but the extreme nature of the 2019–20 season stretched resources across the State,' the final report said. Yet this seems to be sidestepping the central issue – if all indications were that it was always likely be an extreme fire season, what was the sense in preparing for a 'normal' season?

According to the inquiry, the problem was not a lack of resources but one of extreme fires. 'While fire fighting agencies were well prepared and resourced, as the Inquiry heard many times, "all the fire fighters in Australia" couldn't have stopped some of the fires in the 2019–20 season due to their frequency, size, speed and ferocity,' it said. Again, this seems a too-easy explanation. While it is indisputable that some of the most ferocious fire runs of the season were beyond any human intervention once they got going, and the dryness of the landscape combined with extreme weather meant a major fire season was inevitable, this doesn't mean we couldn't have mitigated the destruction with greater resources. Even just a small amount of extra aerial resources – a helicopter to stop a new spot fire becoming a problem for another day, another line-scan plane so residents could be warned a fire was coming, an extra Large Air Tanker to lay down a line of retardant before fire barrelled into an undefended village – could have made a profound difference for many people and their homes. It's hard to see the federal government's fiddling over the ordering of more planes – both in the lead-up to the season and while the country burned – as anything but colossal negligence.

Between them, the two inquiries handed down 156 recommendations – a vast range of actions the country needs to undertake so we're better equipped next time. As the head of the national research centre into bushfires, Dr Richard Thornton, told the NSW Bushfire Inquiry, 'To pursue the same path is tacitly to say that there is an acceptable number of deaths, injuries and property losses from bush fires in Australia each year.'

The NSW Bushfire Inquiry identified a clear pattern to the largest and most damaging fires of the season – one shared by the Currowan fire. Started by lightning in remote forests, they were not tackled early while they were still small, and quickly grew to a size where they were uncontainable.

Lightning sparked nearly 80 per cent of the most significant fires in the state – those responsible for the majority of loss of life, homes and land. By contrast, fires with anthropogenic ignition sources – a human element – contributed to only 6 per cent of houses lost. Why lightning was such a dominant source of ignition requires further study, but what is known is that over the past forty years in southeastern Australia, there has been a trend towards 'dry' lightning conditions: thunderstorms without rain. Meteorologists think this could be an explanation for what happened; it wasn't that there were more storms than usual, just that they came without rainfall. Because the landscape was so dry, these strikes 'caught' easily and fire spread quickly.

The fact that lightning started the vast majority of fires is also interesting in light of comments made by some members of the federal government. During the bushfire crisis, a number appeared in the media promoting the idea that arson was to blame for what was happening. Even the prime minister, at an event for the Australian and New Zealand Cricket teams on the lawns of Kirribilli House on 1 January – just hours after the South Coast was ravaged by two lightning-ignited fires – chose his words carefully to leave open this possibility. 'But the fires do rage on … Whether they're started by lightning storms or whatever the cause may be … it is something that will happen against the backdrop of this Test match,' he said. This attempt to switch the focus from the state of our environment to bad guys with matches can be seen for what it is: a diversion. The last gasps of the climate change wars.

Many of these lightning-ignited fires across the state were not spotted until they were well underway. When I tracked back to the birth of the Currowan fire, I was struck by the blind spot – the fork of lightning responsible for the fire came down around midnight, yet no one saw a thing until nearly fourteen hours later, when it had transformed into an out-of-control bushfire that was chasing the loggers from the forest. It's not possible to know exactly what time the fire escaped from the smouldering tree, but when it was nipping at Dave Howes' heels it had grown to a size of around 12 square kilometres and travelled nearly five kilometres from the point of ignition. The advent of the fire seemed like an accident waiting to happen: a dry lightning storm hitting desiccated forests. Staff from Forestry Corporation were aware of the risk, which is why they were driving around the forests hunting for signs of fire, but a couple of pairs of eyes on the ground were not enough.

Remote sensing technology – sensors attached to drones, balloons, aircraft and satellites, to detect fires in real time – could have led to this fire, and many others, being spotted earlier. The NSW Bushfire Inquiry found that while the RFS does use remote sensing technology – for example, the line-scan

planes that fly over a known fire – 'several of the remote sensing agencies and companies it consulted were surprised that
more sophisticated data fusion and automatic decision-making
tools were not available'. In Australia, both the public and the
private sector has been pioneering this kind of technology for
decades; it just hasn't been widely harnessed to fight bushfires.
The inquiry stated in its recommendations, 'Automatic sensing
of fire for big fire-risk seasons could, and must, be much better,
especially given Australia's strong capabilities in the field.'

I had many *what ifs* about the journey of the Currowan fire
points in time where I wondered if the trajectory could have
been changed. One related to these earliest hours: if it had been
spotted earlier, for example by drone or satellite, could it have
been stopped?

Probably not, I have since learned. This is because unlike
other fire-prone countries – notably Canada and parts of
Europe – Australia doesn't have the systems or resources in
place to aggressively attack remote forest fires as soon as they
start. In these jurisdictions, what's called rapid initial attack is
the norm – specialised aircraft fly in to water-bomb the fire as
soon as it is detected, followed up by remote-area firefighters
who are winched in by helicopter with tools such as rakes and
shovels to extinguish what's left of the fire.

Research shows that upfront investment in rapid initial
attack increases the likelihood a fire will be controlled sooner,
a smaller area will be burnt, and money – potentially millions
of dollars, in the long run – will be saved. Over recent years,
firefighting agencies in both Victoria and South Australia have
introduced protocols to encourage the rapid initial aerial attack
of fires in high-risk areas. At the time of the 2019–20 season,
New South Wales had no such protocol in place. The NSW
Bushfire Inquiry heard evidence that some incident controllers

recognised midway through the season the strategic flaw in not tackling new ignitions early. It was creating a snowball effect, where an unchallenged forest fire would escape and enter populated areas, requiring a heavy investment in resources, which meant there were not enough resources left to deal with the next remote-area fire, allowing it to grow until it too threatened homes.

Attempts to change course, though, were hampered by a lack of access to the specific kind of aircraft used elsewhere to launch these aggressive first attacks. Australia doesn't own any. A fleet of these amphibious water-scooping planes were belatedly ordered from Canada in mid-December 2019 after our prime minister announced his one-off cash injection for aerial firefighting, but this was the order that couldn't be filled because the fleet was grounded by icy conditions. One of the NSW Bushfire Inquiry's recommendations was that the RFS trial this initial aerial-dispatch model and identify the best and most cost-effective mix of aircraft.

The state did use remote-area firefighters during the season. The RFS has a program it runs with National Parks in which specially trained firefighters are deployed by helicopter into inaccessible locations. Among the successes was the saving of a grove of endangered Wollemi pines deep in the Blue Mountains. But sometimes the fire was too extreme to send anyone in, and there were only two helicopters configured for this task.

Evidence given to the royal commission also highlighted a perverse disincentive for state firefighting agencies to water-bomb remote area fires aggressively while they are still small. Federal funding to the states only kicks in once there is an imminent risk to lives and property. This means that if a fire service wants to use aircraft to attack a small fire in a remote area to stop it becoming a megablaze, they'll wear the entire cost themselves – but if the fire escapes and approaches homes, the Commonwealth will pay up to 75 per cent of the costs.

A common perception I heard from many on the South Coast – especially the farmers and bushies who watched the Currowan fire spread – was that fire authorities were 'just letting it go'. In some ways, I think they were correct. Not in any conspiratorial sense that the fire was deliberately allowed to grow, but in the sense that the country wasn't really equipped to do anything but let it go.

In May 2020, I went to speak with Mark Williams, the incident controller for the Currowan fire. By now the country was in the midst of a new disaster – a pandemic – and the fire control centre in Nowra was eerily silent; screens and monitors stared blankly from the walls. Williams and I sat apart, carefully following the new emergency protocol of social distancing.

Williams told me he knew some in the community were still questioning how it got away like it did. 'I hear, "Oh yeah, they should have just wrapped it up on day one."' But he says this was not possible – it was already off and running by the time the helicopter got to it; unstoppable by the time fire trucks arrived. 'It was difficult to get into that area, and by the time our units got anywhere close to the scene, that fire was gone.'

Williams is a pragmatist, less interested in talking about my *what ifs* than how he played the cards he was given. He said in the first week of the Currowan fire, while they were trying to contain it in a box, he only had limited resources. 'I mean, we were requesting stuff,' but RFS headquarters was telling him, 'you're not going to get any more helicopters, they're already earmarked elsewhere'. The long lengths of back-burns and the finite number of fire trucks meant that sometimes shortcuts had to be taken on the blacking-out of the back-burns. 'The patrolling might be a little bit less frequent, or not as detailed. So it would be a drive-by rather than somebody walking on the track having a look at it,' he says. It may have been an imperfectly executed strategy, but he said the risk of doing nothing – of just waiting for it to 'come out on one of those blow-up days with a huge head of steam' – was greater. His attitude at the time was 'we've got to try and do what we possibly can'.

Once the fire escaped the back country, his resources were increased – they surged whenever there were bad blow-up days, depending on the demands across the rest of the state. 'It's very easy to say, "Could we have done more with more?" Yeah, sure we could,' he says. But 'knowing what was going on elsewhere and the resources in place', it just wasn't the reality.

But Williams maintains his greatest adversary by far was the unprecedented dryness of the landscape. This was land that wanted to burn, incited by extreme weather. 'What level of resources would we have needed to hold this on any given day? I couldn't put a figure on it, to be perfectly honest.'

Broad explanations about why the fire season unfolded as it did offer little solace to the many bushfire survivors, who – naturally – have legitimate questions about why certain decisions were taken on their individual fire front.

For many in the community around Conjola, the fact they received so little warning a fire was coming, and barely any assistance once it arrived, fostered a lingering sense of anger and betrayal. While the rest of the state was revelling in a celebration of the RFS – with special concerts and hand-painted placards on the side of the highway saying 'Thank you firies!' – many here viewed this adulation with cynicism. Knowing their views were so out of step with popular perception only deep-ened their sense of estrangement. As one local who lost her home told me, 'My kids would come home from school with all this "how great is the RFS" schoolwork, and I'd just bite my tongue, but I'd be thinking, *Yeah, well, they didn't help us.*'

The greatest source of distress was a widely held suspicion that the back-burns, lit in the hours leading up to the fire, were responsible for the destruction. The story started circulating almost as soon as the smoke had cleared, and before long, the claim that 'a back-burn took out Conjola' became an accepted truth among some locals. No one from the professional ranks of the RFS came forward with any information, so locals resorted to their own amateur sleuthing to figure out exactly where the back-burns were lit and what role they had in the fire runs – much of this taking place on community Facebook pages.

All this talk created fallout for some local National Parks and Wildlife Service (NPWS) rangers. While it was a National Parks team that lit part of the back-burn, what was not initially understood in the grief-stricken community was that they were operating under instructions from the RFS fire control centre in Nowra. One ranger was abused in a local supermarket; others adopted an unofficial policy of not wearing their uni-forms in public or displaying NPWS logos on their vehicles. Similarly, one RFS volunteer who lit another section of the back-burn – again, just doing what he was told – said to me, 'When people say, "It was the back-burn," it feels like it is my fault. It personally hurts me. I've had to seek mental health support. I have more PTSD from the community reaction than from the fire itself.'

There was an intense need for clarity. Ian Stewart, who lost his home and almost his son James in Yatte Yattah, was always certain that the fire which took his property came from the direction of the back-burn. What he found 'galling' and 'hard to accept' was the lack of accountability from the RFS. After the fire, the Stewarts moved into a tiny wooden cabin on their property – improbably, the only structure that survived – and were slowly fixing it up to make it more liveable while they contemplated rebuilding a home. 'Every day I go to look for something and it's not there,' says Ian. 'We are having to deal with a rebuild and clean-up at our stage of life. We have lost so much of what we value. It will be a very long time before we settle into a normal life again.' He believed the RFS 'created mayhem' and 'I want them to be held accountable for that. The days go by, but nothing is easing on that point.'

In May 2020, the RFS finally announced it would hold a community meeting to address the concerns. Because the state was in lockdown due to the pandemic, it was to be conducted via Zoom. Those who still had one joined from their home; many others logged in from whatever temporary lodging they'd managed to secure since the fires. I watched on from a new place in Bawley; we'd had to move again after the first one was sold, our home still not repaired. We were all beamed into a room where Mark Williams was sitting alongside three RFS colleagues – one from another part of the state, who we were told had been appointed to investigate what happened independently of the South Coast team.

Matthew O'Donnell, who works for the RFS in the Hunter region, told us that he'd asked fire-behaviour analysts to conduct something called 'post-fire modelling' – the use of computer software to simulate the path of a fire. Based on this, he had concluded that 'on the balance of probabilities' the spot fire that started the fire run into Conjola 'is likely to have originated from the main fire front', not the back-burn. He said that while 'a spot fire from the back-burn, once the weather conditions had deteriorated, can't be ruled out', it is 'most likely it came from the fire front as it approached the back-burn and met in that area'. The back-burn 'was not believed to have exacerbated the situation'.

O'Donnell explained that weather conditions on 31 December 2019 were worse than forecast. The modelling showed that if they'd been as expected, the back-burn would have been effective in holding the eastern flank. But under conditions that were 'so extreme, and so far away from the forecast', fire was always going to hit the coast – with or without a back-burn in place.

This explanation was almost instantly rejected – angry comments and questions were typed into the chat on the sidebar – and few came away from the meeting with any sense of closure. Another Facebook page was created to continue investigations; emails were written to the RFS. For many in the community, there were a number of problems with the RFS internal investigation. There was scepticism over its independence – in the Zoom meeting, O'Donnell was sitting not even a literal arm's length from Williams, the person who authorised the back-burn. It also appeared to rely heavily on the crunching of computer models – the same kind of modelling that told Conjola residents back on 30 December, via the Fire Spread Prediction Map, that they would not be affected by fire. O'Donnell didn't conduct a physical investigation – 'We were not on the ground, having a look at the physical evidence,' he said – and didn't interview any local witnesses. Some elements of his report contradicted what community members – including local RFS volunteers – claimed to have seen. For example, O'Donnell stated that by around 3.00 am on 31 December the back-burn 'was reported to be blacked out along its entire length and secure with no known threats in the area', whereas eyewitnesses say it was still burning.

Many hoped the NSW Bushfire Inquiry would deliver more answers, but the final report stated that as the fire was the subject of a coronial inquiry, it was 'not appropriate for the Inquiry to make any findings as to the cause'. In an email to a community representative in December 2020, the RFS reiterated it had already 'conducted a thorough investigation' that 'determined that it was likely that the back burn was not responsible for the impact on the Conjola community'.

For a long time, I hoped to be able to give more definitive answers to those around Conjola. The lack of clarity about the events of New Year's Eve seemed such a fundamental part of their trauma – something that distinguished this community from other bushfire-affected places – and it was impossible not to feel this despair seep into my bones too. But as one experienced fire investigator I spoke to told me, trying to determine the role of a back-burn in a fire can be like trying to unscramble an egg.

The back-burn certainly wasn't the only fire in the landscape that day; it is not possible for it to be responsible for everything that happened. Yet it was undoubtedly present – and burning hard.

A satellite image taken around 11.00 am on 31 December 2019 clearly shows the five-kilometre containment line well alight – certainly not blacked-out as the RFS claimed in their inquiry. (In the Zoom meeting, the RFS investigator said he was not aware of this image, which is freely available on a web application.) In the section of the containment line nearest to Ian and Fiona Stewart's home in Yatte Yattah, the back-burn is the only body of fire present. However, in the explosion of fire about to hit Conjola Park, the back-burn is indecipherable from a wave of fire that appears to come from behind it. It is possible that the back-burn impacted some more than others.

Nick Gellie, the Australian fire scientist living in Spain, attempted a fire reconstruction of what happened at Conjola that day. He used satellite images, interviews with residents and any RFS line scans he could obtain – while these are not publicly available, some do have the habit of leaking. His conclusions contained a subtle, but significant, difference to those of the RFS. While the RFS used the 'balance of probabilities' to conclude it was 'most likely' not the back-burn, Gellie's report found 'it is difficult to work out from the information available whether the main fire or the back-burns contributed' to the spot fires that raced into Conjola on New Year's Eve.

It is not hard to understand why some residents still find it hard to accept the back-burn had absolutely no influence on the day. It was a substantial length of fire, burning in a combusting landscape. Equally, it was lit on the eve of dangerous fire weather without adequate resources to control it. Nick Gellie says using 'direct attack' could have been a 'lower-risk fire tactic' than 'implementing a backburn the night before without much community consultation about the potential risks of fire escape'.

One shortcoming of the RFS investigation was that it didn't appear to interrogate the back-burning and dropping of incendiaries that started at Christmas, a little further northwest. At the time, Mark Williams said this was a strategy to 'bring that fire off the escarpment and down to our control line at a controlled rate, rather than the fire coming down under its own steam'. Eyewitness accounts, though, and some imagery indicate that the fire front only came down the escarpment in some places – meaning that in some areas, these original back-burns were the only fire around. The 11.00 am satellite image from 31 December shows a wave of fire exploding in an area that had been extensively back-burned days previously. Of course, this could have been the arrival of the firefront, coming down from the escarpment, but it's not impossible it was a reignition of a back-burn. What is clear – by the RFS's own admission – is that none of these extensive back-burns served their purpose of protecting the coastal villages.

The NSW Bushfire Inquiry received numerous submissions about back-burning; it was one of the most contentious issues, with some arguing for more, others less. Surprisingly for such a high-risk though common strategy, the inquiry discovered the RFS has 'no requirement to record backburns and their outcomes'. The RFS couldn't even provide the inquiry with a complete dataset of all backburns undertaken over the season.

The inquiry found that while many back-burns kept large fires contained during the 2019–20 season, others failed and caused more damage than the fire they were meant to prevent. The RFS told the inquiry it accepted responsibility for the back-burn that escaped into the village of Balmoral, southwest of Sydney, in mid-December, destroying twenty homes. (This was the escape that Nick Gellie knew about when he wrote his Boxing Day letter to the commissioner.) 'The NSW RFS reported that the outcome was highly regrettable and weighs heavily on the NSW RFS senior management and is personally devastating for those directly involved,' the inquiry said.

Both the royal commission and the NSW Bushfire Inquiry received submissions from fire scientists warning of the risks of back-burning when dangerous fire weather is imminent. 'Back-burning under such extreme conditions can often fail – and fail catastrophically,' wrote Professor Jason Sharples. 'In large fires, back-burning often presents itself as the only available option for fire control. However, in certain cases it will not be the right option … The introduction of more fire into the landscape while an extreme bushfire is active can result in further escalation of the event.' Sharples stated that dangerous 'deep flaming' can arise due to the 'overzealous, or ill-informed, use of incendiaries', and that this 'is a major issue that needs to be addressed within the firefighting industry at a national level'. He said that as well as more scientific research into when back-burning is appropriate, 'more training is required to help firefighters understand that back-burning can often have the potential to do more harm than good'.

With extreme weather conditions only going to accelerate, the NSW Bushfire Inquiry agreed that more research and improved protocols and training about back-burning during dangerous fire weather are needed. It recommended that if fire conditions are approaching a fire danger rating of severe or above, an independent review at a state level is conducted before a back-burn is lit.

When the back-burn behind Ian and Fiona Stewart's property in Yatte Yattah was started, late on the afternoon of 30 December, the official fire danger rating for the South Coast on New Year's Eve had been raised to *extreme* – just one below *catastrophic*. This means that under this proposed change, it would have been reviewed before the drip torch hit the ground.

I asked Mark Williams whether, in hindsight, he was comfortable with the decisions he made around these back-burns, and he said he was. 'They [the decisions] were put in place taking everything into consideration: the work of fire behaviour analysts, looking at the weather forecast ... looking at the capability of the resources that we had at the time. Was it a guarantee? No. There was never a guarantee that this thing was going to hold. We had to do something, rather than just sit back and just let it go and come down under its own volition. I wouldn't have been able to sleep at night knowing that we had three or four days to actually try and contain this thing to the west and nothing was done.' The wild weather that day, he says, meant fire was always coming for Conjola. 'That fire was getting into Conjola regardless. If we weren't there, if we hadn't put that line in, that fire was still getting down into Conjola.'

It would be a mistake to conclude that all high-risk back-burns are bad. It was a risky back-burn that got the highway open in the aftermath of New Year's Eve. Another, the same day, saved a coastal village further north of Conjola from almost certain annihilation. Yet one of the biggest lessons of the 2019–20 summer is that under a changing climate, fire is now behaving in ways we don't yet fully understand, and if we fail to adjust, it will be at our peril.

I had my own surprise discovery about back-burning. One night in late summer 2020 when I was speaking with Nick Gellie, he mentioned words to the effect of, *and then that back-burn escaped and that's what got your place.* I wobbled a little – literally – then regained enough composure to hear him out. From RFS line scans he'd obtained he told me he could see that there had been an escape of fire out of the northwestern corner of the original containment box, well before the fire front reached the line, and that is what came charging over the saddle to us. Later, I was given line scans from other sources, which confirmed this to be true. I also learned that it came from the area where the more than ten-kilometre-long back-burn was put in the day before the weather turned, and where the incendiaries were dropped to deepen the burn.

At first, I was shocked. I told Chris, expecting him to feel the same way, but he looked at the map I was showing him and shrugged, saying, 'Yeah, we lit a back-burn there.' Still weary from the long summer, and perhaps more philosophical about mistakes that were made, he went off to bed, while I paced the house for hours, churning. After several months of veering between outrage and acceptance, I too eventually settled on the latter. Knowing the path the fire eventually took, I concluded that it was more than likely coming for us anyway.

I was more perturbed about the discovery of the line scans. The night back in early December 2019 when I was padding around the house on my own, waiting for the fire – having no idea where it was – a line scan already showed the beginnings of the escape. I'd always had this woolly idea that the beekeepers had known to come in at 3.00 am and remove their hives from the forest below us because, well, *they're connected to nature* – but now I think it's more likely that someone tipped them off about the line scan. There were also several line scans taken the day we were hit. While I was sitting at the cricket field trying to guess the movements of the fire, and friends were tearing up hills trying to spot it, two clear images were taken showing the exact location of the fire and the area that was about to be absolutely decimated.

It is true that we had all received an RFS text message alert two days earlier, telling us the fire was approaching. So it can't be said we were not warned. The RFS sends these messages for good reason – to get people out of harm's way. It is arguably the most successful feature of the Australian fire response – without these alerts, the loss of life over the season would have been unfathomable. Yet what of those who choose not to leave? I don't know whether it was an intentional decision not to post every line scan on the Fires Near Me app, or if the systems were just not set up to be so agile, but in a situation where the state can't help everyone with a fire truck, it seems to me that allowing a free flow of information is a way to share the responsibility of the fire effort with those who want it.

In my experience, most people close to the land are keenly interested in protecting themselves. A couple of months after the fire, some of our neighbours who lived along the saddle of the mountain – one of whom lost his home – arranged a meeting with a representative from the Forestry Corporation, and I went along. While the NSW Bushfire Inquiry came to no firm conclusions about the benefits of hazard-reduction burning, finding it 'appears to have reduced fire severity in some instances, but in others it appears to have had no effect on the severity and spread of the fires', these neighbours believed it was essential to keep the fuel loads west of the saddle down. A couple had been asking Forestry Corporation for a burn for years – even offering their own labour – and we could all see that the fire had ripped through the area they'd been worried about. Perhaps if it had been burned earlier, it would have come through slower.

The man from Forestry seemed perplexed as to why we wanted to talk about hazard reduction now, when everything around us was so thoroughly charred. But we wanted to plan ahead – get a commitment for the future, perhaps get some heavy machinery in now to mark out some trails so that in ten or so years' time, burns could be more easily managed. He talked about how it was unlikely, too expensive, and joked about our ten-year timeframe, 'Well, I'll be retired by then,' perhaps not noticing our stony faces. When I persisted, arguing that it wasn't just ourselves we were worried for – there was a telecommunications tower on the ridge and the saddle was a gateway to villages on the coast; *it would be strategic to get this area well managed* – he suggested I try to get it included in our local Bush Fire Risk Management Plan.

I didn't know such a thing existed but raced home to start researching. Under legislation, the RFS is meant to ensure every region in the state has a plan, updated every five years, that identifies critical infrastructure and strategies to reduce bushfire risk. It sounded like a great idea, but when I read the last two plans for our region, I saw that the area near the saddle had already been marked as a strategic zone requiring hazard reduction – it was just that nothing had been done.

Later, I would talk to Mike Gorman from Kangaroo Valley about this. Our areas were both covered by the same bushfire plan, and he'd been over it with a fine-tooth comb, identifying that large parts were just a cut-and-paste from plans for other areas of the state, and that in some areas critical assets were missing. In a submission to the royal commission, Gorman said it was just an 'illusion that effective bushfire risk management planning has been carried out'. (The *Sydney Morning Herald* later conducted an investigation that revealed nearly half the plans in the state were out of date.)

It made me think of the conversation I had with Ian Barnes, where he talked about the inherent laziness in how we manage our land – it's always easier to do nothing.

Everyone needs to get more serious. It's no longer enough for governments and fire agencies to think they can get by on the old ways of doing things. Equally, Australians need to need to adjust our thinking; the days of fire trucks on every corner are long gone. The future will be too intense. If we are going to keep living in these places – which hundreds of thousands of us do, not just in forest-fringed properties, but in towns and villages – we will need to become more resilient, both as individuals and as communities.

CHAPTER 16

SOLASTALGIA

Because I grew up on the South Coast, many people I knew characterised my return to live here as an adult as *coming home*. But it was never quite like that. As a child, I had limited awareness of the uniqueness of the natural landscapes around me. With nothing to compare it to, I simply accepted as a given the bush-covered headlands into which I could disappear for a day with playmates, to construct cubby houses and then climb down the cliff face to poke our fingers in rockpools. As an adolescent, when my family moved away from the beach to a property below the escarpment, I started exploring on horseback the fire trails that led into the ranges with enthusiasm, but my blinkers were gradually coming down – I now owned a world atlas, and trips to Sydney to stay with an uncle had given me a glimpse of the direction I knew I would be going next. By my late teenage years, the vast expanses of bushland served not as places for nature appreciation, but as convenient hideaways where we could share a warm bottle of Passion Pop and a single cigarette someone had nicked from their dad.

When I returned to the South Coast nearly fifteen years later, it was with a new set of priorities – and it was like arriving in a world I'd never been before. Part of my newfound attention to the environment was a necessity: our property was off-grid, so I had to learn the different paths the sun took as it tracked through the sky to know when there was enough power to turn on the washing machine; think about the rain forecast before I ran a deep bath; understand which species of eucalypt would burn all night on the wood fire versus those that started impressively but dissolved by morning. But I also discovered that the landscapes around me offered unlimited possibilities for adventure. Before I moved back to the South Coast I'd spent many years travelling overseas as a video journalist for an international affairs television program, and I'd always enjoyed diving into big cities, such as New York and Cairo, discovering something new around every street corner; perhaps even a hint of danger if you weren't alert. The South Coast contained a different kind of wildness, but the mindset was the same.

In summertime we'd often pull out a topographic map and drive into the back country, searching for a new bend in the Clyde River where we could swim, or a clearing to pitch a tent, marking new discoveries in pencil. Some school holidays we'd haul everything in on bush tracks with a wheelbarrow to camp for weeks on end in Meroo National Park, dropping out of everything but the immediate: the black snake sliding through camp (*best left to move on*), the marauding monitor lizard (*get your distance and hurl a shoe*). On one of these camps, a shaken spearfisherman emerged from the water and threw a huge fish he'd caught onto the sand, explaining that a shark had just bitten off the back third. The kids we were camping with – just in from the ocean themselves – retrieved it eagerly, cooking it up on the campfire for our afternoon tea. One of the members of my book club lived high on a mountain west of us, and I loved the thrill of driving the isolated, narrow dirt road along the spine of the mountain on a wild winter's night – steep drop on one side, wind bending branches over the road to create a tunnel – only to pop out the other side into a warm house filled with books, art and sculpture.

I gained a sharper eye for the natural environment: the delicate native orchids popping up from the understorey of the forests; the vivid red of a Burrawang seed cone bursting out beneath the dark green fronds; the way towards the end of winter, just when you think you can't bear another short cold day, the wattle bursts into yellow bloom as a reminder that you're nearly at the other side. I got used to the busyness of the bush – the sight of lyrebirds darting off into the steep gullies every time I drove a certain road, the sound of a rustle followed by the gentle *thump thump thump* of a hidden wallaby when I walked in the forests at dusk, the squeal of sugar gliders late at night. I was in a full-blown love affair with this newly discovered place – until the arrival of the fire pulled the rug out from under me.

Throughout 2020, I found it gruelling to live amid the utterly transformed landscape, the sense of expansiveness gone. Metal gates came down upon the entrances to the national parks – our favourite playgrounds closed. Evidence of the fire was omnipresent – around 85 per cent of our local government area was burned – and sometimes I'd find myself desperately racking my brain for a local place we could visit that wasn't fire-affected (*what about that little hook up the far end of the inlet?*), but rarely would there be any respite. I remember paddling out in the surf at a quiet little beach just further south one day, feeling good to be in the salt and away from constant vision of charred landscape. When I got out the back and sat on my board and spun around, I realised I'd just afforded myself a clearer view of the burned coastline.

The landscape had taken on a different tenor. Driving to the village of Nerriga for an interview one day, I pulled off the road that runs through the mountain ranges, near to where the pyrocumulonimbus roared through. By now, later in 2020, many of the eucalypts closer to my home were showing signs of epicormic growth, buds underneath the bark sprouting tufts of fuzzy green growth all along the blackened trunks and branches – a stress reaction to being damaged by fire and a last-ditch attempt at survival. But here there was still no green – just endless blackened sticks upright in the ground. In this previously impenetrable area, I could now see into the crevices of every gorge, up the cliff-faces and out across the plateaus for kilometres. I found myself drawn to this vista – similar to the morbid pull that makes you want to look when you drive past a car accident – and I started walking deeper in, passing by the wreckage of a burned-out car. The din of screaming cicadas emanating from this desolate landscape was so loud as to be painful, and I started to imagine they were angry – who wouldn't be, coming out of the ground after seven years to this? The hairs on the back of my neck prickled and, spooked, I turned and ran back to the car.

One afternoon around the same time, I met up with an ecologist to walk through a rainforest reserve near Yatte Yattah. Around 70 per cent of the area's subtropical rainforests – an already fragmented and compromised community – had been fire-affected and I wanted to see what it looked like now. As we descended into a steep gully, we had to push through masses of weeds as tall as we were; the legs of my pants quickly became a mat of burrs. The ecologist had to push aside the intruders to point out the survivors: a mature native quince; a century-old small-leaf fig. When we got to the bottom of the gully, another enormous fig, this one between 200 and 400 years old, lay on the ground. Without its enormous canopy acting as a shield for the rainforest floor, it was inevitable that drier species would move in, the ecologist told me. I kept using the word 'destroyed' to describe what I was seeing, and he corrected me. 'It is still alive,' he said, 'it's changed, the balance disrupted, but not destroyed. Fire is a disturbance, and most natural things have strategies to deal with disturbance.' When I pressed him on when it would come back, he told me not to think in human timeframes – those of the natural world are much longer. So, for my lifetime, this was it.

While I knew immediately after the fires which homes closest to me had been destroyed – there would be no more book club on the mountain, or wine in my neighbour's kitchen – news of other houses, to which I was only tangentially connected, filtered in slowly. More than just physical structures, houses are place-keepers of memories, and I remember feeling inordinately sad when I learned that the sunny cottage where I first met my nephew just hours after he was born was gone, even though it had been well over a decade since his family had lived there. The first time I drove north towards Sydney after the fires, I saw in shock that where a little 150-year-old weatherboard cottage once sat, just off the highway, there was now only a brick chimney. I'd never been inside this home, but since childhood it had been my mental marker – the point at which I was either leaving the South Coast or coming back to it, the building as constant as the certainty that the roses grown in its garden would *always* win first prize at the local show. How could it be gone?

Late in 2020, I spent a week at a writers' retreat in the Blue Mountains along with others writing about climate change, and I learned a new word. In the early 2000s, an Australian philosopher named Glenn Albrecht was thinking about the chronic distress he'd witnessed emerge in the Upper Hunter region of New South Wales as communities grappled with the changes a proliferation of open-cut coalmines had brought to their homes – the changed landscape, the pollution – and was searching for a term for this. He took *solace* and *desolation*, adding the suffix *–algia*, to arrive at *solastalgia* – which he said described 'the homesickness you have when you are still at home'. At last I had a word to describe how I was feeling.

When I went to visit Rae Harvey, the wildlife carer who lost her home in Runnyford, on the banks of the Clyde, I tried to articulate this feeling to her.

'Well, yes, but imagine how it must feel for all the animals,' she said.

After the fire, around twenty of her joeys eventually made their way home – many with burns and wide-eyed with shock. Eastern greys are intensely sensitive creatures – a single episode of fear can kill them – and Rae had barely left their side since. She was living in a tin shed with pouches slung up all around the verandah, and if she had to go into town briefly it would only be after issuing strict instructions for her charges' care to the backpackers camping on her property. Rae lost everything she owned in the fire, but she told me, 'I still haven't cried about the house. I don't give a fuck about it.' She'd decided not to take on any new joeys that year as the survivors needed all her attention, but as it turned out, many wildlife carers on the South Coast were seeing less demand for their services than usual. After the initial, brutal phases of euthanising and emergency care were over, there was simply little wildlife around.

*

Once the rubble was finally cleared – which in some places took at least four months – some turned their attention to starting again, though especially around Conjola, many *For Sale* signs started appearing on empty blocks. Every story of attempting to rebuild comes with its own individual agonies – the discovery of underinsurance, the navigation of building codes, the additional construction costs that come with bushfire attack level (BAL) ratings. Building a house can be arduous at the best of times, let alone after trauma and in the middle of a pandemic.

When I went to see eighty-year-old Frank Condello in Yatte Yattah in late 2020, his block was empty – just a few garden ornaments from his nursery left – and he'd submitted new house plans to council. Only half-jokingly, he said, 'By the time we build this and pretty it up a bit, it'll be a toss-up whether they let me come here or put me in a bloody nursing home.' He told me he still thought a lot about the things he lost in the fire. His beloved dog, who made it through the flames to his car, but had already breathed in too much smoke. His mother's crucifix. His wedding ring, which used to hang on the wardrobe in the bedroom. The two urns in the hallway, containing the ashes of his brother and his granddaughter.

It took us nearly seven months before we could move back home. While our rebuild was not nearly as arduous as constructing a new home, it was an unwanted grind, and we faced constant constraints of supply. Who in Australia *wasn't* ordering a new water tank that year? Life in Bawley Point wasn't all that bad, but with so many cardboard boxes and house moves I was losing track of where everything was. The kids were sick of not being in their own home and the dog just couldn't master his town manners.

Once we moved home, people would often say to me, *What's it like to be back?* It was a question I usually interpreted as meaning, *Are you scared to be living there?* Initially, in the first months after the fire, I did find it hard to imagine ever being comfortable at home again; but over time that feeling started to lift, and by year's end my confidence was fully restored. We installed a built-in fire sprinkler system, the most robust we could afford; for the first time we built a proper concrete-block shed with a fire-resistant door to house the water-pump, instead of sheltering it with a few bricks and a piece of tin. Most of my confidence, though, came from knowledge I gathered along the way – about things we can do to keep fire-proofing our home and property, and especially about 'fire weather' and the influence it has on the behaviour of fire. All this doesn't make me feel more invincible; on the contrary, it makes me more aware of the conditions in which perhaps we could put up a defence if a fire came, and alert to the days where I would leave before there was even a wisp of smoke.

One of my greatest reliefs of the fire season was that my parents' home survived and they weren't facing the upheaval of starting again. When they'd returned the day after being chased out by ember attack, they discovered the gardens were all gone and fire had crept into the wooden pergola attached to their house, but it seemed to have been extinguished. The only clue as to how was the muddy tyre tracks all over their lawn.

It turns out their home was saved by cubies – blokes in utes who turned up without being asked, strangers who spent the better part of the night working to save our family home. Mum tried to track down who they were so she could thank them – but there were so many of them, and they were so humble about claiming credit, it was barely possible. When we were rebuilding our property, one of the workers who knew of my parents only mentioned in the most offhand way, after I'd already spoken to him a dozen times, that he was there.

Of all the damage, the most noticeable was that done to people. In my decades of journalism, I've never experienced so many men crying in front of me during an interview. Once it was my fault; I took a volunteer firefighter back to a location where he'd faced an intense firefight, thinking it would help me to see the place he was talking about, only to realise it was too much for him – we needed to retreat, and I needed to learn to tread more carefully around trauma. It was always humbling, and a disabusing of any stereotypes that Australian men don't talk about their feelings.

Mark Williams told me, 'My firefighters out there, they're hurting. I can see the change in them. I can see the change in me.' When I asked what the impact had been on him, he said, 'Oh, you're probably better off asking my wife. I mean, I don't have problems sleeping at night or anything like that. I think I'm managing my situation well. But I'm quite open, I see a counsellor. I think being able to talk to people, being able to go back and recount what's happened, is certainly second to none.'

Scott McFarlane, who was caught in a firestorm at his home in Woodburn on 4 January – glimpsing his silhouette as his body blocked the embers – told me that for three weeks after the fire he thought he was fine. 'I went to try to go back to work and then somebody asked me about the fire and I started talking about it and then I started shaking and said, "I gotta go home." I took a couple weeks off and talked about it a lot and that helped. Talking brings it out, I'm totally fine talking about it now.'

Everyone had their mental jags. Mine was the WhatsApp messages from the days of the fire at our place – even a year later, going back to check on a detail as I was writing would raise my pulse and make my breathing tight.

For Jen Dudman-Chopping, who was caught on a beach with burning kangaroos south of Conjola, it was one moment on her journey. After she got out of the water and was charging for her life up the beach, she saw a little joey discarded on the sand before her, burnt and curling. 'It was awful,' she says. She wanted to save him, 'but I remember stepping over him and just saying, "Sorry, mate. I can't do it." And that's been one of my struggles to get past, the fact that I left him behind.'

As part of her counselling, in late summer 2020 Jen and her son returned to retrace her steps along the beach. 'I was quite desperate to get back there,' she said. As they walked, she was surprised to find the beach empty. 'I was so pleased to see there were no dead animals on the beach, you know? I didn't feel like I'd left them there behind. I don't know if they'd been cleaned up by the council or washed back into the ocean, but it tells you that it's all okay.'

Late one afternoon in 2021, I was on the phone with Greg Mullins, the former commissioner of Fire and Rescue NSW and the founder of Emergency Leaders for Climate Action. He was out doing some RFS volunteer work – I could hear the trucks reversing in the background – and I'd given him a quick call to get some detail about what kind of aircraft are best for direct initial attack of fires, my head still deep in the question of how we better equip ourselves to fight in future.

At first he patiently answered my questions, but then he said, 'But you know what, in twenty years or so it's not going to matter. It's a new world. It's like the enemy has nukes and we'll just be working with conventional weapons. I have no answers. We're just going to have to harden infrastructure and do mass evacuations while the fire grabs whatever it wants.'

When I hung up, I wondered if I'd just caught him in a bleak moment – but then I realised he was simply being a realist. Scientists have said that even if we slam the brakes on emissions tomorrow, increased warming is locked in for the next twenty to thirty years. Actions we take now will mitigate the severity of what is coming – but the bed is made. As the royal commission put it: 'Catastrophic fire conditions may render traditional bushfire prediction models and firefighting techniques less effective.' We *will* be facing fires where all we can do is flee.

It's hard any longer to describe what happened in Australia over the summer of 2019–20 as a glimpse of the future. It is indisputably part of our present. By 2021, the northern hemisphere was facing its own fire cataclysm, with intense and prolonged wildfires sweeping across vast swathes of North America, Siberia, the Mediterranean and North Africa.

In the United States, the largest fire of the summer started in mid-July, when a tree in a steep, forested gorge in Northern California brushed against a powerline. Several years of drought, combined with many successive days of extreme heat and strong winds, aided the Dixie fire – named after the creek near where it ignited – to evade containment. Over the summer it tormented thousands of people across five counties.

Just after lunchtime, on Wednesday, August 4, it roared in towards Greenville, a gold rush era town on the edge of a valley in Plumas County. The local Sheriff posted a warning on Facebook to the approximately 1,000 residents, 'You are in imminent danger and you MUST leave now!' Once the fire arrived, several hours later, it consumed three-quarters of the town in just half an hour; homes, historic buildings, a petrol station, church, hotel, bar, school and a museum – all reduced to piles of grey ash.

By the time the Dixie fire was officially contained, in October, it had burned nearly 4,000 square kilometres of land, destroyed over 1,300 buildings, and forced the evacuation of nearly 30,000 people from their homes. Its smoke caused the air quality across the west of the United States to plummet to unhealthy levels; one day in early August, Salt Lake City in Utah had the worst air quality in the world. Dixie, though, was just one of over 44,600 fires in the United States in 2021, burning more than 22,600 square kilometres – an area larger than Wales.

In British Columbia, Canada, in the final week of June, a heat dome – created when a high-pressure system traps hot air over land like a lid – descended upon the drought-stricken province, pushing temperatures well above 40 degrees for the entire week; an event with no precedent in recorded history. It was the deadliest weather event ever in Canada, responsible for nearly 600 deaths – including more than 200 on one day alone – and propelled a spate of wildfires.

On Tuesday, 29 June, residents in the little valley-side rural community of Lytton, population 250, suffered through a 49.6°C day – the highest temperature ever recorded in Canada. The following evening, a fire started just south of the town. Residents barely had time to grab any belongings before leaping into their cars to flee as fire swallowed the town. 'It's dire. It took, like, a whole fifteen minutes from the first sign of smoke to, all of a sudden, there being fire everywhere,' said the Mayor. The main street, containing the post office, health centre, ambulance station and numerous shops was levelled, and nearly every home burned to the ground. Two people died.

The behavior of many of the Canadian fires astonished observers. The same day as Lytton was destroyed, a pyrocumulonimbus formed over a forest fire in a mountainous area near Sparks Lake in BC. Scientists watching on from the US Naval Research Laboratory (NRL) and NASA tracked the smoke column rising 16 kilometres upwards into the stratosphere, spreading out to form a storm cell that covered more than 160,000 square kilometres of land – 'absolutely mind blowing' behaviour according to one of the team. This single cloud – which was the largest ever pyrocumulonimbus observed in North America – unleashed over 110,000 bolts of lightning and ignited dozens of fires, some up to 50 kilometres away. A few weeks later, on the border of Saskatchewan and Manitoba province, more than ten pyrocumulonimbus storms simultaneously formed – the largest cluster ever observed on a single day.

In eastern Siberia, fires broke out in the Republic of Sakha (Yakutia) in spring, not long after the snow started melting. This sub-arctic region – Russia's coldest place – had experienced two years of drought and above average temperatures, and by summer, multiple large fires burning through forests that sit atop frozen soil known as permafrost were sending the first ever smoke to the north pole. In the capital Yakutsk, a city of over quarter of a million people, with an average annual temperature of -8°C, residents were warned to stay inside as a thick blanket of toxic smoke enveloped their homes. On one day, analysts found that the levels of PM2.5 – small particles that can enter the blood stream, damaging organs – were more than 40 times the recommended safe levels.

Major wildfires also occurred in Italy, Greece, Turkey, Algeria, Cyprus, Spain, France, Albania, North Macedonia and Morocco over the summer of 2021. On Evia, Greece's second largest island, a fire that started on the northern coastline burned for twenty days, sweeping right across to the southern shoreline. Thousands of people fled on board boats, whilst many villagers stayed to try and save what they could. However, as well as several hundred homes, the fire incinerated nearly 500 square kilometres of land, including olive groves, pine forests used for harvesting resin and bee-keeping, farmland and livestock – leaving many of the island's residents with no future means of livelihood.

Even the United Kingdom, traditionally a haven from the phenomenon of wildfire, burned in 2021. In April, a fire nearly two kilometres long ran through Marsden Moor in Yorkshire. Over three days it destroyed nearly five square kilometres of moorland, in an area known to be habitat for breeding birds like curlews and mountain hares. It was the second serious burn on the Moor in recent years – in 2019, seven square kilometres went up in flames, the same year that a fire in Moray, northern Scotland, raged for over a fortnight across grassland and peat.

While these fires didn't wreak the havoc of those elsewhere in the world, with the duration of heatwaves in the UK significantly increasing since the 1960s – a trend forecast to continue – scientists now consider more wildland fires to be an 'emergent risk' for the United Kingdom. Several British universities are now collaborating on developing the first ever UK-specific fire danger rating system – the kind of tool that has long tracked the rhythm of danger over an Australian summer.

I watched reports of the northern hemisphere burning throughout 2021 with something akin to a morbid fascination;

each story setting off triggers of memory that I both wanted to hide from and dig in to. Photos I saw of the people onboard the ferry evacuating from Evia – the sky an apocalyptic orange, flames licking at the shoreline – elicited a strong feeling of recognition: eyes like dinner plates, hunched shoulders, dogs clutched to chests, masks on faces; a sense of utter helplessness, not unlike the people on the beaches near me back in 2019. It also intensified my fear: if what had happened to us in Australia was some of the most extreme fire behaviour known to humans, then what on earth was this?

Scientists, too, were filled with alarm. 'What stood out as unusual were the number of fires, the size of the areas in which they were burning, their intensity and also their persistence,' said Mark Parrington, a scientist at the European Union's Copernicus Atmosphere Monitoring Service (CAMS). 'Drier and hotter regional conditions caused by global warming increase the risk of flammability and fire risk of vegetation and this has been reflected in the extremely large, fast-developing and persistent fires we have been monitoring.'

CAMS measures carbon emissions from fires, and calculated that July and August 2021 were the worst months globally for wildfires since records began. Over 2021, global wildfires released the equivalent of 6,450 mega-tonnes of carbon dioxide into the atmosphere – nearly 150 per cent more than the total EU fossil fuel emissions in 2020. The conversion of forests from valuable carbon sinks into emitters of potent greenhouse gases is a dangerous form of blowback – potentially turbo-charging climate change.

In Australia, the scientific community was keeping one eye on what was unfolding in the northern hemisphere, whilst still trying to understand the Australian Black Summer. In 2021, a team of researchers finished quantifying the scale of the pyrocumulonimbus outbreaks over Australia in 2019–2020, finding they released the energy of about 2,000 Hiroshima-sized nuclear weapons and injected as much smoke into the stratosphere as a moderately sized volcanic eruption. Because smoke and ash from volcanos has altered the global climate before – having a cooling impact on the atmosphere – and it's long been theorized a large enough atomic explosion could do the same, causing a 'nuclear winter', where smoke and soot block sunlight, the team questioned whether fires could one day do the same. 'Could a series of large pyroCb outbreaks rival the potential climate impacts expected following a nuclear war?' the team asked in its journal article.

The pace of change is almost dizzying. 'Once-in-a-career fire events are becoming normal,' observed Australian fire scientist Professor David Bowman, after watching the extreme fire behaviour first in Australia then the northern hemisphere. 'One needs to consider the global pattern of extreme fire activity. It's a major red flag that the Earth's [climate] system is changing.'

I spent the summer holidays of 2021–2022 camping on a nearby coastal headland with a group of local friends. We were now in a La Niña weather cycle, and most days a steady drizzle of cool rain pattered on the tents – interspersed with moments of sunshine – followed by explosive late afternoon storms that tugged the guy ropes from the muddy ground and sent small rivers rushing through the camp.

Still, it was blissful. All of us had brushed against the Currowan fire in some way – fought it, been wrenched apart from loved ones for terrifying hours, lost property, been plunged into several years of unanticipated rebuilds and tidy ups – and for many of us this felt like it was the first opportunity to really relax since that time.

Sheltering under a large gazebo we passed our time listening to the cricket on the radio and playing cards, watching a magpie frenetically gather worms for her ever-demanding chick, and clambering down the slippery track to the beach for dunks in the foamy sea.

On the first day of 2022, while we were all sitting around the campfire, I was flicking through Twitter on my phone when I saw something that startled me: video of a wildfire, racing through a community on the outskirts of Denver, Colorado. Flames were devouring home after home along with what appeared to be several multi-storey buildings. For a moment I was disoriented; isn't it winter there?

'What are you looking at?' a friend asked, and I handed my phone over. A few others joined the huddle, peering at the video, until someone in the group said sharply, 'Put it away.' One person stood and walked away, and a silence fell over the camp.

It is still raw. Closer than we realise. Looking at the glistening forests sweeping up the hill, undergrowth surging after a summer of rain, we all know what this portends for the next dry spell. None of us believe it will never happen again.

The fact of the climate crisis can be overwhelming. Most days, to stay sane, I try to focus on the small leaps forward – like the way the first boobook owl since the fires has recently returned to our property, sitting unmoving on a low branch outside my studio, pivoting his head to watch me as I walk up the hill at night. How the enormous blue gum that reaches up from the gulley below our house – a tree I thought would certainly die from its scorching – is now bursting into blossom, sending wafts of pale yellow tendrils into every breeze.

But mostly I just think, *what have we done?*

ACKNOWLEDGEMENTS

This book would not have been possible without the many people on the South Coast who generously agreed to share their fire stories with me. Some, but not all, of these stories have been told within these pages, yet I am grateful to have heard every one. Being asked to recount experiences filled with trauma is hard, and I was fortunate to have so many people willing to go back down that road. In hearing these stories, I was consistently in awe of the bravery, quick thinking and fortitude that was displayed during the fires, and this remains a constant source of inspiration for me. All names used in this narrative are real, except in instances where individuals asked not to be identified.

To all my fellow travellers through the period of the fire: thank you. While everyone was facing stress and disruption of their own, I never had any shortage of support and friendship. The list is not exhaustive by any means, but thanks must go to my parents, for housing us at short notice and for constant support over the summer (and always); to Ben, for being a calm presence in my worst moment; and to Donovan, for arriving to help with the hard jobs. To all the members of our WhatsApp group, you were a lifeline (even with the rampant poor punctuation and bad spelling).

To the amazing Bawley crew of friends: you all came through, as always. Special thanks though to Mel for emergency plumbing assistance and events organising to keep our spirits buoyed; to Lisette and Flo Food Van for keeping us in coffee even as everything burned; and to Zora for caring for our wildlife. Colin, Lucille and Finn – turning up with new bicycles (thank you, Trek) was a high point in a grim summer. And Naomi, your prepping skills saved the day while I was unravelling. Thank you to Jo for finding us somewhere to live. And enormous gratitude to Zane – who helped build me a studio to write in even before he started rebuilding his own home.

I will be forever grateful to the Bawley RFS crew who came up to our property the night of the fire: Charlie, Dump, Luci, Joy and Lise. And David for helping get them there.

Thank you to Nick Feik at *The Monthly*, for guidance on transitioning from writing a story about others' fire experiences to my own; to Varuna, the National Writers' House, for the Writing Fire, Writing Drought fellowship; to ABC journalist Anna Henderson, for uncovering vital information through freedom of information; and to ABC journalist Sean Rubinsztein-Dunlop, for his work on the Conjola fire.

Thank you to Chris Feik and Julia Carlomagno at Black Inc. for envisaging this book, skilled eyes, encouragement and patience. Most of all, though, thank you to Chris – for saving our home and for supporting our family as I disappeared for long periods to write this book. And to my children, for being such troopers through it all.

ABOUT THE AUTHOR

BRONWYN ADCOCK is an award-winning Australian journalist and writer. She has worked as a radio current-affairs reporter and documentary maker for the ABC, as a video journalist for SBS's *Dateline* and as a freelance writer, including for *Griffith Review* and *The Monthly*.